"Covenant Keeper"

sj Miller & Leslie David Burns
GENERAL EDITORS

Vol. 3

The Social Justice Across Contexts in Education series is
part of the Peter Lang Education list.
Every volume is peer reviewed and meets
the highest quality standards for content and production.

PETER LANG
New York • Bern • Frankfurt • Berlin
Brussels • Vienna • Oxford • Warsaw

"Covenant Keeper"

Derrick Bell's Enduring Education Legacy

Edited by Gloria Ladson-Billings
and William F. Tate

PETER LANG
New York • Bern • Frankfurt • Berlin
Brussels • Vienna • Oxford • Warsaw

Library of Congress Cataloging-in-Publication Data

Names: Ladson-Billings, Gloria, editor. | Tate, William F., editor.
Title: "Covenant keeper": Derrick Bell's enduring education legacy /
edited by Gloria Ladson-Billings, William F. Tate.
Description: New York: Peter Lang, 2016.
Series: Social justice across contexts in education; v. 3
ISSN 2372-6849 (print) | ISSN 2372-6857 (online)
Includes bibliographical references and index.
Identifiers: LCCN 2016001525 | ISBN 978-1-4331-3035-9 (hardcover: alk. paper)
ISBN 978-1-4331-3034-2 (paperback: alk. paper) | ISBN 978-1-4539-1840-1 (ebook pdf)
ISBN 978-1-4331-3722-8 (epub) | ISBN 978-1-4331-3723-5 (mobi)
Subjects: LCSH: African Americans—Education. | Bell, Derrick, 1930–2011—Influence.
Racism in education—United States. | Discrimination in education—United States.
Critical pedagogy—United States.
Classification: LCC LC2717 .C68 2016 | DDC 371.829/96073—dc23
LC record available at http://lccn.loc.gov/2016001525

Bibliographic information published by **Die Deutsche Nationalbibliothek**.
Die Deutsche Nationalbibliothek lists this publication in the "Deutsche
Nationalbibliografie"; detailed bibliographic data are available
on the Internet at http://dnb.d-nb.de/.

The paper in this book meets the guidelines for permanence and durability
of the Committee on Production Guidelines for Book Longevity
of the Council of Library Resources.

© 2016 Peter Lang Publishing, Inc., New York
29 Broadway, 18th floor, New York, NY 10006
www.peterlang.com

Printed in the United States of America

Contents

Foreword: Critical What What?   vii
   Devon W. Carbado

Introduction   xxiii
   Gloria Ladson-Billings

Section One: Derrick Bell Teaching and Schooling

Chapter One: Continuing to Sacrifice Black Children   3
   Gloria Ladson-Billings

Chapter Two: "Gifted With a Second-Sight": Professor Derrick Bell the Teacher
   Vinay Harpalani   17

Chapter Three: A Critical Race Examination of *McLaurin v. Oklahoma*:
   How Derrick Bell Helped Me Understand George McLaurin's Seat   39
   Daniel G. Solórzano

Chapter Four: The Utility of "The Space Traders" and Its Variations as
   CRT Teachable Moments   57
   Ana Carolina Antunes, Rosie Connor, Kathryn K. Coquemont,
   Kehaulani Folau, Allison Martin, Laura Todd, and Laurence Parker

Section Two: Derrick Bell and Principles of Critical Race Theory

Chapter Five: Derrick Bell, *Brown*, and the Continuing Significance of the
Interest-Convergence Principle   81
Jamel K. Donnor

Chapter Six: The Rules of Racial Standing: Critical Race Theory for Analysis,
Activism, and Pedagogy   91
David Gillborn

Chapter Seven: Letter to My Unborn Daughter: My Career in the
Academy—Reasons for My Mental Breakdown   111
Nicola Rollock

Section Three: Derrick Bell on Theory

Chapter Eight: Derrick Bell's Feminism: Profeminism, Intersection, and the
Multiple Jeopardy of Race and Gender   131
Adrienne D. Dixson

Chapter Nine: In Pursuit of Critical Racial Literacy: An (Auto)ethnographic
Exploration of Derrick Bell's Three Is   141
Keffrelyn Brown

Chapter Ten: Derrick Bell on Race and Memory: From Abolition to
Obama   163
Anthony L. Brown

Afterword: The Ethics of Derrick Bell: Oh How He Loved   181
William F. Tate

Contributors   191

Index   197

Foreword

Critical What What?

DEVON W. CARBADO*

On November 3, 2010, I had the pleasure and honor of delivering the fifteenth annual Derrick Bell Lecture on Race in American Society at New York University School of Law. The event was all the more special to me because it coincided with Professor Bell's eightieth birthday. Little did I know that this would be the last birthday he would celebrate. In 2011, Derrick Bell died. Less than a year after delivering a lecture in his name and presence I was in New York attending a memorial service that beautifully captured and honored the multiple dimensions of his life.

Like all memorial services, Bell's was a difficult one to attend. For no matter how much I told myself that this was a moment in which to commemorate Bell's life, it was also, quite clearly, a moment to mark his departure. This endemic feature of memorial services—that they call upon us to both celebrate life and come to terms with death—is precisely why these services inevitably engender sadness and joy, solemnity and humor, prayer and music.

And, yet, I knew I had to go. My commitment in this regard was not first and foremost about paying my respects to the exemplary and courageous life Professor Bell had lived. There were other ways I could do that. My decision to attend derived from my sense that the memorial service would be a window on facets of Professor Bell's life about which I knew very little. Death is paradoxical in that

---

*Professor of Law, UCLA School of Law. This Foreword draws from an Afterword that appears in volume 44 of the *Connecticut Law Review* (2011).

way. The rituals through which we process death are, quite typically, revelatory biographies of our life.

And so it was with Bell's memorial service. It composed a wonderful picture of his life—the multiple ways in which he performed civil rights, the multiple people with whom he had forged bonds, and the multiple contexts in which his presence—his life—had been felt.

The service also revealed that, even in death, Professor Bell could build a community that transcended and opened up boundaries. Which is to say, the community of people Bell brought together on that day did not otherwise exist as a formation. Bell's death brought that community of people to life.

Eleven months earlier, none of the foregoing was on my mind. Derrick Bell was very much alive. And, his email invitation to me to deliver the Bell Lecture was awaiting my response.

Of course, I could not say no. Nor did I want to. I was deeply honored that he had asked.

But, I was also in a state of worry. More precisely, I felt at least a little bit over my head. To say that Professor Bell helped to found Critical Race Theory (CRT) understates the case. For quite some time his work defined the movement. Moreover, as the CRT literature grew inside and outside of legal discourse, Professor Bell's scholarship helped to chart the multiple trajectories along which the theory would travel. What, then, could *I* possibly say to shape the thinking of a man whose thinking formed and shaped the development of CRT?

Professor Bell wanted to know that as well, though in an altogether different sense. In a series of email exchanges we discussed the areas I might cover in my talk. His engagements with me were not about policing the boundaries of the lecture; there was no litmus test that I had to pass. Nor were those exchanges a kind of interview in which I had to prove to Professor Bell that he had not made a mistake in inviting me to give the lecture. Instead, our discussion reflected a genuine interest on Professor Bell's part in ascertaining the subject matter on which my lecture would be based.

I did not know before writing this Foreword that I kept my email exchanges with Professor Bell. With the permission of Janet Dewart Bell, Professor Bell's widow, I reproduce portions of those emails below. Before doing so, a little context is in order.

When I received the invitation to deliver the lecture I had been working on a book with Mitu Gulati that attempted to pull together some of our work on race as a performative identity. The basic idea is that people experience discrimination based not only on phenotypic markers of race (such as facial features and skin tone) but on performative dimensions of race (such as accent and demeanor). We called our approach a "working identity" theory of race and, in the introduction of our book, we articulated ten implications of our general thesis.

1. Discrimination is not only an inter-group phenomenon, it is also an intra-group phenomenon. We should care both about employers preferring whites over blacks (an inter-group discrimination problem) and about employers preferring racially palatable blacks over racially salient ones (an intra-group discrimination problem).

2. The existence of intra-group discrimination creates an incentive for African Americans to work their identities to signal to employers that they are racially palatable. They will want to cover up their racial salience to avoid being screened out of the application pool.

3. Signaling continues well after the employee is hired. The employee understands that she is still black on stage; that her employer is watching her racial performance with respect to promotion and pay increases. Accordingly, she becomes attuned to the roles her Working Identity performs. She will want the employer to experience her Working Identity as a diversity profit, not a racial deficit.

4. Working Identity requires time, effort, and energy—it is work, "shadow work." The phenomenon is part of an underground racial economy in which everyone participates and to which almost everyone simultaneously turns a blind eye.

5. Working Identity is not limited to the workplace. Admissions officers can screen applicants based on their Working Identity. Police officers can stop, search, and arrest people based on their Working Identity. The American public can vote for politicians based on their Working Identity. Here, too, there are incentives for the actor—to work her identity to gain admissions to universities, to avoid unfriendly interactions with the police, and to gain political office.

6. Working Identity is costly. It can cause people to compromise their sense of self; to lose themselves in their racial performance; to deny who they are; and to distance themselves from other members of their racial group. Plus, the strategy is risky. Staying at work late to negate the stereotype that one is lazy, for example, can confirm the stereotype that one is incompetent, unable to get work done within normal work hours.

7. Working Identity raises difficult questions for law. One can argue that discrimination based on Working Identity is not racial discrimination at all. Arguably, it is discrimination based on behavior or culture rather than race. Therefore, perhaps the law should not intervene. And even assuming that this form of discrimination is racial discrimination, it still might be a bad idea for the law to get involved. Do we really want judges deciding whether a person is or isn't "acting white" or "acting black"—and the degree to which they might be doing so? It is difficult to figure out what role, if any, law should play.

8. Working Identity transcends the African American experience. Everyone works their identity. Everyone feels the pressure to fit in, including white heterosexual men. But the existence of negative racial stereotypes increases those pressures and makes the work of fitting in harder and more time consuming. African Americans are not the only racial minority that experiences this difficulty, though our focus in the book is primarily on this group.

9. Nor is race the only social category with a Working Identity dimension. Women work their identities as feminine or not. Men are expected to act like men. Gays and lesbians are viewed along a continuum of acting straight or not. Racial performance is but part of a broader Working Identity phenomenon.

10. We all have a Working Identity whether we want to or not. Working Identity does not turn on the intentional, strategic behavior of the actor. An employer might perceive an African American as racially palatable even if that person does not intend for the employer to racially interpret her in that way. Irrespective of strategic behavior on the part of the employee, the employer will racially judge her based not only on how she racially looks but also on how the employer perceives her to racially act.[1]

I told Professor Bell that I was going to employ Barack Obama's experiences as president of the United States to explore some of the foregoing issues. Our email correspondence then included, among other exchanges, these:

Professor Bell: *It is so easy to be disappointed that Obama is not speaking out more strongly against his enemies and ours, but then most of us don't do that in our far less important interactions and confrontations with our white faculty colleagues.*

Me: *I think you are right that, in some sense, it's easy to critique Obama. At the same time, it's actually quite hard. There is a kind of closing of ranks in which I confess I sometimes participate. At any rate, my talk will not be a critique of him. It is more about some of the challenges the current moment presents.*

Professor Bell: *Trying to place Obama in his role as president is somewhat like trying to place Jackie Robinson in his first few years in the majors when he took all manner of abuse and kept focusing on the game he played so well. Jackie knew he could play the game. I sometimes fear that Barack is not always sure what game he is playing and were I in his place, I would not know either.*

There is so much humility in Professor Bell's words. As some of you might know, Professor Bell was not always pleased with the way in which President Obama manifested his racial commitments. At the same time, Bell wanted to make clear that, in some ways, President Obama was too easy a target. His point was not that we should eschew criticizing the president. Remember: Professor Bell led a life in which he insisted on confronting authority.[2] Bell's point was that we should hold ourselves, and not just President Obama, accountable. He was urging us to bring our politics home—to "our white faculty and colleagues." Bell understood that politics was not simply "out there" (in, for example, the domain of presidential governance); politics was also "right here" (in, for example, the domains of personal, social, and workplace life).

There is another sense in which Bell's words reflected humility: the due regard he gave to the existential weight of being the first black president. Recall that Professor Bell "would not know" "what game" to play were he president of the United States. His view in this respect was neither apologia for President Obama nor a claim that being the first black president necessarily entails an abdication of one's racial justice responsibilities and commitments. Instead, Professor Bell meant to highlight the enormous constraints—the racial "push" and "pull" factors—under which President Obama undoubtedly operates and raise a question mark about how he (Bell) would negotiate those constraints.

As emails often do, ours eventually trailed off. We moved from the thorny issue of race and Obama to small talk about mutual friends and colleagues. We agreed to stay in touch.

As the date for the lecture neared, we began corresponding again. I do not recall how we got to the title of my presentation. (Regrettably, those emails I do not have.) I do recall telling Professor Bell what I had in mind for the title: *After Obama: Three Post-Racial Challenges*. Bell's response was succinct and pointed: "Do you intend to put post-racial in scare quotes? America is not post-racial."[3]

The truth of the matter is: I had not intended to put post-racial in scare quotes. From where I sat, it went without saying that the United States was *not* post-racial. Surely, Professor Bell knew that I knew that.

However, Bell's intervention was not about what I knew. It was about whether the title of my lecture (at least implicitly) legitimized the ideas around which post-racialism was being organized—including the twin claims that racism was largely a thing of the past and that Obama's presidency proved—once and for all—that the nation had racially overcome. Presumably, Professor Bell was thinking that, against the backdrop of the near normalization of post-racialism as the discourse through which people were beginning to describe and think about American racial politics, it was ideologically dangerous to employ the term without simultaneously interrogating it. Scare quotes were a way of performing that interrogation.

As you might have surmised, I changed the title along the lines Professor Bell suggested. (If only all the feedback I got on my work was that easy to incorporate.) I also changed the title of the book on which the lecture was based. There, too, I interrogated post-racial with scare quotes. Now, every time I see the title—*Acting White? Re-thinking Race in "Post-Racial America"*—I think about Professor Bell. It is a subtle reminder of the vigilance with which he pursued racial justice—down to the very last scare quote.

***

Covenant Keeper: Derrick Bell's Enduring Education Legacy is a more robust and capacious reminder of Professor Bell and his commitment to racial justice. The terrain this book covers is truly remarkable. This should not surprise us. After all, its editors, Gloria Ladson-Billings and William F. Tate, are leading figures in the field on CRT and education, and each of the contributors has written terrific articles in the area. Moreover, the call for the symposium that became the basis for *Covenant Keeper* asked the participants "to select a book, article, chronicle, concept, or principle by Professor Bell that has had direct impact on their work." This call was profoundly generative. It produced a set of engagements with Derrick Bell's work that expands the CRT canon.

The chapters in this book include close readings of: Bell's theory of interest convergence, his structural approach to education, his profound understanding of race as a social construction, his deployment of double jeopardy and intersectionality, his perceptive analysis of legal doctrine, his utilization of narratives and chronicles, and his deep investment in pedagogy and activism.

There is much that I could say about each of the chapters. But this is not a moment for me to be prolix. Besides, Professors Ladson-Billing's and Tate's introduction summarizes and contextualizes each essay. What I will say is that reading the chapters will give you a sense not only of the breadth and depth of CRT in the field of education but also of the breadth and depth of Bell's scholarly agenda, including the interdisciplinary nature and impact of his work.

Given the scope of Bell's work, and the reach of CRT across the disciplines, one might think that that the theory is uncontroversial and well understood. One would be wrong to so conclude. More than 38 years after the publication of Bell's now classic and foundational text, *Race Racism, and American Law*, and more than two decades after the establishment of Critical Race Theory (CRT) as a clearly defined intellectual movement, defining oneself as a Critical Race Theorist can still engender the question: critical what what? When asked, the inquiry is not just about the appellation, though this is certainly part of what engenders the question. For example, when my colleagues and I proposed the establishment of a Critical Race Studies specialization at UCLA School of Law more than a decade ago and mobilized the work of Derrick Bell, among others, to do so, the only push back we got was over the name.

Why Critical Race Studies? Why not Civil Rights? Race and the Law? Anti-Discrimination Studies? Ultimately, we succeeded in persuading our faculty that it made sense for us to trade on and signal a connection to an intellectual movement of which several of us considered ourselves a part and that Derrick Bell helped to found. But the episode suggested that there was something in and about the name. By any other name, our faculty meeting on the matter would have been considerably shorter. To borrow from George Lipsitz, our engagement with our colleagues about this particular institutional naming was a moment of "organization learning."[4]

This should not lead one to conclude that the "Critical what what?" question is only about the name. The query is about the whatness (or, less charitably, the "there there") of CRT as well. What is the genesis of CRT? What are the core ideas? What are its goals and aspirations? What intellectual work does the theory perform outside of legal discourse? What are the limitations of the theory? What is its future trajectory?

This foreword takes up the foregoing questions. I do so because it is critically important that a book that honors Derrick Bell situate his work with respect to the body of literature it helped to produce. As will become clear, my analysis will be decidedly incomplete. Accordingly, you should read this foreword more as a gesture towards answering the questions I raised about CRT than as a definitive answer to them.

One might start by saying that CRT rejects the standard racial progress narrative that characterizes mainstream civil rights discourse—namely, that the history of race relations in the United States is a history of linear uplift and improvement. Of course, America's racial landscape has improved over time, and CRT scholars should be ready to point this out. The problem with the racial progress narrative, however, is that it elides what one might call the reform/retrenchment dialectic that has constituted America's legal and political history.[5]

Consider the following three examples: (1) the end of legalized slavery and the promulgation of the Reconstruction Amendments (the reform) inaugurated legalized Jim Crow and the promulgation of Black Codes (the retrenchment); (2) *Brown v. Board of Education*'s dismantling of separate but equal in the context of K–12 education (the reform) was followed by *Brown II*'s weak "with all deliberate speed" mandate (the retrenchment); (3) Martin Luther King, Jr.'s vision of racial cooperation and responsibility, which helped to secure the passage of the Civil Rights Act of 1964 (the reform), was re-deployed to produce a political and legal discourse that severely restricts racial remediation efforts: colorblindness (the retrenchment). A linear narrative about American racial progress obscures this reform/retrenchment dynamic.

Nor do racial progress narratives make clear that the episodes we celebrate today as significant moments of racial reform (e.g., *Brown*) were moments of national crisis, moments that contested what Lani Guinier has called the "tyranny of the majority,"[6] counter-majoritarian moments, moments preceded by mass political mobilization. Far from reflecting national harmony in which the country as a whole agreed that racial change was in order, racial reform typically has occurred when the equality interest of people of color converges with the interest of powerful elites; and "even when the interest convergence results in an effective racial remedy, that remedy will be abrogated at the point that policy makers fear that the remedial policy is threatening"[7] to the dominant social order. This, of course, is Derrick Bell's theory of interest convergence, which he offers as an explanation for the reform/retrenchment dynamic I have described. The broader point is that one of CRT's key claims is that racial reform and racial retrenchment are defining aspects of American law and politics.

In addition to rejecting the civil rights linear racial progress narrative, CRT repudiates the view that status quo arrangements are the natural result of individual agency and merit. We all inherit advantages and disadvantages, including the historically accumulated social effects of race. I call this "racial accumulation." Racial accumulation is the economic (shaping both our income and wealth),[8] cultural (shaping the social capital upon which we can draw),[9] and ideological (shaping our perceived racial worth). In short, racial accumulation structures our life chances. This does not mean that agency is irrelevant. It means that discussions of agency should not obscure racially accumulated burdens and benefits.

CRT puts those burdens and benefits into sharp relief. The theory exposes the inter-generational transfers of what we might think of as racial compensation. Building up over time to create racial shelters (hidden and protected racial privileges) and racial taxes (hidden and unprotected racial costs),[10] racial compensation profoundly shapes and helps to support the contemporary economies of racial hierarchy.[11] CRT intervenes to correct this market failure and the unjust racial allocations it produces.

One way the theory does so is by challenging two dominant principles upon which American anti-discrimination law and politics rest—to wit, that colorblindness necessarily produces race neutrality and that color consciousness necessarily produces racial preferences. By historically contextualizing existing racial inequalities, CRT is able to both contest the [colorblindness/race-neutrality]/[color-conscious/racial preferences] alignments and reverse them. The theory effectuates this reversal by demonstrating how colorblindness can produce racial preferences and how color consciousness can neutralize and disrupt embedded racial advantages.[12]

CRT also weighs in directly on the very idea of race, rejecting the conception of race as a biologically fixed social category. Part of this effort includes describing race as a performative identity, one whose meanings shift not only from social context to social context but from social interaction to social interaction. Under this view of race, people actively work their identities to shape how others experience them.[13] And even when a person does not intend to manage her identity in this way, the racial meanings others ascribe to her (is she racially assimilationist? is she racially counter-cultural?) will turn at least in part on her performative identity.

Imagine, for example, two black women—one of whom has dreaded hair; the other's hair is relaxed. Neither intends to employ her hair to make a racial statement about herself. Notwithstanding the absence of that intent, both will be racially interpreted (and even interpellated, to draw from Althusser)[14] based at least in part on their hair. As between the two women, people are more likely to "read" the woman with dreads as racially counter-cultural.[15] This is because, as Paulette Caldwell,[16] Angela Onwuachi-Willig,[17] and Margaret Montoya[18] have explained, hair is racially constitutive. Self-presentation or performance more generally is as well. This performative understanding of race suggests that people are not born raced, to re-articulate a point Simone de Beauvoir makes about sex; they become raced, in part through a series of cognizable acts.[19] These acts—which we rehearse, renew, and revise—become consolidated over time, constituting the very thing (race) we imagine to be ontologically prior.[20]

The foregoing were precisely some of the ideas I rehearsed with Derrick Bell as I explored with him the topics I might pursue in the context of delivering the Derrick Bell Lecture. As I indicated earlier, Professor Bell seemed to approve of the analysis, though he wanted to ensure that I interrogated the "post-racial" title under which the work was situated.

CRT rejects the view that race precedes law, ideology, and social relations. Instead, Critical Race Theorists conceptualize race as a product of law, ideology, and social relations. According to CRT, the law does not simply reflect ideas about race. The law constructs race: Law has historically employed race as a basis for group differentiation, entrenching the idea that there are "in fact" different races; law has helped to determine the racial categories (e.g., Black, White, Yellow) into which institutions and individuals place people; law sets forth criteria or rules (e.g., phenotype and ancestry) by which we map people into those racial categories; law has assigned social meaning to the categories (e.g., Whites are superior; Blacks are inferior; Japanese Americans are disloyal); law has employed those meanings to structure hierarchical arrangements (e.g., legalized slavery for inferior people (Blacks) and legalized internment for people who are disloyal (people of Japanese descent)); and those legal arrangements, in turn, have functioned to confirm the social meanings that law helped to create (e.g., the people who are enslaved must be inferior; that is why they are enslaved; the people who are interned must be disloyal; that is why they are interned).[21]

CRT has also focused more specifically on how the law constructs whiteness, thus, for example, Cheryl Harris's arguments about "whiteness as property"[22] and Ian Haney López's white-by-law analysis of the naturalization cases.[23] These efforts are part of a broader body of work demonstrating that, historically, whiteness has functioned as a normative baseline.[24] We are all defined with whiteness in mind. We are the same as or different from whites. Think, for example, about some of our contemporary debates about racial equality. Essentially, two competing paths exist to pursue racial equality in the United States: demonstrate either that people of color are the same as, or different from, whites. To draw from an observation that Catharine MacKinnon makes about sex: "The main theme in the fugue is 'we're the same, we're the same, we're the same.' The counterpoint theme ... is 'but we're different, but we're different, but we're different.'"[25] Both of these conceptions of equality implicitly have whiteness as their reference. Under the sameness framework, people of color are measured in terms of their correspondence with whiteness; under the difference framework, we are assessed according to our non-correspondence.[26]

This sameness/difference dynamic helps to explain how race figures in equal protection analysis. Critical Race Theorists have long criticized what I call the *race per se* approach to equal protection—the presumption that any use of race is constitutionally suspect.[27] As a result of this presumption, the government needs to articulate a compelling justification for incorporating race into its decision-making.[28] To put the point more doctrinally, race-based governmental decision-making must survive strict scrutiny. The baseline effects of whiteness, and the sameness/difference dynamic it produces, provides a *partial* explanation for why this is so. Because we are all (supposed to be) the same as whites—because race is ostensibly nothing but skin color[29]—judges should "strictly scrutinize" instances in which the government treats us differently by relying on race.[30] At the same time, because we (people of color) are said to have different racial experiences than whites and this difference is perceived to facilitate the "robust exchange of ideas," the government may, at least in the context of higher education, invoke diversity to justify relying on race.[31]

At the front end of equal protection analysis, then, the notion is that people of color are *formally* the same as whites (taking race into account treats them differently and thus should be strictly scrutinized)[32]; at the back end of the analysis, the racial experiences of people of color are perceived to be *substantively* different (thus, the government can employ diversity as a compelling justification for affirmative action). Under the strained logic of this sameness/difference approach, people of color are the same as, but have different racial experiences than, whites. One way to make sense of this would be to say that equal protection doctrine reflects a strong imperative that people of color *should be* the same as whites; but, understanding that they are not, the doctrine reflects a weak and instrumental tolerance of their difference.

Neil Gotanda has engaged this problem of sameness and difference by critiquing what he refers to as the Supreme Court's formal approach to equal protection.[33] Under this approach, evidence of formal sameness in treatment precludes the finding of discrimination. Other CRT scholars, such as Charles Lawrence, have linked this problem of racial formalism to intent-centered models of discrimination, models that require evidence of discriminatory intent to sustain an anti-discrimination cause of action.[34] Still other CRT scholars, such as Darren Hutchinson, have demonstrated how the Supreme Court's commitment to treating people formally the same "has effectively inverted the concepts of privilege and subordination; it treats advantaged classes as if they were vulnerable and in need of heightened judicial protection, and it views socially disadvantaged classes as privileged and unworthy of judicial solicitude."[35] Each of these efforts is part of a broader CRT project to articulate racism as a structural phenomenon, rather than as a problem that derives from the failure on the part of individuals and institutions to treat people formally the same.

Informing CRT's structural account of racism is the notion that racism is endemic in society. It is, to put it the way Daria Roithmayr might, "locked-in."[36] This locked-in feature of racism is linked to our very system of democracy. Which is to say, historically, racism has been constitutive of, rather than oppositional to, American democracy. This does not mean that racism is an expression of American democracy. That would be putting the point too strongly. It is more accurate to say that racism was built into the constitutional architecture of American democracy. As Rachel Moran and I explain elsewhere, "[t]he drafters of the Constitution took a sober second look at the rhetoric of radical egalitarianism in the Declaration of Independence, and they blinked. The adoption of the Constitution in 1787 and its ratification one year later depended on a compromise, one that integrated slavery into the very fabric of American democracy."[37] The lingering effects of this foundational moment—or the ongoing relationship between racial inequality and American democracy—are precisely what Gunnar Myrdal referred to racism as an "American dilemma."[38]

In describing racism as an endemic social force, CRT scholars argue that it interacts with other social forces, such as patriarchy,[39] homophobia,[40] and classism.[41] The theory is thus committed to what Kim Crenshaw has called "intersectionality"— and, more specifically, to an intersectional engagement of structural hierarchies.[42] This engagement endeavors not only to "look to the bottom," to borrow from Mari Matsuda[43]; it also seeks to "look to the top."[44] In other words, the theory seeks to make clear that there is a "top" and a "bottom" to discrimination[45] and that, historically, racism has been bi-directional: It gives to whites (e.g., citizenship) what it takes away from or denies to people of color. Framing discrimination in this way helps to reveal an uncomfortable truth about race and power: The disempowerment of people of color is achieved through the empowerment—material or psychological— of whites.[46] There is no disadvantage without a corresponding advantage, no marginalized group without the powerful elite, no subordinate identity without a dominant counterpart. As Guy-Uriel Charles argues, "[l]ooking at the gaping racial disparities [in America] on most socio-economic indicators, there are clearly two classes of citizens: Whites and coloreds."[47] Racism has historically drawn this line, effectuating and maintaining a relational difference that is based on power. CRT attempts to describe the role law plays in producing and naturalizing this racial arrangement.

Critical Race Theorists pursue this project across racial groups,[48] and in the context of doing so try to avoid what Angela Harris might refer to as the pitfalls of essentialism.[49] While some would say CRT scholars *are* anti-essentialist, it would be more accurate to say that we *aspire to be* anti-essentialist. The distinction is important. Because to invoke any social category is already to essentialize, the question is not whether we engage in essentialism but rather the normative work we deploy our essentialism to perform.

Part of that work entails highlighting the discursive frames legal and political actors have employed to disadvantage people of color. These frames include, but are not limited to: "colorblindness,"[50] "illegal alien,"[51] "terrorist,"[52] "reverse discrimination,"[53] "foreigner,"[54] "merit,"[55] "the border,"[56] "citizenship,"[57] "the war on drugs,"[58] and "the war on terror."[59] Even our most celebrated constitutional frameworks, such as "equal protection"[60] and "due process,"[61] can function as repositories of racial power. CRT reflects "a desire not merely to understand ... [these and other] vexed bond[s] between law and racial power but to *change* ... [them]."[62] Committed to grappling with the immediacies of now and the transformative possibilities of tomorrow, CRT reflects both pragmatism and idealism.[63]

***

Clearly, the foregoing ideas do not fully capture CRT. Think of them as a starting point. As you will undoubtedly appreciate upon reading *Covenant Keeper*, scholars of education have pushed the theory beyond its articulations in law—and certainly beyond the redacted account I present in this foreword. *Covenant Keeper* is useful, then, not only for people whose primary field is education. It is useful for scholars in other disciplines as well, including law. To put this point another way, *Covenant Keeper* provides a perfect opportunity for legal scholars to see not only how CRT is travelling in the field of education but also how the theory is being re-articulated and reconstituted in the process.

NOTES

1. Devon W. Carbado & Mitu Gulati, ACTING WHITE? RETHINKING RACE IN "POST-RACIAL" AMERICA" (2013).
2. Derrick Bell, CONFRONTING AUTHORITY: REFLECTIONS OF AN ARDENT PROTESTER (1994).
3. I do not have the email to reproduce the precise quote.
4. George Lipsitz, *"Constituted by a Series of Contestations": Critical Race Theory as a Social Movement*, 43 CONN. L. REV. xxx (2011).
5. *See generally* Kimberlé Crenshaw, *Race, Reform and Retrenchment*, 101 HARV. L. REV. 1331 (1998).
6. LANI GUINIER, THE TYRANNY OF THE MAJORITY (1994).
7. DERRICK BELL, SILENT COVENANTS: BROWN V. *BOARD OF EDUCATION* AND THE UNFULFILLED HOPES FOR RACIAL REFORM 69 (2004).

8. *See, e.g.*, MELVIN L. OLIVER & THOMAS M. SHAPIRO, BLACK WEALTH/WHITE WEALTH: A NEW PERSPECTIVE ON RACIAL INEQUALITY (1997).

9. *Cf.* PIERRE BOURDIEU, OUTLINE OF A THEORY OF PRACTICE, DISTINCTION: A SOCIAL CRITIQUE OF THE JUDGEMENT OF TASTE, AND HOMO-ACADEMICUS (1962).

10. *Cf.* JODY DAVID ARMOUR, NEGROPHOBIA AND REASONABLE RACISM: THE HIDDEN COSTS OF BEING BLACK IN AMERICA (1999).

11. One might also think about this in terms of the racial deficits and racial surpluses we inherit.

12. *See generally* Devon W. Carbado & Cheryl I. Harris, *New Racial Preferences*, 96 CALIF. L. REV. 1139 (2008).

13. *See* Devon W. Carbado & Mitu Gulati, *Working Identity*, 85 CORNELL L. REV. 1259 (2000); Devon W. Carbado & Mitu Gulati, *The Fifth Black Woman*, 11 J. CONTEMP. L. ISSUES 701 (2001); *see also* Mario L. Barnes & Angela Onwuachi-Willig, *By Any Other Name?: On Being "Regarded As" Black and Why Title VII Should Apply Even If Lakisha and Jamal Are White*, 2005 WIS. L. REV. 1283; Frank Rudy Cooper, *Surveillance and Identity Performance: Some Thoughts Inspired by Martin Luther King*, 32 N.Y.U. REV. L. & SOC. CHANGE 517 (2008); Margaret E. Montoya, *Mascaras, Trenzas, y Grenas: Un/masking the Self While Un/braiding Latina Stories and Legal Discourse*, 17 HARV. WOMEN'S L.J. 185 (1994). Scholars outside of the field of CRT have also drawn on this insight. *See, e.g.*, KENJI YOSHINO, COVERING: THE HIDDEN ASSAULT ON OUR CIVIL RIGHTS (2007).

14. According to Althusser:

    There are individuals walking along. Somewhere (usually behind them) the hail rings out: "Hey you there!" One individual (nine times out of ten it is the right one) turns around, believing/suspecting/knowing that it is for him, i.e., recognizing that "it really is he" who is meant by the hailing. But in reality things happen without succession. The existence of ideology and the hailing or interpellation of individual as subject are one and thus the same thing.

    LOUIS ALTHUSSER, *Ideology and Ideological State Apparatuses*, *in* LENIN AND PHILOSOPHY AND OTHER ESSAYS 174–75 (Ben Brewster trans., 1971).

15. *See generally* Carbado & Gulati, *The Fifth Black Woman*, *supra* note 13 (discussing these dynamics).

16. *See* Paulette M. Caldwell, *A Hair Piece: Perspectives on the Intersection of Race and Gender* 1991 DUKE L.J. 365 (1991).

17. *See* Angela Onwuachi-Willig, *Another Hair Piece: Exploring New Strands of Analysis Under Title VII*, 98 GEO. L. REV. 1079 (2010).

18. Margaret Montoya, *Mascaras, Trenzas, y Grenas: Un/Masking the Self While Un/Braiding Latina Stories and Legal Discourse*, *supra* note 13.

19. SIMONE DE BEAUVOIR, THE SECOND SEX 12–13 (Constance Borde & Sheila Malovany-Chevalier trans., Knopf 2009) (1949).

20. *Cf.* Judith Butler, *Performative Acts and Gender Constitution: An Essay in Phenomenology and Feminist Theory*, 40 THEATRE J. 519, 523 (1988) ("[T]he body becomes its gender through a series of acts which are renewed, revised and consolidated through time."). *But see* BRUCE WILSHIRE, ROLE PLAYING AND IDENTITY: THE LIMITS OF THEATRE AS METAPHOR (1982) (arguing that gender is not a performance)

21. Devon W. Carbado, *Discrimination on the Basis of Racial Orientation* (draft on file with author).

22. *See* Cheryl Harris, *Whiteness as Property*, 106 HARV. L. REV. 1707, 1713 (describing "whiteness" as a "valuable asset" that whites seek to protect).

23. IAN HANEY LÓPEZ, WHITE BY LAW: THE LEGAL CONSTRUCTION OF RACE (2006).

24. *See, e.g.*, CRITICAL WHITE STUDIES: LOOKING BEHIND THE MIRROR (Richard Delgado & Jean Stefancic eds., 1997); STEPHANIE WILDMAN ET AL., PRIVILEGE REVEALED: HOW INVISIBLE PREFERENCE UNDERMINES AMERICA (1996). Feminists have made similar points about gender. *See* Martha Minow, *Feminist Reason: Getting It and Losing It*, 38 J. LEGAL EDUC. 47, 48 (1988) ("The norms and the dynamics of the natural world—the way its biological, evolutionary, and even chemical and physical properties are explained—embody unstated male reference points."); *see also* Janet E. Ainsworth, *In a Different Register: The Pragmatics of Powerlessness in Police Interrogation*, 103 YALE L.J. 259, 316–17 (1993) (noting that "the law's incorporation of a male normative standard may be invisible but it is not inconsequential"). One can, of course, advance similar claims about heterosexuality. *See* Devon W. Carbado, *Straight Out of the Closet*, 15 BERKELEY WOMEN'S L.J. 76 (2000).

25. CATHARINE A. MACKINNON, FEMINISM UNMODIFIED: DISCOURSES ON LIFE AND LAW 34 (1987); *see also* Carbado, *Straight, supra* note 24 (drawing on MacKinnon's sameness/difference analysis).

26. Here, too, I am merely re-articulating a point MacKinnon makes about sex. *See* Carbado, *Straight, supra* note 24.

27. Devon W. Carbado, *A Strict Scrutiny of Strict Scrutiny* (draft on file with author).

28. *See Adarand Constructors, Inc. v. Pena*, 515 U.S. 200 (1995). Race-based classifications must also be narrowly tailored, which, roughly, means that even when the government has a compelling reason for incorporating race into its decision-making, the means by which it does so should be carefully thought out and narrowly circumscribed.

29. *Shaw v. Reno*, 509 U.S. 630 (1993). According to the Court:

   A reapportionment plan that includes in one district individuals who belong to the same race, but who are otherwise widely separated by geographical and political boundaries, and who may have little in common with one another but the color of their skin, bears an uncomfortable resemblance to political apartheid. It reinforces the perception that members of the same racial group—regardless of their age, education, economic status, or the community in which they live—think alike, share the same political interests, and will prefer the same candidates at the polls. We have rejected such perceptions elsewhere as impermissible racial stereotypes.
   Id. at 647–48.

30. *Adarand*, 515 U.S. 200.

31. *Grutter v. Bollinger*, 539 U.S. 306 (2003).

32. *Adarand*, 515 U.S. at 239 (Scalia, J., dissenting) ("[U]nder our Constitution there can be no such thing as either a creditor or a debtor race. ... In the eyes of government, we are just one race here. It is American."); *see also Parents Involved in Cmty. Schs. v. Seattle Sch. Dist. No. 1*, 377 F.3d 949, 987 (9th Cir. 2004) (quoting *Adarand* for the same proposition); *Bass v. Bd. of Cnty. Comm'rs, Orange Cnty., Fla.*, 256 F.3d 1095, 1103 (11th Cir. 2001) (same); *Equal Open Enrollment Ass'n v. Bd. of Educ. of Akron City Sch. Dist.*, 937 F.Supp. 700, 710 (N.D. Ohio 1996) (same); *U.S. v. Adair*, 913 F. Supp. 1503, 1513 (E.D. Okla. 1995) (same); *Clarke v. City of Cincinnati*, 1993 WL 761489, *27 (S.D. Ohio, 1993) ("[W]e are all members of one and only one race, the human race.").

33. Neil Gotanda, *A Critique of "Our Constitution Is Colorblind,"* 44 STAN. L. REV. 1 (1991).

34. Charles R. Lawrence, III, *The Id, the Ego, and Equal Protection: Reckoning with Unconscious Racism*, 39 STAN. L. REV. 317 (1987).

35. Darren Lenard Hutchinson, *"Unexplainable on Grounds Other Than Race": The Inversion of Privilege and Subordination in Equal Protection Jurisprudence*, 2003 U. ILL. L. REV. 615 (2003) [hereinafter Hutchinson, *Unexplainable*].

36. *See generally* Daria Roithmayr, *Barriers to Entry: A Market Lock-In Model of Discrimination*, 86 VA. L. REV. 727 (2000).

37. DEVON W. CARBADO & RACHEL F. MORAN, *Introduction* to RACE LAW STORIES 8 (Rachel F. Moran & Devon W. Carbado eds., 2008).

38. GUNNAR MYRDAL, AN AMERICAN DILEMMA: THE NEGRO PROBLEM AND MODERN DEMOCRACY (1944).

39. *See generally* Angela P. Harris, *Race and Essentialism in Feminist Legal Theory*, 42 STAN. L. REV. 582 (1990).

40. *See generally* Devon W. Carbado, *Black Rights, Gay Rights, Civil Rights*, 47 UCLA L. REV. 1467 (2000); Darren Lenard Hutchinson, *Out Yet Unseen: A Racial Critique of Gay and Lesbian Legal Theory and Political Discourse*, 29 CONN. L. REV. 561 (1997); Russell K. Robinson, *Racing the Closet*, 61 STAN. L. REV. 1463 (2009).

41. *See generally* Trina Jones, *Race, Economic Class, and Employment Opportunities*, 72 LAW & CONTEMP. PROBS. 57 (2009).

42. *See generally* Kimberlé Crenshaw, *Mapping the Margins*, 43 STAN. L. REV. 1241 (1991).

43. Mari J. Matsuda, *Looking to the Bottom*, 22 HARV. C.R.-C.L. L. REV. 323 (1987).

44. *See generally* Devon W. Carbado, *Race to the Bottom*, 49 UCLA L. REV. 1283 (2002).

45. *See id.*

46. Of course, whiteness is not a monolithic identity category. Class, sexual orientation, among other aspects of person, shape how whites experience their whiteness. Understood in this way, whites have differential access to the privileges of whiteness. *See id.* at 1297; *see also* Camille Gear Rich, *Marginal Whiteness*, 98 CALIF. L. REV. 1497 (2010). At the same time, whites across differences can nevertheless trade—if only psychologically—on their whiteness. Du Bois's notion of the wages of whiteness speaks precisely to this idea. Du Bois argued that "the white group of laborers, while they receive a low wage, were compensated in part by a sort of public and psychological wage." W. E. B. DU BOIS, BLACK RECONSTRUCTION IN AMERICA: AN ESSAY TOWARDS A HISTORY OF THE PART WHICH BLACK FOLK PLAYED IN THE ATTEMPT TO RECONSTRUCT DEMOCRACY IN AMERICA 1860–1880, at 700 (1965). Du Bois's point was that, notwithstanding the material deprivations that working class whites historically have experienced, they were able to draw on the psychological wages of whiteness, which they treated as a material resource over and against the instantiation of black inferiority. *See* DAVID ROEDIGER, THE WAGES OF WHITENESS: RACE AND THE MAKING OF THE AMERICAN WORKING CLASS (1991).

47. Guy-Uriel Charles, *Towards a New Civil Rights Framework*, 30 HARV. J. L. & GENDER 353 (2007).

48. *See, e.g.*, ROBERT CHANG, DISORIENTED: ASIAN AMERICANS, LAW, AND THE NATION-STATE (1999); Sumi K. Cho, *Converging Stereotypes in Racialized Sexual Harassment: Where the Model Minority Meets Suzie Wong*, 1 J. GENDER RACE & JUSTICE 177 (1997); Francisco Valdes, *Queers, Sissies, Dykes, and Tomboys: Deconstructing the Conflation of "Sex," "Gender," and "Sexual Orientation" in Euro-American Law and Society*, 83 CALIF. L. REV. 1 (1995).

49. On the problem of essentialism in feminist legal theory, see generally Angela Harris, *Race and Essentialism in Feminist Legal Theory*, 42 STAN. L. REV. 581 (1990).

50. *See, e.g.*, Gotanda, *supra* note 33.

51. *See, e.g.*, Kevin R. Johnson, *The Intersection of Race and Class in U.S. Immigration Law and Enforcement*, 72 LAW & CONTEMP. PROBS. 1 (2009) (discussing racialization of illegal aliens).

52. Leti Volpp, *The Citizen and the Terrorist*, 49 UCLA L. REV. 1575 (2002).

53. Luke Charles Harris & Uma Narayan, *Affirmative Action and the Myth of Preferential Treatment: A Transformative Critique of the Terms of the Affirmative Action Debate*, 11 HARV. BLACK-LETTER L.J. 1 (1994); *see also* Kimberlé W. Crenshaw, *Framing Affirmative Action*, 105 MICH. L. REV. FIRST IMPRESSIONS 123 (2007), http://www.michiganlawreview.org/assets/fi/105/crenshaw.pdf.

54. Keith Aoki, *"Foreign-Ness" & Asian American Identities: Yellowface, World War II Propaganda, and Bifurcated Racial Stereotypes*, 4 ASIAN PAC. AM. L.J. 1 (1996); Robert S. Chang, *Dreaming in Black and White: Racial-Sexual Policing in the Birth of a Nation, the Cheat, and Who Killed Vincent Chin?*, 5 ASIAN L.J. 41 (1998).

55. *See* Lani Guinier, *Admissions Rituals as Political Acts: Guardians at the Gates of Our Democratic Ideals*, 117 HARV. L. REV. 113 (2003); Harris & Narayan, *supra* note 53.

56. *See* Kevin R. Johnson, *Race, the Immigration Laws, and Domestic Race Relations: A "Magic Mirror" into the Heart of Darkness*, 73 IND. L.J. 1111 (1998); Kevin R. Johnson, *Race Matters: Immigration Law and Policy Scholarship, Law in the Ivory Tower, and the Legal Indifference of the Race Critique*, 2000 U. ILL. L. REV. 525; George A. Martínez, *Race and Immigration Law: A Paradigm Shift?* 2000 U. ILL. L. REV. 517.

57. *See* HIROSHI MOTUMURA, AMERICANS IN WAITING: THE LOST STORY OF IMMIGRATION AND CITIZENSHIP IN THE UNITED STATES (2006); Linda Bosniak, *Constitutional Citizenship Through the Prism of Alienage*, 63 OHIO ST. L.J. 1285 (2002); Linda Bosniak, *Citizenship Denationalized*, 7 IND. J. GLOBAL LEGAL STUD. 447 (2000).

58. *See* PAUL BUTLER, LET'S GET FREE: A HIP-HOP THEORY OF JUSTICE 43–36 (2009); Paul Butler, *Retribution, for Liberals*, 46 UCLA L. REV. 1873 (1999).

59. *See* Muneer I. Ahmad, *A Rage Shared by Law: Post-September 11 Racial Violence as Crimes of Passion*, 92 CALIF. L. REV. 1259 (2004).

60. *See* Cheryl I. Harris, *Equal Treatment and the Reproduction of Inequality*, 69 FORDHAM L. REV. 1753 (2001).

61. *See* Jane Rutherford, *The Myth of Due Process*, 72 B.U. L. REV. 1 (1992).

62. *See* CRITICAL RACE THEORY: THE KEY WRITINGS xiii (Kimberlé Crenshaw et al. eds. 1995).

63. *See* Mari J. Matuda et al., WORDS THAT WOUND: CRITICAL RACE THEORY, ASSAULTIVE SPEECH, AND THE FIRST AMENDMENT 3 (1993) (describing CRT as "both pragmatic and utopian").

Introduction

GLORIA LADSON-BILLINGS

On Tuesday night, October 11, 2011, I was up late working on a lecture I was scheduled to deliver as the speaker for the American Educational Research Association's
8th Annual Brown Lecture in Washington DC. The lecture was titled, "Through a
Glass Darkly: The Persistence of Race in Education Research" (Ladson-Billings,
2012). But, as I was working I was reflecting on two significant losses. The previous week the Reverend Fred Shuttlesworth of Birmingham, Alabama, had died.
Rev. Shuttlesworth was known as "the most dangerous Negro in Birmingham" for
his work co-founding the Southern Christian Leadership Conference (SCLC)
and his persistence in fighting for the cause of justice for Black people in Alabama.
Earlier that same evening I learned that Silicon Valley innovator and entrepreneur
Steve Jobs had succumbed to the cancer that had ravaged his body. Despite all
of his alleged quirks and eccentricities I thought Jobs was a genius. It had been
a sad week. Just as I was about to retire for the night I received a text that read,
"Derrick Bell just died!" Those four words came over me like a cloud. The man
who could rightly be called "The Father of Critical Race Theory" had died. Like
Jobs, Derrick Bell was an innovator. He did things with the law that others had
not thought possible, and one of the fields that he invigorated by his creative use
of the law was education.

Derrick Albert Bell was the first African American to earn tenure at the
Harvard Law School.[1] Before arriving at Harvard, Bell attended Duquesne Uni-
versity, served in the United States Air Force for 2 years, and enrolled in the
University of Pittsburgh Law School, where he received his law degree in 1957.

After law school Derrick Bell took a position in the Civil Rights Division of the United States Department of Justice. In 1959 his superiors in the Justice Department asked him to resign his membership of the NAACP because they believed it compromised his objectivity and made the Department look biased. Bell refused to relinquish his NAACP membership and chose to resign from the Justice Department. Soon after, he took a position as an assistant counsel for the NAACP Legal Defense Fund.

At the Legal Defense Fund Bell worked with prominent civil rights attorneys such as Thurgood Marshall, Constance Baker Motley, and Robert L. Carter. His initial assignment was to Mississippi, where he oversaw some 300 school desegregation cases—one of which was the James Meredith case leading to the integration of the University of Mississippi. In the 1960s Bell was appointed to the law faculty of the University of Southern California, and by 1969 the fervent protests of students at Harvard Law School over the lack of faculty diversity made him the prime candidate to join the Harvard faculty. He earned tenure at Harvard in 1971.

Bell established a new course in civil rights law and produced what has become a famous casebook titled, *Race, Racism, and American Law* (Bell, 1973/2008), which is currently in its 6th edition. In it he perfected his use of counter-storytelling to illustrate legal principles concerning race and racism. Through the use of "chronicles," Bell and his students produced a prodigious number of law review articles. Over the span of his career Derrick Bell would be known for both his scholarship and activism.

In 1980 Bell became one of the few African Americans to lead a major law school when he became dean of the Oregon Law School. In that same year Bell (1980) published, "*Brown v. Board of Education* and the Interest-Convergence Dilemma," in which he argued that White Americans would only support racial and social justice to the extent that it benefits them. He further argued that the *Brown* decision was driven by anti-Communist concerns rather than an attempt to redress the centuries of unequal education Black people had endured.

In 1986 Derrick Bell resigned his position at Oregon because the faculty refused to hire an Asian American female professor. He returned to Harvard, but soon after returning to Cambridge he staged a 5-day sit-in to protest the school's failure to grant tenure to two women of color. In 1990 he took unpaid leave from Harvard after years of activism around hiring more faculty of color, especially women faculty of color. After a 2-year leave Harvard dismissed Professor Bell and he accepted a position at New York University. At NYU Bell displayed his love of teaching and taught classes in a style very different from most law classes. Instead of the Socratic question-and-answer style, Bell fashioned courses that employed a more Freirean approach using participatory learning designed to empower the students.

My connection with Derrick Bell came as a result of reading a column he wrote in the *Chronicle of Higher Education* that described his "Chronicle of the Divine

Gift"—a classic saga of affirmative action. Although I had never spent time trying to read and understand law review articles I was intrigued by Bell's allegory and decided to purchase the book from which the Chronicle was excerpted. His book *And We Are Not Saved: The Elusive Quest for Racial Justice* (Bell, 1987) changed my sense of what legal scholarship could be. More importantly, I had a rather interesting near "close encounter" with Professor Bell in 1986.

Derrick Bell spent the 1985–1986 academic year as a visiting professor at Stanford Law School. I was teaching at Santa Clara University and living in Palo Alto, California, about a quarter of a mile south of Stanford University. Professor Bell was at Stanford to teach the "Contracts" course—one of the central courses for law students. Because of his innovative teaching strategies and his insistence on merging issues of race with law, a number of White students decided to boycott his class and organized an alternate contracts course where they invited in a series of White law professors. Their protest made the local newspapers. A few weeks later a White woman wrote a scathing op-ed piece insisting that the White students had every right to protest Professor Bell. Interestingly, within a paragraph or two the writer began talking about how Professor Bell did not deserve to teach at Stanford and how an African American female judge totally unrelated to the Stanford Law students boycott did not deserve to be on the county bench.

The move to critique Professor Bell's position (rather than the course), along with the jurist, seemed curious to me so I did some digging. I learned that the woman was an Assistant County District Attorney who had attempted to get a teaching position at Stanford and did not succeed. I also learned that she had tried to get appointed to a judgeship and lost out to the African American woman. Professor Bell was the first African American tenured at Harvard Law and the African American judge was a graduate of Stanford Law and was the only bilingual (English-Spanish) judge in the entire county. Their credentials were impeccable, and for some reason her op-ed angered me enough to write a letter to the editor about the holes in her argument. Imagine my surprise when I saw my critique in print the following week. I was even more surprised to learn that the woman was the wife of one of the Hoover Institution's most prominent Black conservatives. His entire career was based on attempting to destroy affirmative action and his wife was merely mimicking his rhetoric—even when it was indefensible.

By the time I moved to Madison, Wisconsin, some 5–6 years later I had read several of Derrick Bell's writings. I came across his "*Brown vs. Board of Education* and the Interest-Convergence Principle" chapter in the book *Shades of* Brown (Bell, 1980). In it, Bell argued that *Brown* was not an education decision but rather a Cold War strategy designed to encourage non-aligned nations to align with the US and western nations instead of the Eastern-bloc Soviet states. Black children were merely a pawn in the international drama. Later, in a conversation with co-editor William F. Tate, I learned of Kimberlé Crenshaw's work. Professor Crenshaw

XXVI | GLORIA LADSON-BILLINGS

(1988) wrote the path-breaking *Harvard Law Review* piece, "Race, Reform, and Retrenchment: Transformation and Legitimation in Antidiscrimination Law." I later learned that Crenshaw was a former student of Derrick Bell's and one of the founders of a budding radical movement in the law called "Critical Race Theory" (CRT). The more Tate and I talked about this work the more intrigued we became with its possibilities for education. But, before venturing into this area we committed to immersing ourselves in the law literature so we could speak with some authority about the implication of CRT for explaining education inequity.

Our conversations and "makeshift" law education resulted in the production of what has become a seminal piece in CRT and education, "Toward a Critical Race Theory of Education" (Ladson-Billings & Tate, 1995). In the process of reading CRT law articles and learning about the CRT movement we were pleasantly surprised to learn that much of the work and formation of CRT happened right on our campus at the University of Wisconsin-Madison. The first split from Critical Legal Studies (CLS) occurred at Wisconsin. The subsequent summer, CRT workshops happened in Wisconsin. Besides Crenshaw (who was a Hastie Fellow), scholars such as Richard Delgado, Patricia Williams, Linda Greene, all worked at Wisconsin for a time. Indeed, Wisconsin had become a leader in diversifying law school faculty due primarily to the hard work of Professor Jim Jones (Crenshaw, 2011).

The "Toward a Critical Race Theory" article was one of the pieces of scholarship my review committee decided to send to our university divisional committee, and unbeknown to me, Derrick Bell was one of the people they chose as an external reviewer. Had I known Bell was on the list I would have begged the committee to reconsider their decision. I knew my work was not worthy of someone as significant as Professor Bell. On the other hand, I think if I had known that he was on the list I would have assumed that Bell would have been too busy to do the review. However, I was very wrong. Professor Bell may have been busy but he still took the time to write a letter on my behalf.

Because of Wisconsin's incredible open records law, when I received my tenure dossier after the decision I got the opportunity to read all of the letters in my file. I had received letters from some of the most eminent scholars in education research. But the letter that left the most profound impact on me was a rather brief one by Derrick Bell. Professor Bell began his letter by apologizing for the lateness of his letter. He had been traveling and was just getting through his mail. He wrote that he hoped it was not too late to weigh in as an external reviewer. And then, in typical Derrick Bell fashion, he wrote the words I will never forget: "Professor Ladson-Billings reminds me of the words of the 60s soul song, 'She may not be the one you want, but she sho' nuf is the one you need!'" That letter humbled me more than one can imagine.

In 2008 Derrick Bell was named the W. E. B. Du Bois lecturer for the Research Focus on Black Education (RFBE) of the American Education Research

Association. I had the privilege of introducing Dr. Bell at that lecture and the opportunity to personally thank him for everything he had done for our field and for my career, specifically. Professor Bell regaled the audience with an interpretation of a short story Du Bois had written that proved to be a perfect example of a CRT chronicle.

All of the contributors of this volume have their own Derrick Bell memories. When Professor Bell died several of them sent me text messages about their profound sadness and the incredible influence he had over their scholarly inquiry. Within a few days we agreed that as education researchers we needed to do something to mark his powerful impact on our field. Unfortunately, his death occurred past the deadline for submissions to the annual meeting of our professional association, the American Educational Research Association (AERA). However, we made an appeal to the leadership and were granted a Presidential Session to reflect on Derrick Bell's legacy.

The directions for participating in the presidential session were for participants to select a book, article, chronicle, concept, or principle by Professor Bell that has had direct impact on their work. Adrienne Dixson, Jamel Donnor, David Gillborn, Daniel Solórzano, William F. Tate, and I participated in the session and we received such positive and enthusiastic feedback that we thought it made sense to try to create something, perhaps a special issue of a journal, where we could share our work on Professor Bell. However, when we began discussing what to include we realized that we could expand the work to include additional scholars—enough scholars to comprise a volume. Thus, what is contained here is the assemblage of a group of scholars with deep commitment to the path-breaking work of Professor Derrick A. Bell, a scholar, a teacher, an activist, a mentor, and a covenant keeper.

We chose the title "Covenant Keeper" as a way to honor Professor Bell's notion that White supremacy was being maintained by silent covenants, but he saw his primary responsibility as a scholar, a teacher, and a Black man, to keep the covenant he entered into with Black people in their quest for justice and equality. No matter what others decided to do, Derrick Bell would keep his covenant, even if it meant losing a position or leaving a job. His integrity would remain intact.

The volume is organized around three themes: Derrick Bell on teaching and schooling, Derrick Bell and the principles of Critical Race Theory, and Derrick Bell on Theory. In the "Teaching and Schooling" section Vinay Harpalani, a legal scholar, describes what it was like to be Professor Bell's teaching fellow and to witness his pedagogical approach. Daniel Solórzano explores the landmark *McLaurin v. Oklahoma* education case and how Professor Bell's work helped him understand the position (both physical and metaphorical) that the law placed Mr. McLaurin in. In a compilation of counter-stories, Laurence Parker and his students discuss one of Professor Bell's most cited stories "The Space Traders" as a powerful teaching tool that can be interpreted from multiple perspectives for teaching. And, Ladson-Billings uses Bell's "Chronicle of the Sacrificed Black Children" to look at how education—the "great equalizer"—is regularly and systematically denied to Black children both then (during the desegregation era) and now (during this hyper-segregation era).

In the "Principles of Critical Race Theory" section Jamel Donnor uses Bell's "Interest Convergence" Principle as a rubric for understanding the iconic *Brown v Board of Education* Supreme Court decision and explores its ongoing significance in education legislation. UK scholars David Gillborn and Nicola Rollock each explore specific examples of CRT. Gillborn draws from Bell's "Rules of Racial Standing" to demonstrate how profound Professor Bell's CRT insights are and the depth of their impact on novice CRT students. Nicola Rollock draws directly on the notion of counter-story to break the scholarly writing boundaries, much like Bell did throughout his career, by writing a letter to an unborn daughter.

In the third section, "Derrick Bell on Theory," scholars write in ways that describe how expansive Bell's scholarship was and how powerfully malleable CRT has become as it incorporates gender, positionality, and racial memory. Adrienne Dixson delves into Bell's work on feminism and intersectionality. Keffrelyn Brown employs the tools of autoethnography to explore critical racial literacy, and Anthony Brown draws on the work of historical memory to describe how race and memory operate over time and space.

Co-editor William F. Tate provides an "Afterword" that reminds readers of Professor Bell's exceedingly high ethical stance. He never let his detractors bring him down to their levels. He never took his eye off the prize and he never compromised on his love of humanity. Indeed, this is the mark of a covenant keeper.

Together, the authors in this volume made it our goal to ensure that Derrick Bell's contribution to education research and scholarship is made clear. His work paved an important path for scholars invested in justice and equity, especially in the field of education. In this volume we honor the covenant.

NOTE

1. Biographical information on Derrick Bell retrieved from http://professorderrickbell.com/

REFERENCES

Bell, D. (1980). *Brown v. Board of Education* and the interest-convergence dilemma. *Harvard Law Review, 93*, 518–553.

Bell, D. (Ed.). (1980). *Shades of* Brown: *New perspectives on school desegregation.* New York, NY: Teachers College Press.

Bell, D. (1987). *And we are not saved: The elusive quest for racial justice.* New York, NY: Basic Books.

Bell, D. (2008). *Race, racism, and American law* (6th ed.). New York, NY: Aspen (Original work published 1973)

Crenshaw, K. W. (1988). Race, reform, and retrenchment: Transformation and legitimation in anti-discrimination law. *Harvard Law Review, 101*(7), 1331–1387.

Crenshaw, K. W. (2011). Twenty years of Critical Race Theory: Looking back to move forward. *Connecticut Law Review, 43*(5), 1253–1352.

Ladson-Billings, G. (2012). Through a glass darkly: The persistence of race in education research. *Educational Researcher, 41*(4), 115–120.

Ladson-Billings, G., & Tate, W. F. (1995). Toward a critical race theory of education. *Teachers College Record, 97,* 47–68.

Derrick Bell Teaching
AND Schooling

CHAPTER ONE

Continuing TO Sacrifice Black Children

GLORIA LADSON-BILLINGS

"America eats its young"

—FUNKADELIC, BEANE, CLINTON, & WORRELL (1972)

It is incredibly difficult to select just one piece of Derrick Bell's work as having a profound impact on me. I loved the entire volume, *And We Are Not Saved: The Elusive Quest for Racial Justice* (Bell, 1987). It was my introduction to Bell's creative and playful approach to the legal scholarship. It was clear that he wanted his readers to understand the law from the inside out. It was my first exposure to Critical Race Theory and I did not even know it. I just knew I was reading an engaging, critical, insightful look at race in a distinctly different way. His work was provocative and cutting-edge. No sooner had I completed that volume than I started looking for other things written by Derrick Bell and I have spent my scholarly career absorbing as much of his work as I could.

For those who regard Bell as someone who merely "translates" law to the broader public, I would challenge you to peruse a copy of Bell's (2008) classic legal text, *Race, Racism and American Law*, which is in its sixth edition. For more than 35 years this has been the seminal text on race and law in the United States. Those who want to understand Bell as a legal scholar are obligated to read this incredible assemblage of legal cases that detail how race operates in our legal system. Of particular interest to me as an education researcher is Chapter 3, "The Quest for Effective Schools," which includes examinations of the Seattle-Louisville decision, 19th-century and early-20th-century struggles for equal education, the *Brown* decision, the *Swann* decision, single-race schools, charter schools and vouchers, and Black colleges and desegregation.

MY BELL SELECTION

Forced to select just one Bell piece I would have to say my favorite chronicle is in *And We Are Not Saved* and is titled, "The Chronicle of the Sacrificed Black Children." It is a story of school desegregation where the White community mounts vehement opposition to the court's school desegregation order. On the first day of school all of the Black children mysteriously disappear. Naturally, their parents are frantic. They search everywhere but the children are nowhere to be found. On the other side of town the White community is ecstatic. Their precious children will not have to attend school with Black children! However, after days and then weeks of searching for the Black children their absence begins to have implications for the White community.

The school desegregation order required the White school district to do several things in preparation for receiving the Black students. First and foremost they needed to order school buses, which was an extensive capital outlay. And, the buses could not drive themselves. Thus, the school district needed to hire drivers and be prepared to increase their personnel costs. In addition to transporting the Black students to their new schools the district needed to hire new teachers to avoid overcrowded classrooms. The teachers and administrators would need training to cope with their changed environment. The training came as a result of federal school desegregation funds that paid for the cost of professional development specialists.

There were also "out of school" costs that school desegregation incurred. With hundreds of new students coming into the area, the local stores increased their inventory of candy and snacks in anticipation of many more customers. More students meant possibly more athletes, artists, and musicians. This would mean more sports uniforms, more instruments, and more of every possible school supply.

Initially, when the Black children disappeared, the White community celebrated its victory. They did not worry about where the Black children were; they had achieved their immediate goal. The Black parents, on the other hand, were inconsolable. Where were their precious children? They were using every resource at their disposal to try to locate them. Their pain over their loss and unaddressed anger toward the White parents made their lives unbearable. What on earth could they do?

Within the month the White community's joy began to fade. They realized they could not afford those newly purchased school buses, but sending them back was nowhere near as easy as they had imagined. The buses were painted with the district's name, and the moment they drove them off the lot they had depreciated. The district could not recoup the price they paid for them. The district also had to lay off the bus drivers it had hired and release the additional teachers it had hired. It had to return the funds the federal government had sent for professional development. By the time the district comptroller sat down with the books the news was very bad. Without a levy that would substantially increase the local property taxes the district would have to severely cut programs and personnel that had made it a model school district. Once this news was disseminated to the wider community the White parents figured out the one thing that could save them. They had to find those Black children and enroll them in their schools. The chronicle closes with Black and White parents and community members searching everywhere for the missing Black children.

Bell created this chronicle to demonstrate that civil rights law always benefits and serves White interests. This concept is the basis of the "Interest-Convergence" principle (Bell, 1980). Bell contended that the *Brown* decision was a result of an interest convergence, not a civil rights imperative. Despite its reliance on the fanciful, the point of the chronicle is clear—Black people's value is linked to how serviceable they are to Whites. From a Critical Race Theory perspective, civil rights decisions are never about the benevolence or altruism of the nation state but always about how granting civil rights converges with the interest of Whites.

WHAT I DID WITH THE CHRONICLE

Many years after reading the "Chronicle of the Sacrificed Black Children" I was asked to give a keynote presentation at a joint Education School/Law School Conference on Education Equity at the University of North Carolina at Chapel Hill. My presentation was titled, "Can We At Least Have *Plessy*?" and I talked about what schools for Black children might be like if there was a "real" *Plessy* (separate but truly equal) rather than a "fake" *Brown* (a pretense at integrated and equal schooling). Many of the educators at the conference were appalled at the mere suggestion of "separate but equal" as a standard, but many of the legal scholars were willing to explore the concept. They agreed that the reality of schooling for students in US schools was more intense segregation than the 1960s, and maybe the path to equal outcomes was through funding equity rather than desegregation. That address ultimately became a *North Carolina Law Review* article (Ladson-Billings, 2007) that enabled me to craft what I called "The Chronicle of the Sacrificed Black Children, part 2."

In that chronicle I (Ladson-Billings, 2007) painted a scenario of city leaders—politicians and business people—who were plotting the transformation of the city. Under the plan to revitalize the city they offered corporations generous tax breaks while those same corporations offered meager salaries and limited benefits to those who did the most menial jobs—custodians, food service workers, low level clerks, etc. They also schemed to remove the poor from the city by destroying public housing and putting high-priced condominiums in its place. This pushed the poor and low-income residents to first-ring suburbs where they struggled to earn a living because of the limited employment choices. Most had to rely solely on service jobs as clerks and fast food workers. While the city fathers were making these elaborate plans they realized that their one stumbling block was the inadequacy of the public school system. Cleaning up the city, providing jobs for corporate executives, creating upscale housing, along with all the creature comforts of city living would all be for naught if upper middle class people had nowhere to send their children to school.

The public schools had a terrible reputation, so to signal to their new constituency that things were really changing the schools instituted a series of draconian measures that included high-stakes testing, a stripped-down back-to-basic curriculum, and insistence on retaining any students who did not pass the tests. At the same time, the plotters convinced the state legislature to draft laws allowing for the creation of private school vouchers and the expansion of public charters. The overall plan was to financially starve the public schools so they would be ineffective and ultimately collapse. By privatizing the schools, providing tax breaks for the rich, and reducing public services for working class and poor people, the city fathers could create a city environment that served the needs of their biggest donors and most influential citizens. The primary casualties of all this "urban renewal" would be the children. This was the "Chronicle of the Sacrificed Black Children, part 2."

WHAT THE CHRONICLE CAN MEAN IN THE 21ST CENTURY

The relevance of the "Chronicle of the Sacrificed Black Children, part 2" is that unlike Bell's (1987) initial chronicle it looks at the school as a site of the problem rather than as the solution to the problem. This is a common point of disagreement between lawyers and educators. Often lawyers understand the need to get people *to* a service or resource, but educators recognize how deeply problematic schools are. They recognize that for far too many students of color school is a place that either initiates or exacerbates problems. In Bell's chronicle, the task was to give Black students access to higher quality schools in hopes of ensuring they received a higher quality education. In my chronicle I attempted to point out how the power brokers actually wanted to destroy (or, at minimum, cripple) public schools to fit in with their business model and serve the city's moneyed interests.

This chronicle is set in the context of a neoliberal agenda that sees privatization as the highest good. Bell's (1987) chronicle describes a time when people on both sides of the political divide believed that government should provide some basic public services—health, social security, public transportation, education. Now we have transitioned to a period where many believe that everyone (especially the poor) should provide for themselves. This belief relies on a sense that all community social services function better if they are privatized—transportation, housing, health services, and education.

The original chronicle was written at a time when no one could imagine charter schools and voucher programs as alternatives to public education. But today we are in a very different context that demonizes public education—its teachers, its administrators, its curriculum, and its students. Indeed, the enmity aimed at public school extends to the entire education enterprise. For example, we now hear in rightist discourse that teacher education is unnecessary and without intellectual substance. Unfortunately, even those on the left seem to have become seduced by quick pathways to the classroom (see, for example, Strauss, 2013) and participate in the denigration of teachers, parents, and teacher education.

For the first time in recent history we are witnessing what can only be described as a backlash against teachers. In both Wisconsin and Ohio the conservative governors and legislatures offered legislation designed to curtail (or totally eliminate) the power of teachers' unions and create a wedge between public employees (e.g., teachers, state workers, prison guards, etc.) (Greenhouse, 2014). This move sparked massive protests in Wisconsin and a recall effort against the governor. In Ohio, where the state has a referendum process, voters rejected the governor's policy. In Wisconsin, the recall effort failed, and some would argue that the governor became more emboldened to push even more conservative policies. In the subsequent year the Wisconsin governor expanded voucher programs allowing public dollars to flow to private schools despite no evidence that students are performing at higher levels. The first school districts impacted by the voucher programs were those that served large numbers of Black students—Milwaukee, Beloit, Racine, and Kenosha.

In addition to diverting monies from public to private schools, another tactic of sacrificing Black children is through staffing their schools with inadequately prepared young, mostly White, teachers who are unfamiliar with the students and their cultures and communities (Strauss, 2013). While few would doubt the devotion of these young people to pursue teaching as a way to serve the community and make a difference in the lives of the neediest students, many of the programs are exploiting the desperation of the school districts and the animus the community now seems to feel toward veteran teachers. So-called education reformers have appropriated the language of civil rights to make a case for these neoliberal reforms. For example, Michelle Rhee (Lemann, 2013) talked about this course of alternatively certified new teachers as victims of seniority who end up as the last hired and first fired—similar to what was said about Black workers without access to employment.

The idea of turning civil rights legislation on its head so that it ends up disadvantaging those it was originally crafted to serve is not a new idea. Affirmative Action went from serving people of color to mostly serving White women. In the *Parents Involved in Community Schools (PICS) vs. Seattle School District No.* 1 (2007) case, voluntary school desegregation/integration efforts in Seattle, Washington, and Louisville, Kentucky, voluntarily used individualized racial classifications to achieve diversity and/or avoid racial isolation through student assignment. The Supreme Court asserted that seeking diversity and avoiding racial isolation are compelling state interests. However, the Court struck down both school districts' assignment plans, finding that the plans were not sufficiently "narrowly tailored," a legal term that essentially suggests that the means or methods being employed (in this case, a student assignment plan based on individualized racial classifications) are closely and narrowly tied to the ends (the stated goals of achieving diversity and/or avoiding racial isolation). In *PICS*, the Court used *Brown* to assert the rights of the White families. Today, many conservatives will quote Martin Luther King, Jr.'s (1963) words from his iconic "I Have a Dream" speech, particularly the line that reads, "I have a dream that my four little children will one day live in a nation where they will not be judged by the color of their skin but by the content of their character." They use this language to suggest that we cannot look at institutional and systemic forms of racism but must consider each person as an individual rather than a member or representative of a group.

THE CONTINUING SACRIFICE

Today the 24-hour news cycle and ubiquitous social media have made it possible for us to know more about everyday acts of racism than ever before. Names such as Trayvon Martin, Oscar Grant, Eric Garner, Michael Bell, Jr., Jordan Davis, Rekia Boyd, Tamir Rice, Sandra Bland, and nine praying Black people in Charleston, South Carolina's Emanuel AME Church, and countless others are evidence of the low regard the nation seems to have for Black humanity. When communities mobilize to assert "Black Lives Matter", the push back is "All Lives Matter" and "What about Black on Black crime?" But, if Black on Black crime IS the issue where are White people in the fight to combat it, especially if "ALL lives matter"? Statistically, people commit crime within their racial and ethnic group because most violent crimes are intimate crimes, i.e., people assault and/or kill people they know. Our segregated lives mean the person who is likely to perpetuate a crime against you is more likely to look just like you.

Before the explosion of social media we tended to call acts of racism "isolated incidents," but when the Federal Bureau of Investigation (2013) reported almost 6,000 single-bias hate crimes in 2013, with 48.5 percent of them being racially motivated (and another 11.1 percent being ethnically motivated), we know that this represents systemic racism. Something deeply entrenched in the fabric of American life makes racism, as CRT scholars have contended, "normal, not an aberration" (Delgado & Stefancic, 2013, p. 2).

Anti-blackness is fundamental to understanding how the sacrifice of Black children continues to occur. The entire system of racial segregation is based upon a pathological and virulent negative response toward Black people (Lawrence, 1980), and that response is instantiated in our laws, customs, mores, and folkways. Our system is organized around race as a concept, or, as Smedley and Smedley (2012) argued, as a worldview. Writer and cultural critic Ta-Nehisi Coates (Demary, 2015) underscored the way anti-blackness represents a paradigm that links blackness and death together in ways that make them synonymous. No good life outcomes are associated with blackness. Although the documenting of this instantiation throughout American culture is beyond the scope of this chapter, I will focus on how it functions in schooling.

School Segregation

Although we are more than 60 years past the landmark *Brown v. Board of Education* case Black children still find themselves attending segregated schools. In the cities of Cleveland, Washington, DC, Milwaukee, and Detroit the rate of concentrated Black student enrollment ranges from 71 percent to 88 percent. These concentrations of Black students are conjoined with concentrations of poverty (Rothstein, 2013) since the poverty rate for Black children is three times that of their White counterparts.

Post-Secondary Outcomes

Even if Black students persist and complete high school they still experience an 18 percent unemployment rate, twice that of White high school graduates. Even before the 2008 recession, unemployment for Black college graduates was 50 percent higher than for Whites; by 2011, over 8 percent of Black college graduates remained unemployed, compared with 4.5 percent for Whites (Mishel, Bivens, Gould, & Shierholz, 2012).

School Suspensions

According to a recent report of the Center for the Study of Race & Equity in Education (Smith & Harper, 2015), 1.2 million Black students were suspended from K–12 public schools in a single academic year, and the overwhelming proportion

(55 percent) occurred in 13 Southern states. Increasingly, we are seeing a strong correlation between school suspensions and later incarceration. The U.S. Office of Civil Rights (2014) reported that although Black students were 18 percent of preschool enrollment they were 48 percent of out-of-school suspensions.

School Expulsions

Smith and Harper (2015) also reported that Black students experience high rates of school expulsions. Again, the Office of Civil Rights (2014) indicated that Black students are suspended and expelled at three times the rate of White students. The increased implementation of zero-tolerance policies has resulted in Black students experiencing over-surveillance and over-policing in schools similar to that they and Black adults experience in their neighborhoods from the police.

Privatization of Public Schools

This piece of the sacrifice is both complicated and complex. Black families have suffered from substandard education for centuries. Their initial fight was to gain access to the quality education they believed existed in schools serving White children. After decades of fighting to desegregate public schools and subsequent decades fighting the rollback of school desegregation they find themselves in more segregated schooling—what scholars call hyper-segregated schools (Ladson-Billings, 2004). All of the evidence suggests that Black and Brown children are more likely to attend schools with teachers who are unqualified or under-qualified. They are more likely to be taught by mathematics and science teachers who are unqualified.

The case of Pinellas County, Florida, is instructive (Fitzpatrick, Gartner, & LaForgia, 2015). In a deliberate act of re-segregation, the Pinellas County School Board returned to what is now called "neighborhood schools," which is a euphemism for re-segregation. This decision created five Black schools that are failing in every category measured by the state. Teacher turnover in these schools is outrageous, with some students having a dozen teachers in 1 year. In 2014 more than half of the teachers in these five schools asked to transfer out. At least three teachers walked off the job without notice (Fitzpatrick et al., 2015). However, instead of focusing on the devastating impact this re-segregation has had on Black children in Pinellas, one school board member, Peggy O'Shea, who voted for the re-segregation in 2007, was quoted as saying, "This is a nationwide thing, not just us. You hear school districts everywhere talking about this. It's an issue that's everywhere, unfortunately. … We only talk about it in black schools, but we re-segregated white schools as well" (Fitzpatrick et al., 2015).

The "this" O'Shea referenced is poverty, which has become the default answer to every question concerning why Black children are struggling in schools. One of the most popular books in urban schools is *A Framework for Understanding Poverty* (Payne, 1996), which equates Black culture with the social condition of poverty. Teachers are told that the problem with the students is they lack "middle class" values and must be taught to defer gratification, comply with rules and authority, develop verbal skills to solve conflict, and sit down and eat dinner together, along with a whole host of socially acceptable behaviors (Kunjufu, 2006). What Payne (1996) did not consider or explain is the fact that middle class Black children also experience similar educational disparities as their poor and low-income counterparts (Reardon, Fox, & Townsend, 2015; Wells et al., 2014; White, 2015).

Given the dismal record of Black students in public schools it is no surprise that Black families seek other options. For many years middle-class-to-affluent Black families sought to educate their children in private and parochial schools (see, for example, Irvine & Foster, 1996). However, neo-liberal school reforms have opened up the modern phenomenon of charter schools and private vouchers as an option to traditional public schooling.

The dilemma for those who are fighting for quality education is making sense of the agony individual parents are experiencing while advocating for wholesale improvement and maintenance of a public good—public education. This means we may find ourselves sympathetic to the cries of a specific family that has the opportunity to send its children to a much better school versus watching the siphoning of public resources and leaving millions of other Black children behind.

It is much easier to challenge the case of voucher schools that transfer money from public to private schools. Currently, 12 states and the District of Columbia offer voucher programs to students. Some are specific to students within income limits and some are limited to students with documented special needs (see National Conference of State Legislatures website: http://www.ncsl.org/research/education/voucher-law-comparison.aspx).

The question here is why the state does not re-invest dollars into the public schools to ensure the upgrading of services for all students. The charter school option is more complex. Since charter schools are public schools the public monies remain under the purview of a public institution and governing body. The original concept of the charter school as promoted by United Federation of Teachers president Albert Shanker was to create a public entity that would enable teachers to be free from the onerous rules and regulations of the state so that they might use their pedagogical knowledge and expertise to experiment with new ideas about curriculum, teaching, learning, and administration. The charter school was not to be positioned as a way to destroy the traditional public system. Rather, charter schools were to serve as incubators for new ideas to improve the traditional public schools. Unfortunately, those who were more interested in the destruction of public schools have used the charter school laws to do just that.

New Orleans, Louisiana, has become the "poster-child" for charter schools. Because of the disastrous floodwaters from Hurricane Katrina that engulfed the city of New Orleans (particularly the poorer sections where Black people lived), public schooling in the city was literally washed away. Within a few months after the storm, Louisiana Governor Kathleen Blanco called a special session of the Louisiana legislature. Here they passed Act 35, which changed the definition of a "failing" school and allowed the state-run Recovery School District to assume control of 107 of 128 public schools in Orleans Parish, enabling charter expansion on a scale never before attempted in Louisiana or elsewhere (Buras, 2014). Later in the year officials announced that all New Orleans Public School employees would be fired. So, in addition to losing their homes, these public servants were now without a livelihood. This decision decimated New Orleans' Black middle class.

Today, for all practical purposes, New Orleans is the nation's first all-charter school district (there are a few schools outside of the Recovery School District considered to be traditional public schools). This means that there are no neighborhood schools and schools must compete for students. In most instances the charter schools are administered by Educational Management Organizations (EMOs) such as Knowledge Is Power Program (KIPP), Choice Foundation, Capital One-New Beginnings, First Line Schools and ReNew Schools. These schools have the opportunity to pick the students they want to enroll and reject those who do not conform to the behavior standards and are likely to lower their test scores. And, there are stories from students and family members that describe draconian approaches to classroom management. For example, in some schools students were told they were not automatically entitled to a desk and had to sit on the floor for days until they "earned" the privilege of sitting at a desk. In other schools students were required to walk on a black line painted on the floor whenever they passed in the hall. In addition to the line the students were required to walk with their hands folded in front of them. The only other place that polices the human body like this is a prison, and it is not surprising that these prison-like approaches are used in schools serving predominately Black students.

Teachers in New Orleans' new schools tend to be young, White, and ill-prepared for urban teaching. Many come from innovative alternative teacher certification programs, and while no one can fault their energy and enthusiasm to try to make a difference in children's lives, the children they serve can ill afford to be subjected to experimentation and inexperience. Historically, New Orleans was a city where African Americans were the majority. Most of the teachers were Black. Today, the demographics are shifting and new residents to the city are White, young, and forcing the cost of living to rapidly rise. Similar to the removal of Black teachers as a cost of school desegregation in 1960s New Orleans, Black teachers have been summarily dismissed without a second thought (Ladson-Billings, 2004).

Neo-liberal reformers tout New Orleans as the template for urban school reform. While there are some signs of improved test performance one must remember that New Orleans really had no way to go but up. It was one of the worst performing school districts in one of the worst performing states. Its so-called improvement is relative. Test scores are going up, but compared to national averages New Orleans' students continue to lag far behind. Most of the class of 2014 graduating from the 100-percent-charter New Orleans Recovery School District scored so low on the national ACT test that they did not meet the minimum requirements for Louisiana's colleges. The district's test scores were extremely low prior to Hurricane Katrina and the charter school conversion, but despite Governor Jindal's claims of "remarkable gains," there has been only a 2-point improvement in New Orleans' Recovery School District ACT scores since 2005. The class average is now 16.4, one of the lowest in Louisiana (Ollstein, 2015).

New Orleans is being touted as the model all urban school districts should follow, and cities such as Chicago, Detroit, Memphis, and Philadelphia seem to be doing just that. Frustrated by poor-performing schools, parents are now being forced to try to find other options, which lack transparency in governance and administration and seem openly hostile to experienced Black teachers. In an attempt to seek quality education, parents find themselves sacrificing their children once again.

CODA

The history of education of African Americans in our public schools is one fraught with disappointments—from lack of access to lack of quality. From his early days as an attorney for the NAACP Legal Defense and Education Fund Derrick Bell understood that education, especially public education, was the vehicle that Black people would need to move toward equity and justice. By supervising over 300 school desegregation cases Bell said he learned "a lot about evasiveness, and how racists could use a system to forestall equality" ("Derrick Bell," n.d.).

The education of Black children almost certainly will continue to require sacrifice. Parents, family, and community members will need to continue to fight for quality teachers, enhanced curriculum, and increased access to honors and gifted programs. Black families must revisit the history of Black education that tells how valiantly their ancestors fought for decent education. The stories of Linda Brown (Topeka, Kansas), the Little Rock Nine (in Arkansas), Ruby Bridges (New Orleans), Boston School desegregation, the Ocean-Hill/Brownsville school strike (New York), the Philadelphia (Pennsylvania) Black History walkout, *Larry P. v*

Riles (CA), and the scores of individual school district fights to get Black students fair, equitable, and quality education.

For so many years Black people have fought primarily for access. They have marched, protested, and litigated to get into the school. Today, the fight is more complex. Equal access is not the same as equal outcomes, and true equality can only come when Black children can expect to post academic gains equal to or better than those of White children. Black students will need to graduate and experience much lower special education assignments, suspension, and expulsion rates for us to be able to acknowledge that we are no longer sacrificing Black children. When the early fights for educational equity began, Black families, communities, and their advocates saw the existing schools as separate and unequal. The task was to get Black children into the better-resourced schools that Whites across town attended. When the litigants were finally able to access those schools, Whites began leaving the city schools and either attending private schools or moving to suburban school districts. Today, as Black children find themselves in increasingly segregated urban schools, their families also find that cities and municipalities are retreating from providing any kind of public schooling at all.

Cities such as Chicago, Philadelphia, and Detroit are closing schools in neighborhoods serving Black students. In some instances the closed schools are being sold at minimal cost to Educational Management Organizations (EMOs) where young, inexperienced people are recruited to be teachers. Once again, Black children are subject to experimentation when their futures are placed in jeopardy. Experienced Black teachers are discouraged from remaining in urban schools and most Black children are being taught by teachers whose race, ethnicity, language, and backgrounds are radically different from their own.

The challenge of the 21st century is how to educate Black students not only in basic skills and approved school curricula but also in what Paulo Freire (2014) called how to read the word and the world. Black people in the United States are at a pivotal point in their American sojourn. There are increasing concerns of over-policing and mortal threat to unarmed citizens in Black communities. And these concerns have spawned a new activism. The "Black Lives Matter" movement reflects a broad coalition of youth from all races and ethnicities. These coalitions are filled with new energy and are making greater demands that our government and elected officials be more responsive to the needs of Black and other communities of color. This generation seems determined to halt the sacrifice of Black children.

REFERENCES

Beane, H., Clinton, G., & Worrell, B. (1972). America eats its young [Recorded by Funkadelic]. On *America eats its young* [Record]. Detroit, MI: Westbound Records.

Bell, D. (Ed.). (1980). *Brown* and the Interest Convergence dilemma. In D. Bell (Ed.), *Shades of* Brown: *New perspectives on school desegregation* (pp. 90–106). New York, NY: Teachers College Press.

Bell, D. (1987). *And we are not saved: The elusive quest for racial justice.* New York, NY: Basic Books.

Bell, D. (2008). *Race, racism and American law* (6th ed.). New York, NY: Aspen.

Buras, K. (2014, December 26). Charter schools flood New Orleans. *The Progressive.* Retrieved from http://www.progressive.org/news/2014/12/187949/charter-schools-flood-new-orleans

Delgado, R., & Stefancic, J. (Eds.). (2013). *Critical Race Theory: The cutting edge* (3rd ed.). Philadelphia, PA: Temple University Press.

Demary, M. (2015, July 14). A grand theory of anti-blackness: The unflinching and profound terror in Ta-Nehisi Coates's "Between The World and Me." *Salon.* Retrieved from http://www.salon.com/2015/07/14/a_grand_theory_of_anti_blackness_the_unflinching_and_profound_terror_in_ta_nehisi_coates_between_the_world_and_me/

Derrick Bell. (n.d.). In *Wikipedia.* Retrieved August 22, 2015, from https://en.wikipedia.org/wiki/Derrick_Bell

Federal Bureau of Investigation. (2013). *Hate crime statistics, 2013.* Washington, DC: Author.

Fitzpatrick, C., Gartner, L., & LaForgia, M. (2015, August 14). Failure factories. *Tampa Bay Times.* Retrieved from http://www.tampabay.com/projects/2015/investigations/pinellas-failure-factories/5-schools-segregation/

Freire, P. (2014). *Pedagogy of the oppressed: 30th anniversary edition* (M. Bergman Ramos, Trans.). New York, NY: Bloomsbury Academic.

Greenhouse, S. (2014, February 22). Wisconsin's legacy for unions. *The New York Times*, Business 1.

Irvine, J. J., & Foster, M. (Eds.). (1996). *Growing up African American in Catholic schools.* New York, NY: Teachers College Press.

King, M. L., Jr. (1963, August 28). I have a dream [speech]. Retrieved from http://www.american-rhetoric.com/speeches/mlkihaveadream.htm

Kunjufu, J. (2006). *An African centered response to Ruby Payne's poverty theory.* Chicago, IL: African American Images.

Ladson-Billings, G. (2004, October). Landing on the wrong note: The price we paid for *Brown*. *Educational Researcher, 33*, 3–13.

Ladson-Billings, G. (2007). Can we at least have *Plessy*? The struggle for quality education. *North Carolina Law Review, 85*(5), 1279–1292.

Lawrence, C. (1980). One more river to cross—Recognizing the real injury in *Brown*: A prerequisite to shaping new remedies. In D. Bell (Ed.), *Shades of Brown: New perspectives on school desegregation* (pp. 48–68). New York, NY: Teachers College Press.

Lemann, N. (2013, May 20). How Michelle Rhee mislead education reform. *The New Republic.* Retrieved from http://www.newrepublic.com/article/113096/how-michelle-rhee-misled-education-reform

Mishel, L., Bivens, J., Gould, E., & Shierholz, H. (2012). *The state of working America* (12th ed.). Ithaca, NY: Cornell University Press.

Ollstein, A. (2015). New Orleans' all-charter school system is struggling, but Bobby Jindal wants it to be a model. *Think Progress.* Retrieved from http://thinkprogress.org/education/2015/02/09/3620799/nola-bobby-jindal-school-plan/

Parents Involved in Community Schools v. Seattle School District No. 1, 551 U.S. 701 (2007).

Payne, R. (1996). *A framework for understanding poverty* (3rd ed.). Highlands, TX: aha! Process.

Reardon, S., Fox, L., & Townsend, J. (2015). Neighborhood income composition by household race and income 1990–2009. *Annals of the American Academy of Political and Social Sciences, 660*, 78–97.

Rothstein, R. (2013, August). *For public schools, segregation then, segregation since: Education and the unfinished march.* Washington, DC: Economic Policy Institute.

School voucher laws: State-by-state comparison. (n.d.). Retrieved from the National Conference of State website: http://www.ncsl.org/research/education/voucher-law-comparison.aspx

Smedley, A., & Smedley, E. (2012). *Race in North America: The origin and evolution of a worldview.* Boulder, CO: Westview Press.

Smith, E. J., & Harper, S. R. (2015). *Disproportionate impact of K–12 school suspensions and expulsions on Black students.* Philadelphia, PA: Center for the Study of Race & Equity in Education.

Strauss, V. (2013, October 16). The debt deal's gift to Teach for America (yes, TFA). *The Washington Post.* Retrieved from http://www.washingtonpost.com/blogs/answer-sheet/wp/2013/10/16/the-debt-deals-gift-to-teach-for-america-yes-tfa/

U.S. Department of Education, Office for Civil Rights. (2014). *Civil rights data collection, 2011–12.* Washington, DC: Author.

Wells, A. S., Ready, D., Fox, L., Warner, M., Roda, A., Spence, T., … Wright, A. (2014). *Divided we fall: The story of separate and unequal suburban schools 60 years after* Brown v. Board of Education. New York, NY: The Center for Understanding Race & Education, Teachers College, Columbia University.

White, G. (2015, January 19). How Black middle-class kids become poor adults. *The Atlantic.* Retrieved from http://www.theatlantic.com/business/archive/2015/01/how-black-middle-class-kids-become-black-lower-class-adults/384613/

CHAPTER TWO

"Gifted With a Second-Sight"

Professor Derrick Bell the Teacher

VINAY HARPALANI

INTRODUCTION: A TEACHER FIRST AND FOREMOST

As one of the founding figures in Critical Race Theory (CRT), the late Professor Derrick Albert Bell, Jr. (1930–2011) influenced generations of scholars and activists. He was well known for his pioneering scholarship and for principled protests against the exclusion of women of color from the legal academy (Delgado & Stefancic, 2005). His writings had a salient impact not only in his chosen field of law but also in a variety of other disciplines. Scholars in the field of education have particularly embraced CRT in the last 20 years (Lynn & Dixson, 2013; Parker, Deyhle, & Villenas, 1999; Tate, 1997) ever since Professors Gloria Ladson-Billings and William F. Tate (1995) introduced CRT to an audience of education scholars. Two decades later, and five years after his passing, it is particularly fitting now to examine the contributions of Professor Bell[1] to education.

While Professor Bell is widely cited and celebrated for his academic and activist work, less has been written about his own classroom teaching style and philosophy—his direct interest in education and especially in pedagogy. Professor Bell himself did author several articles about legal education, including general commentary and critiques (Bell, 1980b, 1982; Bell & Edmonds, 1993) and more specific details about his classes and the teaching methods he employed (Bell, 1997b, 1998). His teaching philosophy was rooted in Paulo Freire's (1968/1993) critical pedagogy, and he (Bell, 1998) described it as a "participatory approach to teaching" that strived for the "Freire ideal … that students become teachers and teachers become learners." A few other scholars also discussed Professor Bell's classroom teaching (Garden, 2013; Harpalani, 2013; Radice, 2012) and linked it to his scholarship (Lynn, Jennings, & Hughes, 2012). All of these works show how Professor Bell brought humanity into the classroom, aiming to create a dynamic, innovative, and supportive learning atmosphere in the competitive environment of law school (Bell, 1998; Harpalani, 2011, 2013; Radice, 2012).

Nevertheless, there is more to be said about Professor Derrick Bell the teacher. As one who knew Professor Bell personally and worked with him closely to develop and teach his constitutional law classes (Harpalani, 2013), I can confidently say that he thought of himself as a *teacher* first and foremost—even more so than as a scholar or an activist (Harpalani, 2011). Moreover, although Professor Bell is best known as a critical race scholar and activist, his "radical humanist" pedagogy transcended ideology and perspective (Harpalani, 2013). At its core, his pedagogy aimed to teach students to grapple with the tensions and challenges inherent not only in constitutional law but also in life more generally. Ultimately, Professor Bell wanted his students to look within themselves, find the courage to confront the challenges they faced (Bell, 1994), and determine for themselves how to live an ethical and ambitious life (Bell, 2002).

In this chapter, I aim to illustrate how Professor Bell went about teaching these lessons. In many ways, I view Professor Derrick Bell as the post-Civil-Rights era heir to the great African American scholar and activist, W. E. B. Du Bois (1868–1963) (Hackney, 1998; Harpalani, 2015). Professor Bell's scholarship problematized civil rights and integration (Bell, 1976, 1980b, 1987, 1992) in the same manner that W. E. B. Du Bois (1903/2006) had critiqued Booker T. Washington's (1901/1965) accommodation of White political rule. Both W. E. B. Du Bois (1935) and Professor Bell (1976, 2004) were critical of overemphasis on integration and had battles with the NAACP over this issue: in fact, Professor Bell frequently cited Du Bois in support of his own views (e.g., Bell, 1977). Beyond these scholarly and activist parallels, however, I also see Professor Bell's teaching itself as a manifestation of "double-consciousness" (Du Bois, 1903/2006, p. 9)—the tension between "warring ideals" and "unreconciled strivings" that characterizes the most important questions in constitutional law, and in life more generally. As Du Bois (1903/2006) eloquently stated:

> After the Egyptian and Indian, the Greek and Roman, the Teuton and Mongolian, the Negro is a sort of seventh son, born with a veil, and *gifted with second-sight* in this American world—a world which yields him no true self-consciousness, but only lets him see himself through the revelation of the other world. It is a peculiar sensation, this *double-consciousness*, this sense of always looking at one's self through the eyes of others, of measuring one's soul by the tape of a world that looks on in amused contempt and pity. One ever feels his two-ness—an American, a Negro; two souls, two thoughts, two unreconciled strivings; two warring ideals in one dark body, whose dogged strength alone keeps it from being torn asunder. (pp. 8–9)

Like many African American intellectuals, Professor Bell grappled with this tension in his scholarship (Bell, 1976) and throughout his life (Bell, 1994, 2002). He also believed that making students grapple with double-consciousness—by employing the participatory approach—led to the best possible education for law and life. Professor Derrick Bell was "gifted with a second-sight" when it came to teaching—and perhaps even more importantly, he gifted his students with that same "second-sight" as he strove to teach students how to address the real-world problems posed by constitutional law and by life more generally.

By combining Du Bois's notion of double-consciousness and Professor Bell's own innovative method of storytelling (e.g., Bell, 1987, 1992), I aim to tell the story of Derrick Bell the teacher—in my own words and those of his students. My analysis shows the evolution in Professor Bell's thought. Most of his own works on his teaching were published in the 1980s and 1990s (Bell, 1980b, 1982, 1998; Bell & Edmonds, 1993), but until the end, Professor Bell continued to experiment with different teaching methods and to develop his own life philosophies, and part of this process included sharing his developing views with students. Professor Bell himself quoted Paulo Freire to underscore that "[k]nowledge emerges only through invention and re-invention, through the restless, impatient, continuing, hopeful inquiry [men and women] pursue in the world, with the world, and with each other" (Bell & Edmonds, 1993, p. 2025; Freire, 1968/1993, p. 53). I show here in part how these ideas applied to Professor Bell himself.

Additionally, to illustrate my various points, I use direct quotes and examples (with permission) from students I supervised in Professor Bell's classes—many of whom I keep in touch with. These anecdotes convey the richness of the interactions and relationships that Professor Bell had with his students, which were central to his radical humanist pedagogy (Harpalani, 2012, 2013). Although the analysis herein is mine, it is supported not just by my observations of Professor Bell, but also through the voices of Professor Bell's constitutional law students.[2] In a sense, these narratives parallel the many stories that Professor Bell himself often told in his scholarship (e.g., Bell, 1987, 1992).

As such, this chapter is organized as a series of short narratives, reflecting my stories of Professor Bell and of the lessons he taught in his class. First, I briefly describe my relationship with Professor Bell, as a New York University (NYU) law student and then as the 10th and final Derrick Bell Fellow—my first job out of law school. I cover my role in planning and co-teaching his courses, which led to all of my insights into his pedagogy (Harpalani, 2011, 2012, 2013). Next, I discuss Professor Bell's courses in constitutional law, the subject he taught for the last two decades of his career (with the exception of a Critical Race Theory seminar in the spring of 2011—the very last course he was able to teach in full). After briefly covering the structure of the courses and the participatory method, I discuss four aspects of Professor Bell's pedagogy and illustrate these through anecdotes about his teaching: (1) His approach to constitutional law ("The Constitution is like roach power"); (2) His view on Critical Race Theory and critical perspectives more generally ("It just means telling the truth …"); (3) His incorporation of life lessons into the classroom ("Don't let the perfect be the enemy of the good"); and (4) His efforts to "humanize the law school experience." I conclude with a poignant, personal story about Professor Bell's last days—one that illustrates his dedication to teaching and to his students until the very end.

MY FIRST JOB OUT OF LAW SCHOOL

Fig 1: Vinay Harpalani, 2009–10 Derrick Bell Fellow, with Professor Derrick Bell, at New York University School of Law, on January 11, 2010.

My first job out of law school was the best one I could have possibly imagined. I got to share an office with my professional role model: the person whose career I most strived to emulate. Each year, Professor Derrick Bell hired one recent graduate as the "Derrick Bell Fellow"—to assist him in organizing, teaching, and administering his classes. Professor Bell had come to NYU Law in 1991, after leaving Harvard Law in protest of its failure to hire women of color faculty. He retained a position continuously as a visiting professor at NYU Law until his passing in 2011, having negotiated with the law school to hire a Bell Fellow beginning in the late 1990s. The fellowship lasted 1 year, and Professor Bell hired 10 such fellows over the years, primarily to help teach his two courses: the Current Constitutional

Issues seminar in the fall semester and large Constitutional Law course in the spring.

I began my tenure as the 10th and final Derrick Bell Fellow in August 2009, shortly after I had graduated from NYU Law School and completed the New York Bar Exam. Previously, I had taken Professor Bell's Current Constitutional Issues seminar in fall 2008, and I had served as a teaching assistant for his large Constitutional Law course in spring 2009—that is how we got to know each other.

My background is also relevant here. Before law school, I earned my PhD in Education from the University of Pennsylvania, focusing on racial identity and academic achievement. I had taught three undergraduate courses at Penn before enrolling at NYU Law. During my time in graduate school, I had read Professor Bell's groundbreaking works in Critical Race Theory (Bell, 1980a, 1987, 1992), and they had inspired me to try and follow in his footsteps, as best I could (Harpalani, 2009). I came to law school because I wanted to be a law professor who focused on race and law. I was in my early 30s when I started, and many of my law school classmates saw me as a "quasi-professor" even in my first year. I was explicit about my career goals and much less intimidated by law school than most: I knew what I wanted out of the experience, and having been in academia, I had a good sense of how to pursue it. After my first year, I made the *NYU Law Review*, and I was also very active in student-of-color organizations as a law student, serving on the boards of both the Black Allied Law Students Association (BALSA) and the South Asian Law Students Association (SALSA) (Harpalani, 2009). Many of my classmates—and particularly my fellow students of color—looked up to me as an academic mentor. Needless to say, this was, and continues to be, a role that I value and cherish.

Professor Bell was aware of all this, and given my teaching experience and relative maturity, he had a lot of confidence in me. He entrusted me with a large amount of responsibility in designing and administering his courses. He also told Richard Revesz, the then Dean of NYU Law School, that if he ever became ill, there was no doubt that I could teach the classes by myself—something that was very important to Professor Bell. He allowed me to make independent decisions about course content and structure (D. A. Bell, personal communication, February 5, 2010), so long as I followed the basic model he had developed for years. Of course, I always informed him of my decisions, and he carried full veto power, but rarely did he exercise it. Instead, he left most of the details to me, so that he could focus on making students grapple with the tensions posed by constitutional law and by larger life questions in the real world.

He did this through the student-centered, participatory approach that constituted the format of all of his courses (Garden, 2013; Harpalani, 2013; Lynn, Jennings, & Hughes, 2013; Radice, 2012). Professor Bell believed, in Freire's words, that "[e]ducation must begin with the solution of the teacher-student contradiction, by reconciling the poles of the contradiction so that both are simultaneously teachers *and* students" (Bell & Edmonds, 1993, p. 2025; Freire, 1968/1993, p. 53). He (Bell, 1998) believed that "students do vastly more work, and learn more from, an engaged teaching methodology, one which requires that they perform very much like the lawyers they will soon become" (p. 1044).

As such, Professor Bell's courses did not involve lecturing, or the cold-calling and Socratic questioning usually associated with law school classes (Bridges, 1973). He would occasionally ask students their opinions on matters of controversy but not in a manner where the student could be wrong or feel embarrassed. But most of the time, his classes were not instructor-centered, nor did they have exams. Rather, in both the seminar and the larger course, students argued hypothetical cases designed by Professor Bell and me, or real cases pending before the federal courts.

These courses occurred in the context of the "Court of Bell"—which was his classroom. Each week, two student advocates argued a case in moot court format, after preparing appellate briefs that were distributed to the entire class several days earlier. Prior to the oral argument, a third student, acting as "Chief Justice," prepared a bench memo for the class that was distributed with the students' appellate briefs, presented the basic issues prior to the argument, and then presided over questioning during the argument itself. These three students constituted a team for the given case and worked together on it. The rest of the students in the class acted as "Associate Justices"—they were appellate judges whose role was to ask questions during the oral argument. The format simulated a real appellate argument, although of course the panel of questioners was not three appellate judges or even nine, but, rather, close to 90 (including students, teaching assistants, Professor Bell, and me—all of whom could ask questions during argument). At the end of the argument, the Associate Justices voted on the case.

After the class, the student Associate Justices wrote short op-ed papers (500–1000 words, although some might be longer) on the given case and posted these online, and student advocates and the Chief Justice would review and respond to the op-eds and lead a discussion of them for the first half of the next class. Prior to the next class, some students also responded back-and-forth online to each other's op-eds, setting the tone for the class discussion. Students were also allowed to write a certain number of op-eds—dubbed "global op-eds"—on topics of their choice, including social and political issues not discussed in class. Discussion of op-eds took place during the first half of each class; after break, the second half of class was devoted to the subsequent oral argument. Also, the final class of each semester was a celebration and talent show, where students would organize and perform skits, songs, poetry, and other performances that reflected constitutional law themes or parodied aspects of the course.

Fig 2: Program for the end-of-the-year celebration and talent show in Professor Derrick Bell's spring 2009 Constitutional Law course.

Thus, students largely ran the class sessions, with supervision from Professor Bell, me, and our student teaching assistants (TAs) who had taken one of Professor Bell's courses in the prior year. For the seminar class of about 30 students we had six teaching assistants to help supervise and evaluate the class activities, while for the large course of about 75 students we had 15 teaching assistants to do the same. TAs were assigned two or three teams to work with during the course of the semester and aided in all aspects of preparation for the oral arguments and subsequent discussions.

My job was to do background research for the hypothetical cases and to help write them; to coordinate the logistics of all of the oral arguments; to make sure students understood what was required of them and that they completed tasks on time; to assist students in preparing for the oral arguments, and, as necessary, in writing their briefs and op-eds; to supervise TAs in working with the student teams; and to assist the TAs and Professor Bell in grading.

Grading itself was a cumbersome and enlightening process. Professor Bell did not merely give letter grades to students. He insisted that each student receive a "grade memo" of five or more pages that evaluated every aspect of course performance: written briefs/bench memos, op-eds and responses, oral argument/Chief Justice presentation, and also level of participation as a questioning Associate Justice. Students appreciated receiving this amount of personal attention. For example, Tania Schrag, NYU Law '11, wrote to us after the semester:

> Thank you so much for your incredible grade memo. It's been a long time (if ever) that I've felt so recognized and appreciated for who I am, my writing, my speaking. ... I almost started crying reading the memo, as it was so touching. (T. Schrag, personal communication, June 15, 2010)

In the classroom itself, Professor Bell would largely stay in the background and defer to students. At the beginning of class, he would offer a few comments and questions about the cases or about world affairs or life more generally. He would take part in the discussion of op-eds (which was led by the students who had argued the given case), and he would often also ask one or two questions during the oral arguments—particularly towards the end after students had the opportunity. Professor Bell typically limited himself to one lecture per semester. After he and the Bell Fellow did a mock oral argument in the first class and then went over the course requirements and cases for the semester, he would lecture in the second or third class of the semester. He designed this one lecture to provocatively elicit student participation and invoke the "double-consciousness" that characterized his "critical" constitutional pedagogy (Harpalani, 2013).

"THE CONSTITUTION IS LIKE ROACH POWDER"

During his one lecture in the large constitutional law class, Professor Bell argued, essentially, that the U.S. Constitution is a useless document. As was often the case, he invited students, TAs, and the Bell Fellow to challenge him. When I was a TA in spring 2009, Professor Bell asked me to come to the front of the class and challenge him as he gave the lecture. He talked for 15 minutes about how the Constitution is unnecessary because the Justices vote their personal preferences in most important cases (Harpalani, 2013, p. xxiv). He delved into his theory of "interest-convergence" (Bell, 1980a), which he had used to explain the Supreme Court's 1954 decision in *Brown v. Board of Education* (1954) in terms of promoting U.S. foreign policy interests in Africa and Asia—where the portrayal of domestic segregation in the media embarrassed the U.S. government (Dudziak, 2000).

I then interrupted him and asked:

Professor, I can see what you are saying about interest convergence—it is like political process, and that is what Footnote 4 of *U.S. v. Carolene Products* (1938) recognized. But doesn't the Constitution provide a nice structure for interest convergence? Don't federalism, separation of powers, etc., allow different political interests to become aligned, such that minority group interests can be served? And in that sense, isn't the Constitution a useful document? (Harpalani, 2013, p. xxiv)

Professor Bell stopped and looked at me for a second, almost as a grandparent would look at a small child who just said something silly. He then responded:

When I was a kid, we had cockroaches in the house, but we didn't have roach powder. So we killed the roaches by stomping on them. What the Justices do is stomp on the roaches, and then spray them with roach powder. The Constitution is like the roach powder. (Harpalani, 2013, p. xxv)

Students in the class laughed aloud in response. But they also grasped the "roach powder" analogy and wrote global op-eds about the lecture—with their own critical reactions. For example, Monique Robinson, NYU Law '10, wrote:

Justices, as humans ... use their feet to step on the roaches ... [and] ... it seems that feet make more of impact than roach powder when it comes to killing a roach. So, why not just use feet? Well, because we do have a constitution and a constitution represents democracy. There can only be legitimacy in our process of judicial review and in our democracy if we use the roach powder. (M. V. Robinson, personal communication, March 30, 2012; Harpalani, 2013, p. xxv)

Monique's op-ed expresses precisely the lesson that Professor Bell intended to convey with his provocative lecture. Professor Bell (1998) believed that "[t]he challenge in teaching Constitutional Law is to teach the doctrine while puncturing the myths ... [which] is not an easy task" (p. 1040). In spite of his "roach powder" analogy and well-known legal realist critiques of constitutional doctrine (e.g., Bell, 1980a, 1987), Professor Bell's Spring 2010 Constitutional Law syllabus stated that "many if not most op-ed postings [which were the primary basis for students' grades] should reflect ... awareness and understanding of applicable legal precedent" (D. A. Bell, personal communication, January 7, 2010; Harpalani, 2013, p. xxv). His prior syllabi included similar guidelines, and Professor Bell described his constitutional law courses as "almost entirely doctrinal, and very practitioner-oriented" (Bell & Edmonds, 1993, p. 2037). He wanted students to learn constitutional doctrine thoroughly and to apply it. But he also wanted them to critique it and to understand how personal ideologies, formed in the context of individual experiences and real world social and political pressures, affected application of constitutional doctrine.

Such "double-consciousness" was a hallmark of Professor Bell's "critical" constitutional pedagogy (Harpalani, 2013), and of his thought, more generally

(Hackney, 1998; Harpalani, 2015). He wanted students to explore and consider all sides of an issue, including perspectives that he disagreed with. And he wanted students to grapple with contradictory views and come to the best resolution they could, knowing that there was no perfect solution. Such is usually the case for the most significant constitutional questions. Moreover, this critical engagement extended far beyond the "roach powder" analogy and even beyond constitutional law. Professor Bell wanted to teach broader life lessons through his classes.

"IT JUST MEANS TELLING THE TRUTH"

Professor Bell used to half-jokingly say about Critical Race Theory (of which he was a founding figure): "I don't know what that is. To me, it just means telling the *truth*, even in the face of criticism" (Harpalani, 2013, p. xxv). But while he had strong and pointed views on many issues, Professor Bell also recognized that being "critical" meant analyzing all perspectives—particularly those that were marginalized in the mainstream discourse. Although he did share his personal views in class, Professor Bell did not expect students to accept his views uncritically—quite the opposite. As the "roach powder" story illustrates, he encouraged rebuttals to his critical commentary. In this sense, Professor Bell accepted the relativity of "truth." He strove to tell his own version, and he strongly believed in it—but as a teacher, he also recognized other versions and held a "double-consciousness" with respect to truth.

In fact, Professor Bell's method here paralleled that of W. E. B. Du Bois (1973), who once stated to the NAACP Board of Directors, "I have not always been right, but I have been sincere, and I am unwilling ... to be limited in the expression of my honest opinions" (p. 478). Essentially, Professor Bell acknowledged that he might not be right, but that he was sincere. Moreover, beyond the "truth" itself, he encouraged students who were unwilling to be limited in expressing their sincere opinions. The second part of Professor Bell's quote on Critical Race Theory—"even in the face of criticism"—was even more important to him than the "truth." Professor Bell (1994) wrote an entire book entitled *Confronting Authority*, which he took quite seriously as a philosophy of life. He actually wanted students to confront *his* own authority in the classroom—to sincerely tell their own version of the "truth," even when they knew that he and others would oppose them.

During my tenure working with Professor Bell, the student who most often took up Professor Bell on this challenge was Tommy Haskins, NYU Law '09. Tommy was a White male from Mississippi, and he professed to hold conservative political views and to support the Republican Party (Harpalani, 2013, p. xxvi; T. Haskins, personal communication, September 24, 2012). He was the type of student one might expect to clash with Professor Bell, and they did often clash—but out of those clashes grew mutual respect and deep friendship. Tommy described his initial interaction with Professor Bell:

> Professor Bell was discussing the various policies enacted by the George W. Bush adminis-
> tration. Shortly into his lesson, he began intimating that the administration was operating
> more like a dictatorship than the head of a republic. Almost involuntarily, I found myself,
> voice raised, interrupting him to tell him how off-base and destructive his opinion was.
> After finishing my own mini-rant, I remember a voice inside my head saying that I may
> have gone too far, that raising my voice to (really *at*) a professor was probably not the best
> move. Professor Bell's response, however, told me differently, and evinced that there was
> something radically different about his brand of radicalism. In his characteristic calm tone,
> Professor Bell looked at me, smiled broadly, and said "yea, you're probably right." Thus
> began what was, and remains, one of the most intellectually honest and open relationships
> I've ever been a part of. (T. Haskins, personal communication, January 12, 2013)

Tommy continued about this relationship with Professor Bell:

> While Professor Bell and I disagreed on nearly every major issue in which we engaged in a
> debate, we also seemed in each case to hit a level of understanding that allowed us to walk
> away knowing we had a more complete picture and appreciation of the issue, and each
> other. It seemed that the more we disagreed, and the more heated our debates became, the
> better friends we were left.
>
> I don't think that the America Professor Bell saw was an accurate portrayal of where the
> country is. The prescriptions he offered for what he saw as ailing the country are not, and
> would not, in my opinion, be effective in the ways he believed. Many of the positions he
> held on the most important issues of the day are positions that I believe would lead us in
> the wrong direction. But, I think Professor Bell's approach to discourse is one that is both
> radical and transformative. Professor Bell engaged, he challenged, and he encouraged. He
> was genuinely interested in knowing where it was I believed his positions to be off-base;
> he wanted to be convinced by a different perspective. He understood, and taught, that if
> you take a person's opinions, political leaning, or positions on the big issues, and use those
> to assign value to that person, that you were doing nothing but stunting your own growth,
> your own knowledge, and indeed working against the advancement of your own opinions
> and positions. You have to understand the person, you have to understand their core values,
> you have to understand what makes them tick.
>
> Professor Bell's legacy is that of a man who desired intellectual and emotional honesty and
> openness, and of a man who was willing to be the first to offer it, even if it resulted in great
> backlash. (Harpalani, 2013, pp. xxvi–xxvii; T. Haskins, personal communication, 2013)

In fact, when his more liberal classmates—who far outnumbered the conservatives—criticized Tommy for expressing his conservative views, Professor Bell came
to Tommy's defense, noting his own deep admiration for students who had the
courage to challenge him or any other authority figure (Harpalani, 2013, p. xxvii).
Tommy became a TA for the large Constitutional Law class the following year and

continued his debates with Professor Bell. The two even made light of their battles. At the end-of-the-year celebration, Tommy and Professor Bell played a video boxing match on the screen at the front of the classroom, where Tommy dubbed Professor Bell "Communist" and himself "JesusFreak," and they battled it out as the other students watched and cheered (T. Haskins, personal communication, September 10, 2012).

What is noteworthy here is that as part of his double-consciousness, that "sense of always looking at one's self through the eyes of others" (Du Bois, 1903/2006), Professor Bell could see himself in Tommy Haskins. Just as he became a founding figure in CRT by confronting authority (Bell, 1994) and by "just … telling the truth" (Harpalani, 2013, p. xxv), Professor Bell wanted his students to stand up to authority and tell their own truth, even in the wake of criticism, and even if he disagreed with them. When I later interviewed Professor Bell publicly, as part of a student event at NYU Law, one of the questions I posed to him was whether a person could be ethical and morally upstanding and still hold politically conservative views that he strongly disagreed with. His initial response was "You mean like Tommy Haskins"— and then he smiled, sighed, and said in begrudging but jocular fashion, "I guess so."

It was clear that Professor Bell respected Tommy Haskins, in spite of their vast ideological differences, because Tommy was honest and willing to speak his truth, even in the wake of criticism. And rather than converting students to his own views, Professor Bell's focus in class was getting students to understand various versions of the "truth" and to develop and articulate their own version.

"DON'T LET THE PERFECT BE THE ENEMY OF THE GOOD"

Professor Bell's double-consciousness about law and life also came through his own kernels of wisdom—the life advice that he shared in the classroom. His book *Ethical Ambition* (Bell, 2002) focused on balancing the "warring ideals" of ambition and personal ethics—a tension that he delved into through his personal stories. He spoke frequently of his happy marriage to Ms. Janet Dewart Bell (and also to his first wife, Jewel Hairston Bell, who passed away in 1990) and encouraged students to find healthy relationships, but his ambivalence also came through. He talked about how difficult it was to live with another person and stated, tongue-in-cheek, that a marriage was successful if it did more good than harm—and that was the goal to strive for. Another half joking, half serious lesson that Professor Bell often recounted was that he had learned not to trust anyone who was on television more than two or three times a year.

But Professor Bell's favorite aphorism, during his last years, was "Don't let the perfect be the enemy of the good"—usually attributed to the French philosopher Voltaire (although different versions of the saying can also be traced to

Aristotle, Confucius, and Shakespeare). Professor Bell frequently referred to this saying in class during his last 2 years of teaching, when I worked with him. Indeed, it captured his view on marriage—a far from perfect institution. Professor Bell also referenced "don't let the perfect be the enemy of the good" when discussing the political challenges that President Barack Obama faced—although true to his double-consciousness, he was also critical of many of Obama's policies. Professor Bell was writing a book on the Obama Presidency at the time (D. A. Bell, personal communication, September 5, 2009), employing his concept of interest convergence (Bell, 1980a). During his later years, he seemed to take a pragmatic turn with respect to interest convergence, which was one of the founding concepts of Critical Race Theory (Delgado & Stefancic, 2001). In class, he would discuss how one might use interest convergence to advance small changes for the better, rather than trying to bring about large sweeping changes at once. His comments on President Obama reflected this view, and it became his focus in his later years—particularly when teaching students how to grapple with real world challenges.

Yet, Professor Bell continued to espouse his well-known critiques of *Brown v. Board of Education* and school integration (Bell, 1976, 2004). When I once asked him in class about *Brown*, he maintained that he would have decided it differently and focused on equal funding and resources for schools rather than the slow, stalled path of integration (Bell, 2004). I never heard him waver in any of the radical views for which he is known—his own version of the "truth"—such as his critiques of emphasis on integration (Bell, 1976, 2004) and diversity (Bell, 2003, 2008), and his belief in the permanence of racism (Bell, 1987). Part of Professor Bell's double-consciousness was that he could be highly critical on one hand—in telling the "truth"—and then completely pragmatic on the other—espousing that the perfect should not be the enemy of the good. More than anything else, he aimed to teach students to do the same and develop this second-sight.

In fact, even the "roach powder" story has another side. In analogizing the Constitution to roach powder, Professor Bell was essentially supporting his own contention that it is a useless document because the Justices vote their personal preferences in the most important cases. But in fitting irony, by stating repeatedly that the perfect should not be the enemy of the good, Professor Bell was articulating the very principle that Benjamin Franklin had relied upon some 225 years earlier, when urging his colleagues to ratify the same Constitution. In his speech of September 17, 1787, at the Constitutional Convention in Philadelphia, Franklin noted:

> I agree to this Constitution with all its faults, if they are such; because I think a general Government necessary for us. ... [W]hen you assemble a number of men to have the advantage of their joint wisdom, you inevitably assemble with those men, all their prejudices, their passions, their errors of opinion, their local interests, and their selfish views. From such an assembly can a perfect production be expected? (Franklin, 1787)

Professor Bell did not reference these remarks by Benjamin Franklin, but as a constitutional law professor, he knew well the history of compromises that occurred in the drafting of the Constitution. He formed many of his ideas by analyzing these compromises and their implications for the rights of people of color (Bell, 1987, 1997a; Delgado & Stefancic, 2005). Thus, he was aware of the broader implications of "don't let the perfect be the enemy of the good" for our constitutional history. Ironically, by implicitly contradicting his own roach powder analogy, Professor Bell exhibited his second-sight for students and modeled the critical engagement that he expected from them.

"HUMANIZING THE LAW SCHOOL EXPERIENCE"

All of this critical engagement made Professor Bell's courses more challenging for students—particularly those who were motivated to perform to their potential. Because his courses occurred in the midst of the competitive, stressful, and demanding law school experience, Professor Bell exhibited another facet of "double-consciousness": he balanced the challenging dilemmas posed in class with several efforts to, in his own words, "humanize the law school experience" (Harpalani, 2012, 2013).

For Professor Bell, this meant balancing another set of "warring ideals" (Du Bois, 1903/2006): the rigorous and competitive nature of law school and the desire to maintain a sense of humanity in his classroom. He did this in many small ways that made students feel like he respected them and cared about them personally.

For example, during the break in the middle of every class, Professor Bell made sure to provide snacks for students (Radice, 2012). Sometimes the Bell Fellow and TAs would arrange this, while other times student advocate teams were responsible and were reimbursed for purchasing snacks of their choice. Every student who wanted them could have refreshments at the break of every class. Additionally, for the student team arguing a case for a given class, Professor Bell would take the student team, along with the Bell Fellow and TA, out to dinner after class, using his budget from NYU Law School that he negotiated for this purpose. The dinner was an opportunity for students to chat with Professor Bell in a small group setting, which they very much appreciated. Brittany Jones, NYU Law '11 recounted: "I remember my small group dinner fondly, as it was the ONLY time that a law school professor ever offered to get to know me outside of a classroom context" (B. D. Jones, personal communication, June 29, 2015). Brittany would go on to serve as a TA for Professor Bell's final full course, Critical Race Theory, in spring 2011.

Professor Bell took other measures to bring a sense of humanity to the classroom. During spring 2009 he decided to have a class song, the first verse of "Morning Has Broken"—a Christian hymn by Cat Stevens (Islam, 1971).

Together with Andy Artz, NYU '09—a TA in the class—Professor Bell would lead the students in singing at the beginning of each class (D. A. Bell, personal communication, January 13, 2009; Radice, 2012). The first time I heard Professor Bell use the phrase "humanize the law school experience" was when he explained to the students why he wanted to have a class song. It was also an extension of his broader interest in music: each year, Professor Bell would conduct a gospel concert at the law school for the entire NYU community. Moreover, the class song was not the only singing in Professor Bell's classes. In any given class, if he knew that a student or TA had a birthday, he would often have the entire class sing "Happy Birthday" to that person.

Professor Bell sometimes even combined academic debate with his efforts to humanize the law school experience. For example, a student once challenged the appropriateness of using a Christian hymn as the class song for a group of students with diverse religious views, and his classmates defended the choice and criticized him. Nevertheless, Professor Bell welcomed the discussion and encouraged students who objected to speak up, noting again that he appreciated such challenges and the courage it takes to raise them. Also, for orthodox Jewish students in his class, Professor Bell organized a separate dinner at a kosher restaurant. He would have a pleasant and jovial conversation with the students, but then just as readily ask their opinions on charged issues such as the Israel-Palestine conflict. Professor Bell understood that humanizing law school would enable students to delve into controversial issues in constitutional law and world politics with greater depth, comfort, and sincerity. His efforts to humanize really aimed "to break down traditional barriers between student and teacher, and even among students themselves" (Radice, 2012, p. 47), so that honest discourse on charged topics could take place, and so that students could critically assess all versions of the "truth."

There were many other ways in which Professor Bell aimed to resolve the "teacher-student contradiction" (Bell, 1998; Bell & Edmonds, 1993) and humanize the law school experience. His day-to-day interactions with students exemplified this. For example, at the 2009 Faculty of Color Appreciation Dinner at NYU Law, Maneka Sinha, NYU '09, recounted her personal story in a speech honoring Professor Bell:

As a 1L, I was called on a bunch of times in class and not once did a professor make an attempt to pronounce my name correctly. Monica, Maneeka, Maneequa—I got the works. So when I landed in Professor Bell's class my second year, I expected nothing different. So early in the semester, I'm sitting in class, minding my business—just trying to learn some conlaw and I hear, "Maneeka Sinka?" And so I blush a little, put my hand up and say, "yes Professor Bell?" But instead of moving on to his question, he asks me if he said it right. Of course, he didn't, so I correct him and we move on. So, I'm feeling pretty good—Professor Bell—Derrick Bell!—knows my name! So next class, I sit down feeling pretty pleased and I hear

"Monica Singh?" and at this point I'm a little confused—new class, new pronunciation? So I tell him again and with his characteristic warm grace, he apologizes and corrects himself. But this goes on all semester in class and even when he ran into me outside of the classroom—Professor Bell desperately trying to remember how to pronounce my name and despite his best attempts—getting it more amusingly wrong each time. Until we got to the very end of the semester when, I sit down in class and this time I know it's coming. My face is already red, I've got my hand over my face, cringing in anticipation. And I hear, "Maneka Sinha!" Not a question this time—an exclamation. And I look up—I sort of shake my ears out to see if I heard right and I see Professor Bell with this giant grin on his face—he got it right. And since that day, Professor Bell has never once forgotten it again.

The reason I tell you this is not just because it is a very rare opportunity to be able to embarrass Professor Bell a little bit, but because it was important for him to *know* me. It was a way for him to engage me in a little banter, a little back and forth and a way to start a conversation with me. And although the way he did it with me was unique—he does it with all of his students—the way he teaches, the way he runs his class. Just the way he interacts with us. He finds a way to create meaningful personal relationships with his students, in an environment where we don't expect to have that with our professors. (Harpalani, 2013, p. xxvi; M. Sinha, personal communication, March 25, 2009)

Fig 3: Professor Derrick Bell, with NYU Law students Vinay Harpalani and Maneka Sinha, at the Faculty of Color Appreciation Dinner, March 25, 2009.

Maneka's reflection here is one of literally hundreds of unique stories that students could tell about Professor Bell. More than any professor I have known— from undergraduate to graduate to law school—Professor Bell enjoyed getting to know students on a personal level, developing a level of comfort with them—often through gentle teasing and humor—and then drawing upon that comfort to challenge them and further their education.

Such was the brilliance of his "radical humanism" (Harpalani, 2012, 2013). But Professor Bell's humanism extended to much more serious situations as well. Mark Goldfeder, NYU Law '11, was a very able student and an outstanding writer in the large Constitutional Law class in spring 2010. However, he was going through a difficult family crisis during the semester and missed several classes. Nevertheless, Mark made up the assignments that he had missed, and he did very well in the class. He stayed in touch with Professor Bell after the class, and shortly after Professor Bell passed away in October 2011, Mark sent me an e-mail with the following message, asking for Ms. Janet Dewart Bell's address:

> Professor Bell … not only wrote me a recommendation, but always, whenever I would see him, would take the time to stop and chat and ask me how I was and how things were going. His small acts of kindness were actually quite profound and meant a lot to me, and I wanted to write his wife a note just expressing that, and my condolences on her loss and what an incredible person he was. (M. Goldfeder, personal communication, October 26, 2011; Harpalani, 2013, p. xxvii)

Mark also recently began his academic teaching career and later wrote and told me that his Law and Religion course is modeled on his "most memorable law school class; Con Law, with Professor Bell and you" (M. Goldfeder, personal communication, January 17, 2013; Harpalani, 2013, p. xxvii).

In sum, Professor Bell's teaching philosophy was about much more than learning the law or even the real world pressures that influence constitutional decisions. At its core, it was a reflection of how he lived his own life, and of the challenges and contradictions of life itself (Bell, 1994, 2002).

CONCLUSION: A TEACHER UNTIL THE VERY END

All of the above stories show how Professor Derrick Bell was "gifted with a second-sight" when it came to teaching—and how he gifted his students with that same "second-sight," by incorporating broader life lessons into his constitutional law pedagogy. And I can only conclude this chapter with one more salient personal story that illustrates Professor Bell's dedication to teaching until the very end.

In the summer of 2010, I left NYU Law School for a position as the Korematsu Teaching Fellow at Seattle University School of Law. Professor Bell had decided not to hire another fellow for the following year, opting instead for time on leave and a reduced teaching load. At nearly 80 years of age, he felt that he could not keep up with a rigorous schedule of teaching with the level of dedication that he insisted upon. He took his leave in fall 2010 and then returned to teach a Critical Race Theory seminar in spring 2011. He became ill during that semester, as the carcinoid cancer that he had lived with for years, and which eventually took his life (Bernstein, 2011), began to recur. Although he was inactive and in bed during much of that summer (D. A. Bell, personal communication, June 20, 2011), Professor Bell still planned to teach his Current Constitutional Issues seminar in fall 2011 and Critical Race Theory again in spring 2012 (again, he would not hire a Bell Fellow because he was not teaching the large Constitutional Law course). As the summer progressed, I felt confident that Professor Bell would be okay: he had battled carcinoid cancer for over a decade, and it had slowed him down before, but he had always recovered. Indeed, such resilience was another hallmark of Professor Bell's life (Bell, 1994, 2002).

Professor Bell was still in poor health as the summer ended; yet he was determined to move forward with his classes. He invited me to give a guest lecture on the constitutionality of race-conscious admissions in his seminar course on Wednesday, September 14, 2011, when I would be back in New York City for other reasons. Although he was wheelchair-bound, he still prodded me with questions after my presentation. In spite of his health, he insisted on coming to class, being as engaged and involved as possible, and making sure that his students got the most out of his classes.

On Tuesday, September 27, I wrote to his wife, Ms. Janet Dewart Bell, to ask if Professor Bell was well enough to write a letter of recommendation for me. I asked her explicitly not to request this from him if she thought it would add to his stress level, but she told me that he would be delighted to do it (J. D. Bell, personal communication, September 27, 2011). He went to his last class the next day, Wednesday, September 28, and I heard he was again asking tough questions in class, in spite of still being in a wheelchair.

Then, on Friday, September 30, Professor Bell's health took a turn for the worse. I received a phone call from Ms. Bell early the next morning, Saturday, October 1. She told me that the prognosis was not good. Professor Bell had been hospitalized; he was unconscious, and his body was slowly shutting down. Doctors did not expect him to live past the weekend. Ms. Bell held the phone up to his ear and allowed me to speak to him. I was in shock and could hardly come up with words to say. She then told me that she would send my letter of recommendation off on Monday. Professor Bell wanted it to be done and insisted on it. Needless to say, I was amazed.

I stayed in a state of shock for much of the weekend: for some reason, I had not anticipated this happening—given Professor Bell's resilience. It dawned on me that I had seen him for the last time ever, just a little over 2 weeks earlier. While I could not help Professor Bell's health, I determined that I could at least assist with his class on Wednesday, October 5, which I knew would be very important to him. So I planned to fly from Seattle to New York City on Tuesday night, October 4, and to go to his class on Wednesday. I even canceled a scheduled presentation at the Latino Critical Legal Theory (LatCrit) conference in San Diego to do so.

Professor Bell was not expected to make it until then. Several other former Bell Fellows were also helping with his class: Joy Radice, Taja-Nia Henderson, Anjana Samant, and Cynthia Monaco. I figured that together we would have to break the sad news to the students (if they had not heard already), have a memorial for Professor Bell, and then press on just as he would have insisted. I spent the weekend planning all of this in my mind.

But the weekend passed, and Professor Bell lived on. On Monday night, I decided that as soon as I landed in John F. Kennedy (JFK) Airport on Tuesday evening I would take a cab over to St. Luke's Hospital in Harlem and go see Professor Bell, who was hanging on longer than doctors had expected. I sent a text message to Ms. Bell to see if this was okay, and she said that it definitely was fine and that she would be glad to see me. My plane arrived in JFK Airport at 10 p.m. on Tuesday, October 4. I rushed to Ground Transportation, hopped in a cab, and got to St. Luke's Hospital by 11 p.m. Professor Bell was unconscious and non-responsive, but still alive, and I got see him once again. Ms. Bell was very strong under the circumstances: she had been inundated with phone calls and hosted numerous visitors who had come to see Professor Bell. She greeted all of them patiently, explained the protocol for visiting Professor Bell, asked them to sign the guestbook, and then talked to them cheerfully about Professor Bell. She also gave me some time alone to speak to him, and I thanked him for everything he had meant to me, and to all of his students. I told him that his classes and his legacy would go on. I was overcome with emotion and just so glad I got to see him one last time.

Professor Anthony Thompson of NYU Law came to the class on Wednesday, which started at 4 p.m. He announced that his friend Professor Bell was ill, and that he would be taking over the class for as long as necessary. Professor Thompson would teach not only the Current Constitutional Issues seminar in fall 2011, but also the Critical Race Theory seminar scheduled for spring 2012 (Thompson, 2012). That is the way Professor Bell would have wanted it—he would not have wanted his classes canceled due to his health.

My presence in that Wednesday's class turned out to be unnecessary, at least for pedagogical purposes. Professor Thompson and the other former Bell Fellows who were there ran the class very well. But coincidentally, Ms. Valerie Cabral, an NYU administrator who was a good friend of Professor Bell, also came to class unannounced that day, hoping to see Professor Bell. She was unaware that he had been hospitalized and was not expected to live. I had met Valerie in spring 2010, when I was the Bell Fellow. At her request, I had arranged for several NYU undergraduate students to visit Professor Bell's large Constitutional Law classes—an experience they enjoyed immensely. She gifted me a tie in gratitude. I was wearing that very tie in class on Wednesday when Valerie came up to me and asked me where Professor Bell was. I realized that she was unaware of the circumstances, and I stepped outside the classroom with her and explained what had happened. I also told her that she should go see Professor Bell right now; that although unconscious, he was still alive—but he could pass away at any time. I assured her that Ms. Bell, who was staying at the hospital all day, would welcome her visit. Valerie later recounted to me that she did go straight to St. Luke's Hospital; that Ms. Bell welcomed her; and that she made it in time to see Professor Bell while he was still alive. She was immensely grateful to have had the opportunity to do so (V. Cabral, personal communication, October 7, 2011). So while my presence in class was unnecessary for teaching, it served a greater purpose.

In a sense, this small but important episode symbolized Professor Bell's impact, both inside and outside the classroom. I was wearing the tie that Valerie gave to me for welcoming her undergraduate mentees to his classroom. That set the stage for this day, as I was the only person present who knew Valerie and would know to inform her of Professor Bell's condition and whereabouts. It reminded me of how Professor Bell used the classroom to teach about larger issues of life, and now of death. Everything was coming full circle. I learned about Professor Bell by reading his academic work, and I had the opportunity to take his classes and to teach with him. And now, in his final days, Professor Bell's spirit was humanizing the law school experience and life more generally.

Quite poignantly, after outliving doctors' predictions by several days, Professor Bell passed away at about 7:15 p.m. that very same Wednesday evening, October 5—right after his class ended at 7 p.m. True to form and always dedicated to teaching, he was not going to go until his class was over, and until we made sure that it would continue as planned. Neither I nor his other students would expect anything else of Professor Derrick Bell. Rest in peace, Professor. You live on through all of us.

ACKNOWLEDGMENTS

I would like to thank the late Professor Derrick Bell and Ms. Janet Dewart Bell for their support over the years, Professor William F. Tate for inviting me to contribute this chapter, Professor Gloria Ladson-Billings for coordinating this project, and the many former students of Professor Bell whose experiences and stories contributed to this work. Also, the Fred T. Korematsu Center for Law and Equality at Seattle University School of Law and Chicago-Kent College of Law provided support for this work, along with Savannah Law School.

NOTES

1. Although he invited students and others to refer to him as "Derrick," I usually called him "Professor Bell" or just "Professor," and that is how I refer to him throughout this chapter.
2. Where I have e-mail or written documentation, I cite the stories and statements from Professor Bell, his students, and others as "personal communication." However, many of my personal memories are undocumented, and I tell those without citation, except where they were noted in prior publications.

REFERENCES

Bell, D. A. (1976). Serving two masters: Integration ideals and client interests in school desegregation litigation, *Yale Law Journal, 85*, 470–516.

Bell, D. A. (1977). The legacy of W. E. B. Du Bois: A rational model for achieving public school equity for America's black children. *Creighton Law Review, 11*, 409–431.

Bell, D. A. (1980a). *Brown v. Board of Education* and the interest convergence dilemma. *Harvard Law Review, 93*, 518–533.

Bell, D. A. (1980b). Humanity in legal education. *Oregon Law Review 59*, 243–247.

Bell, D. A. (1982). The law student as slave. *Student Lawyer, 11*, 18–22.

Bell, D. A. (1987). *And we are not saved: The elusive quest for racial justice.* New York, NY: Basic Books.

Bell, D. A. (1992). *Faces at the bottom of the well: The permanence of racism.* New York, NY: Basic Books.

Bell, D. A. (1994). *Confronting authority: Reflections of an ardent protestor.* Boston, MA: Beacon Press.

Bell, D. A. (1997a). *Constitutional conflicts.* Cincinnati, OH: Anderson Press.

Bell, D. A. (1997b). A pre-memorial message on law school teaching. *New York University Review of Law & Social Change, 23*, 205–215.

Bell, D. A. (1998). Constitutional conflicts: The perils and rewards of pioneering in the law school classroom, *Seattle University Law Review, 21*, 1039–1051.

Bell, D. A. (2002). *Ethical ambition: Living a life of meaning and worth.* New York, NY; London, England: Bloomsbury.

Bell, D. A. (2003). Diversity's distractions. *Columbia Law Review, 103*, 1622–1633.

Bell, D. A. (2004). *Silent covenants:* Brown v. Board of Education *and the unfulfilled hopes for racial reform.* New York, NY: Oxford University Press.

Bell, D. A. (2008). What's diversity got to do with it? *Seattle Journal for Social Justice, 6*, 527–532.

Bell, D. A., & Edmonds, E. (1993). Students as teachers, teachers as learners. *Michigan Law Review, 91*, 2025–2052.

Bernstein, F. A. (2011, October 7). Derrick Bell, pioneering law professor and civil rights advocate, dies at 80. *The New York Times*, p. A18. Retrieved from http://www.nytimes.com/2011/10/06/us/derrick-bell-pioneering-harvard-law-professor-dies-at-80.html

Bridges, J. (Writer/Director). (1973). *The paper chase* [Motion picture]. United States: 20th Century Fox. Brown v. Bd. of Educ., 347 U.S. 483 (1954).

Delgado, R., & Stefancic, J. (2001). *Critical Race Theory: An introduction.* New York, NY; London, England: New York University Press.

Delgado, R., & Stefancic, J. (Eds.). (2005). *The Derrick Bell reader.* New York, NY; London, England: New York University Press.

Du Bois, W. E. B. (1935). Does the Negro need separate schools? *The Journal of Negro Education, 4*, 328–335.

Du Bois, W. E. B. (1973). In H. Aptheker (Ed.), *The correspondence of W. E. B. Du Bois: Selections, 1877–1934*. Amherst, MA: University of Massachusetts Press.

Du Bois, W. E. B. (2006). *The souls of Black folk*. Hazelton, PA: Electronic Classics Series (Original work published 1903)

Dudziak, M. L. (2000). *Cold War civil rights: Race and the image of American democracy*. Princeton, NJ: Princeton University Press.

Franklin, B. (1787, September 17). Benjamin Franklin to the Federal Convention. *The Founders' Constitution, 4*(7), Document 3. Retrieved from http://press-pubs.uchicago.edu/founders/documents/a7s3.html

Freire, P. (1993). *Pedagogy of the oppressed* (M. B. Ramos, Trans.). New York, NY: Continuum (Original work published 1968)

Garden, C. (2013). Bell labs: Derrick Bell's inspirational pedagogy. *Seattle University Law Review, 36*, xx–xxii.

Hackney, J. R. (1998). Derrick Bell's re-sounding: W. E. B. Du Bois, modernism, and critical race scholarship. *Law & Social Inquiry, 23*, 141–164.

Harpalani, V. (2009). Ambiguity, ambivalence, and awakening: A South Asian becoming "critically" aware of race in America. *Berkeley Journal of African-American Law & Policy, 11*, 71–83.

Harpalani, V. (2011, October 16). Tributes in memory of Professor Derrick Bell. Retrieved from http://professorderrickbell.com/tributes/vinay-harpalani/

Harpalani, V. (2012, March 22). Professor Derrick Bell: "Radical humanist." *The Black Commentator, 464*. Retrieved from http://www.blackcommentator.com/464/464_bell_harpalani_guest_share.html

Harpalani, V. (2013). From roach powder to radical humanism: Professor Derrick Bell's "critical" constitutional pedagogy. *Seattle University Law Review, 36*, xxiii–xxviii.

Harpalani, V. (2015). The double-consciousness of race-consciousness and the Bermuda Triangle of university admissions. *University of Pennsylvania Journal of Constitutional Law, 17*, 821–854.

Islam, Y. (née Stevens, C.). (1971). Morning has broken. On *Teaser and the firecat* [record]. Santa Monica, CA: A&M.

Ladson-Billings, G., & Tate, W. F., IV (1995). Toward a Critical Race Theory of education. *Teachers College Record, 97*(1), 47–68.

Lynn, M., & Dixson, A. D. (Eds.). (2013). *Handbook of Critical Race Theory in education*. London, England: Routledge.

Lynn, M., Jennings, M. E., & Hughes, S. (2013). Critical race pedagogy 2.0: Lessons from Derrick Bell. *Race Ethnicity and Education, 16*, 603–628.

Parker, L., Deyhle, D., & Villenas, S. (Eds.). (1999). *Race is … Race isn't: Critical Race Theory and qualitative studies in education*. Boulder, CO: Westview Press.

Radice, J. (2012). Derrick Bell's community-based classroom. *Columbia Journal of Race & Law Special Feature, 2*, 44–48.

Tate, W. F., IV (1997). Critical Race Theory and education: History, theory, and implications. *Review of Research in Education, 22*, 195–247.

Thompson, A. (2012). In remembrance of Professor Derrick Bell. *New York University Review of Law & Social Change, 36*, 1–4.

U. S. v. Carolene Products, 304 U.S. 144 (1938).

Washington, B. T. (1965). *Up from slavery*. New York, NY: Avon Books (Original work published 1901)

CHAPTER THREE

A Critical Race Examination OF *McLaurin v. Oklahoma*

How Derrick Bell Helped Me Understand George McLaurin's Seat[1]

DANIEL G. SOLÓRZANO

INTRODUCTION

When one reads the works of Derrick Bell one is stuck with how he engages us in conversations about theory, concepts, and pedagogy. This is especially true when you read and use his casebook, *Race, Racism, and American Law* (Bell, 2008) and accompanying *Teacher's Manual: Race, Racism, and American Law* (Bell & Radice, 2008).[2] This happened to me in the spring of 2004 in Washington, DC. I was attending a meeting and during an afternoon break I made my way to the American History Museum. I came across an exhibit on the 50th anniversary of the 1954 *Brown v. Board* Supreme Court decision titled "SEPARATE IS NOT EQUAL: *Brown v. Board of Education*." Little did I know that in 48 hours I would begin a journey to better understand issues of Critical Race Theory, everyday racism in the form of racial microaggressions, and critical race pedagogy. This chapter is the story of how Derrick Bell helped guide me in that journey.

The story begins with the case of Mr. George McLaurin, who in 1948 applied for, and was denied, admission in the doctoral program in Educational Administration at the University of Oklahoma. In this chapter I illustrate how this racial history can help us better understand the racialized experiences of Students of Color in higher education today. I start by telling a story of how I came to understand the legal case *McLaurin v. Oklahoma State Regents for Higher Education* (1950) (hereafter *McLaurin v. Oklahoma*). Next, using a Critical Race Theory framework, I lay out my working definitions of race, racial microaggressions, institutional racism, and white supremacy, and build a model to examine the experiences of Students of Color in higher education. Then, I examine the legal history of *McLaurin v. Oklahoma*. Finally, I use the photo of Mr. McLaurin at the University of Oklahoma to examine the role of racial microaggressions, institutional racism, and white supremacy as a pedagogical case study.

To help facilitate that conversation I employ Derrick Bell's (1992) concept of "racial realism" to describe the permanence of racism in the U.S. Derrick Bell (1993) defined racial realism in the following way:

> Black people will never gain full equality in this country. Even those herculean efforts we hail as successful will produce no more than temporary "peaks of progress," short-lived victories that slide into irrelevance as racial patterns *adapt* in ways that maintain white dominance. This is a hard-to-accept fact that all history verifies. We must acknowledge it, not as a sign of submission, but as an act of ultimate defiance. (p. 573) (emphasis added)

Bell continued on to state:

> it is not a matter of choosing between the pragmatic recognition that racism is permanent no matter what we do, or an idealism based on the long-held dream of attaining a society free of racism. Rather, it is a question of both … the futility of action … that action must be taken. … Our triumph is assured at the moment we rise to that challenge. (p. 587)

In his work, Bell alerts us that institutional racism speaks to a systematic positioning of race and racism in the U.S. that leads to racial realism. The story of *McLaurin v. Oklahoma* is the story of how a Black professor, a Black civil and legal rights organization, and Black communities "rise to that challenge" of confronting and challenging institutional racism.

HOW I CAME TO KNOW *McLAURIN V. OKLAHOMA*

In the fall of 2004, I was in Washington, DC at the National Museum of American History and came across the exhibit of the 50th anniversary of *Brown v. Board of Education* (see Figure 1).

As I walked through the *Separate Is Not Equal*: Brown v. Board of Education exhibit, I came across a section titled "A Turning Point in 1950" (see Figure 2). This portion of the exhibit focused on two legal cases decided in 1950 by the U.S. Supreme Court that were important precursors to the 1954 *Brown v. Board of Education* case—*Sweatt v. Painter* (1950) and *McLaurin v. Oklahoma* (1950).

As I followed the history of these legal cases along the wall, I came across a photo of an African American man sitting outside a classroom (see Figure 3). It was a picture of Mr. George McLaurin, a doctoral student in Education Administration at the University of Oklahoma.[3] After Mr. McLaurin was initially denied

Fig 1: *Separate Is Not Equal*: Brown v. Board of Education—exhibit entry. National Museum of American History, 2004.

Source: author's photo archive.

Fig 2: *Separate Is Not Equal*: Brown v. Board of Education—"A Turning Point in 1950." National Museum of American History.

Source: Author's photo archive.

admission to the doctoral program based on his race, the National Association for the Advancement of Colored People (NAACP) entered into a series of legal battles in the U.S. Federal Court to get Mr. McLaurin admitted to the University of Oklahoma. In 1948 Mr. McLaurin was finally admitted to the university under conditions of "Jim Crow"—legal segregation. The photo was provided as evidence in the trial showing him sitting outside the classroom and separated from the white students. The only source notation on the photo mentioned the NAACP Archives at the Library of Congress. This reference started me on a journey to find out more about the *McLaurin v. Oklahoma* case and its role in the 1954 *Brown v. Board* litigation and later educational equity and affirmative action cases leading to the most recent U.S. Supreme Court case—*Schuette v. Coalition to Defend Affirmative Action* (2014); *Fisher v. University of Texas et al.* (2016).[4]

Fig 3: *Separate Is Not Equal*: Brown v. Board of Education—*McLaurin v. Oklahoma*, 1950. George McLaurin Seated Outside the Carnegie Hall Classroom 104, 1948. National Museum of American History.

Source: Author's photo archive.

The next day I went to the Library of Congress and began examining the NAACP Archives[5] to piece together a story of George McLaurin—a 68-year-old education student who, when finally admitted to the doctoral program, was forced to sit in an alcove outside the classroom (University of Oklahoma, Carnegie Hall, Classroom 104).[6] Our story continues with my examination of this photo and the NAACP documents that framed the legal case. I use the tools of Critical Race Theory to define the concepts needed in this analysis.

CRITICAL RACE THEORY AND THE WORKING DEFINITIONS OF RACE, RACISM, RACIAL MICROAGGRESSIONS, INSTITUTIONAL RACISM, AND WHITE SUPREMACY

The exercise of analyzing the photo of George McLaurin and related legal documents begins by using Critical Race Theory (CRT) to define race, racism, racial microaggressions, institutional racism, and white supremacy. In the two decades plus that CRT has been utilized in the field of education, this framework has provided powerful insights into the ways oppressive mechanisms mediate the lived experiences of People of Color within and beyond educational institutions. I define Critical Race Theory in Education (CRTE) as the work of scholars who are developing an explanatory framework that accounts for the role of race and racism in education. CRTE works toward identifying and challenging racism in its historical and contemporary forms as part of a larger goal of identifying and challenging all forms of subordination. In addition, CRTE has led to the development of conceptual "tools" that reveal, disrupt, and work toward dismantling racist ideologies and practices that marginalize, subordinate, and exclude People of Color in education (see Ladson-Billings & Tate, 1995; Parker, Deyhle, & Villenas, 1999; Solórzano, 1997). Three of these conceptual tools that I use in this article are racial microaggressions,[7] institutional racism, and white supremacy.

According to James Banks (1993), Eurocentric versions of U.S. history reveal the concept of race to be a socially constructed category, created to differentiate racial groups and to show the superiority or dominance of one race over another. This definition leads to the question: Does the dominance of a racial group require a rationalizing ideology? One could argue that dominant groups try to legitimize their position through the use of an ideology (i.e., a set of beliefs that explains or justifies some actual or potential social arrangement). Because racism is the ideology that justifies the dominance of one race over another, we must ask, how do we define racism? For our purpose, Audre Lorde (1992) may have produced the most concise definition of racism as "the belief in the inherent superiority of one race over all others and thereby the right to dominance" (p. 496). Manning Marable (1992) also defined racism as "a system of ignorance, exploitation, and power used to oppress African-Americans, Latinos, Asians, Pacific Americans, American Indians and other people on the basis of ethnicity, culture, mannerisms, and color"

(p. 5). Marable's definition of racism is important because it shifts the discussion of race and racism from a Black-White discourse to one that includes multiple faces, voices, and experiences. Embedded in the Lorde and Marable definitions is how an ideology of white supremacy is foundational to definitions of racism. Indeed, they provide at least three important insights: (1) one group deems itself superior to all others, (2) the group that is superior has the power to carry out the racist actions, and (3) racism benefits the superior group while negatively affecting other racial and/or ethnic groups. The Marable and Lorde definitions take the position that racism is about institutional power, and People of Color in the history of the United States have never possessed this form of power.

Racial microaggressions are one form of a systemic everyday racism that are layered, cumulative assaults used to subordinate People of Color based on race, gender, class, sexuality, language, immigration status, phenotype, accent or surname (see Pérez Huber & Solórzano, 2015a; Pérez Huber & Solórzano, 2015b; Pierce, 1970, 1988, 1995; Solórzano, 1998; Solórzano, Ceja, & Yosso, 2000; Solórzano & Pérez Huber, 2012; Yosso, Smith, Ceja, & Solórzano, 2009). These assaults can be verbal and non-verbal and are often carried out in automatic and unconscious ways by the perpetrator. They are often subtle, but can also be blatant. Finally, microaggressions are cumulative assaults that take a physiological, psychological, and academic toll on People of Color (Pérez Huber & Cueva, 2012; Pierce, 1970, 1988, 1995). I argue that the concept of racial microaggressions is a "tool" useful for research on race, racism, and the everyday experiences of People of Color because it enables us to identify the often subtle acts of racism that can emerge in schools, college campuses, classrooms, and in everyday conversations and interactions. In this chapter, I use racial microaggressions synonymously with everyday racism. At another level, institutional racism can be understood as the formal or informal structural mechanisms, such as policies and processes that systematically subordinate, marginalize, and exclude non-dominant groups and mediate their experiences with everyday racism.

Finally, white supremacy is the set of beliefs and/or ideologies that guides a system of racial domination and exploitation where power and resources are unequally distributed to privilege Whites and oppress People of Color. This ideology also justifies actual or potential social arrangements that legitimize the interests and/or positions of a dominant group (i.e., Whites) over non-dominant groups (i.e., People of Color). My use of white supremacy in the context of the *McLaurin v. Oklahoma* case stems from the observation of the NAACP attorney Robert Carter (1988), who argued the case before the Supreme Court and later reflected on the persistence of race-based educational inequity following the landmark 1954 *Brown v Board of Education* decision.[8] He stated:

> the NAACP lawyers erred. The lawyers did not understand then how effective white power could be in preventing full implementation of the law; nor did they realize at the time that

the basic barrier to full equality for blacks was not racial segregation [institutional racism], a symptom, but white supremacy, the disease. (p. 1095)[9]

These concepts of racial microaggressions, institutional racism, and white supremacy serve as our guides as we embark upon our examination of the photo of George McLaurin sitting outside of the classroom in 1948 (see Figure 3). For instance, I will argue that racial microaggressions take place within the context of institutional racism, and both are made possible within an ideology (and related structures) of white supremacy.

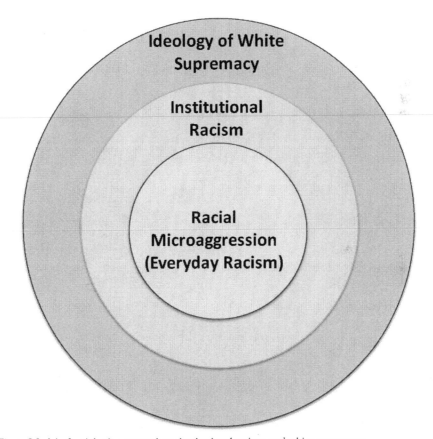

Fig 4: Model of racial microaggressions, institutional racism, and white supremacy.

McLAURIN V. OKLAHOMA LEGAL HISTORY

In 1948 Mr. George McLaurin, a professor at Langston University in Oklahoma—an Historically Black College—applied to, and was denied admission to, the

doctoral program in Educational Administration in the College of Education at
the University of Oklahoma. The reason given for the denial was a 1941 Oklahoma
law titled, "Oklahoma Statutes, Title 70, Section 455."[10] It stated that it was a
misdemeanor, punishable by a fine of not less than $100 nor more than $500, for
"any person, corporation or association of persons to *maintain or operate a college,
school or institution* [emphasis added] of the State where persons of both white and
colored races are received as pupils for instruction."[11] With the legal and political support of the NAACP, Mr. McLaurin challenged this Jim Crow statute. In
1948 the Federal District Court (see *McLaurin v. Oklahoma State Regents*, 1948),
found that:

> The school authorities were required to exclude him [Mr. McLaurin] by the Oklahoma
> statutes (Title 70 Oklahoma Statutes (1941) sections 455, 456, 457) which made it a
> misdemeanor to maintain or operate, teach or attend a school at which both whites and
> Negroes are enrolled or taught.

The Court went on to conclude that:

> The court is of the opinion that insofar as any statute or law of the State of Oklahoma
> denies or deprives this plaintiff admission to the University of Oklahoma for the purpose
> of pursuing the course of study he seeks, *it is unconstitutional and unenforceable* [emphasis
> added].

This meant that the University of Oklahoma had to admit Mr. McLaurin to the
doctoral program in Educational Administration. However, the Court provided an
opening. It went on to state that, "This does not mean, however, that the segregation laws of Oklahoma are *incapable of constitutional enforcement* [emphasis added].
We simply hold that insofar as they are sought to be enforced in *this particular
case*, they are *inoperative*" [emphasis added]. This language provided the University with at least five policy options to meet the mandate of the Court. First, the
University could set up a "separate but equal" school/program (see *Missouri ex rel.
Gaines v. Canada*, 305 U.S. 337, 1938; and *Sweatt v. Painter et al.*, 339 U.S. 629,
1950). For instance, a "separate and equal" doctoral program in Education Administration could be established at the nearby Historically Black College/University
(HBCU)—Langston University in Oklahoma. Second, the state of Oklahoma
could send (and financially support) Mr. McLaurin to another state that would
admit African American students. Third, it could close the Historically White
Institution (HWI)—University of Oklahoma. Fourth, it could let Mr. McLaurin
attend the University of Oklahoma as an equal. Fifth, it could admit Mr. McLaurin
into the University of Oklahoma and segregate him. The University chose the
fifth option—admit him and segregate him. Indeed, when Mr. McLaurin was
finally admitted to the doctoral program, he was forced to sit in an alcove outside
the classroom (i.e., Carnegie Hall, Classroom 104), sit at separate tables at the

university's Bizzell Library,[12] sit at a separate table and specific time in the cafeteria, and use separate bathroom facilities.

Mr. McLaurin and his NAACP attorneys challenged the ruling, and in 1949 the Federal Court of Appeal decided that:

> The segregation condemned in *Westminster School District v. Mendez*, 9 Cir., 161 F.2d 774, was found to be *"wholly inconsistent"* [emphasis added] with the public policy of the State of California, while in *our case* [emphasis added] the segregation based upon racial distinctions is in accord with the *deeply rooted social policy of the State of Oklahoma* [emphasis added].[13]

The Court argued that Jim Crow laws are deeply rooted in the lives and history of the State of Oklahoma. It continued on to state:

> We conclude therefore that the classification, based upon racial distinctions, as recognized and enforced by the regulations of the University of Oklahoma, rests upon a *reasonable basis*, having its foundation in the *public policy of the State, and does not therefore operate to deprive this plaintiff of the equal protection of the laws*. The relief he now seeks is accordingly *denied*. (see *McLaurin v. Oklahoma State Regents for Higher Education*, 1949) [emphasis added]

Again, the Court found that the laws governing Jim Crow segregation "rest on a reasonable basis" based on longstanding public policy in the state and did not violate Mr. McLaurin's 14th Amendment or "equal protection" rights.

The NAACP appealed for relief to the U.S. Supreme Court. On April 3rd and 4th 1950 the case was argued before the Supreme Court.[14] On June 5, 1950, the Court ruled in favor of Mr. McLaurin (see *McLaurin v. Oklahoma State Regents for Higher Education*, 1950). In a unanimous opinion the Court stated:[15]

> We conclude that the conditions under which this appellant is required to receive his education *deprive him of his personal and present right to the equal protection of the laws* [emphasis added]. ... We hold that under these circumstances the Fourteenth Amendment precludes differences in treatment by the state based upon race. Appellant, having been admitted to a state-supported graduate school, *must receive the same treatment at the hands of the state as students of other races* [emphasis added]. The judgment is *Reversed*.

The Supreme Court also took into account "intangible factors," such as "his ability to study, to engage in discussion and exchange views with other students, and, in general, to learn his profession" to strike down these Jim Crow *conditions* and find that a separate program of study of this sort can never be equal. These intangible factors (i.e., Jim Crow conditions) were one of the legal and social cornerstones in the 1954 *Brown* case. In fact, these *intangible factors* continued to be used as a legal strategy to argue in favor of subsequent educational equity and affirmative action cases such as *Bakke v. Board of Regents* (1978), *Gratz v. Bollinger* (2003), *Grutter v. Bollinger (2003), Fisher v. Texas* (2013), and *Schuette v. Coalition to Defend Affirmative Action* (2014).

The NAACP team in *McLaurin v. Oklahoma*, headed by Thurgood Marshall and Robert Carter, felt that this decision (along with *Sweatt v. Painter*) was the beginning of the "End of Jim Crow." In fact, in an NAACP press release dated June 5, 1950, Marshall maintained that these cases now provided a legal road-map to defeat racial segregation in all segments of the educational pipeline (see Figure 5).

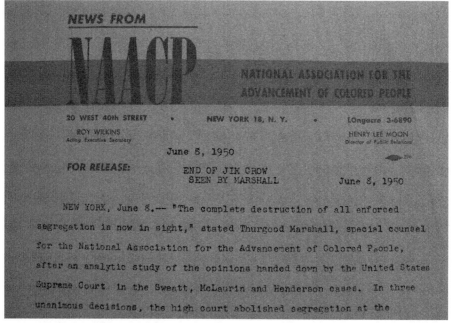

Fig 5: "End of Jim Crow Seen By Marshall," NAACP Press Release, June 8, 1950.
Source: Library of Congress. Manuscript Division, NAACP Archives.

This brief legal history of *McLaurin v. Oklahoma*[16] has shown how Mr. McLaurin and the NAACP challenged Jim Crow segregation laws in the state of Oklahoma.[17] It is the story of how Mr. McLaurin was initially denied admission solely based on his race, was then admitted but segregated based on Jim Crow laws of the state, and finally admitted as an "equal" to the university. It is the story of the racial microaggression of everyday racism living in Jim Crow conditions. It is the story of the institutional racism of Jim Crow policies, processes, and laws. It is the story of the ideology of white supremacy that explains and justifies the everyday and institutional racism.

USING THE TOOLS OF RACIAL MICROAGGRESSIONS, INSTITUTIONAL RACISM, AND WHITE SUPREMACY TO ANALYZE THE MCLAURIN PHOTO

Let's go back to the photo of Mr. McLaurin that began our journey and analyze it using the tools of racial microaggressions, institutional racism, and white supremacy (see Figure 6). In 1948 at least 17 states had Jim Crow (de jure) segregation laws for various public services, accommodations, and race relations (i.e., schools, movie theatres, restaurants, use of textbooks, libraries, inter-racial marriage, etc.).[18] So the very act of Mr. McLaurin sitting outside of the classroom is a form of racial microaggression as everyday racism—circa 1948. In 2015 there are no Jim Crow (de jure) laws that keep People of Color out of schools, classrooms, or other public or private facilities. However, educational institutions have *adapted* (i.e., racial realism) with educational policies (i.e., language policies, curricular policies, disciplinary policies), and in everyday practices that in fact (de facto) keep Students of Color out of, or limit, certain schools/majors or other educational opportunities.[19]

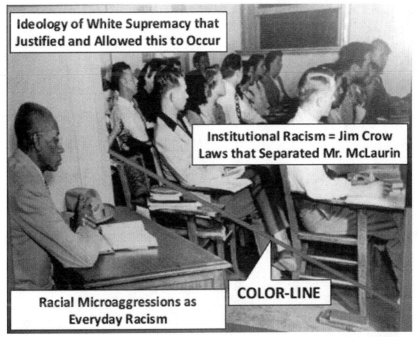

Fig 6: *Separate Is Not Equal: Brown v. Board of Education—McLaurin v. Oklahoma*, 1950. "George McLaurin Seated Outside the Carnegie Hall Classroom 104, 1948." National Museum of American History.

Source: Author's photo archive. Author's annotations.

The next part of the analysis of the photo is the fact that racism in the everyday is often maintained by systems of institutional racism. In the case of Mr. McLaurin, we have the Oklahoma State Statutes (i.e., 455, 456, 457) that made it legal to keep him out of the university and maintain racial segregation by the letter of the law. Today, we don't have codified Jim Crow laws, but we have efforts by states to pass laws that, in fact, keep Students of Color on the margins of various institutions within society. For instance, anti-affirmative action laws in states such as California, Michigan, Washington, Arizona, and others send the message that Students of Color are not wanted or are not qualified for admission to their colleges or universities. Also, anti-immigrant legislation in Arizona, Georgia, Alabama, and other states sends a message to the immigrant community (often Latina/o) that they are not wanted in many aspects of social life—including education.

Finally, the last part of the analysis examines the ideology that Jim Crow laws needed in order to justify keeping Mr. McLaurin out of the University, and, when forced to admit him, to segregate him in various parts of campus life. The ideology of white supremacy is written all over Jim Crow laws; the ideology that whites are superior to African Americans or other People of Color, who, because of their inferiority, need to be separated from whites (Solórzano, 1997). Over the years, we find the ideology of white supremacy embedded in the "cultural deficit" frameworks used to explain why African American and Latina/o students don't do well in school and then to justify separating them into different schools and programs within schools (Solórzano, 1997; Solórzano & Solórzano, 1995; Valencia, 1997; Valencia & Solórzano, 1997).

CONCLUSION

In this chapter, I attempted to use the tools of Critical Race Theory, everyday racism in the form of racial microaggressions, and critical race pedagogy to analyze and understand the 1950 U.S. Supreme Court case of George McLaurin, a 68-year-old doctoral student in Educational Administration at the University of Oklahoma. As the story comes to an end, I want to leave you with two findings—one pedagogical and one theoretical.

First, I want to pay special attention to the importance of Paulo Freire's (1970a, 1970b) methods of critical pedagogy when teaching racism (whether institutional or interpersonal) in and out of the classroom. Freire's concept of generative codes is one of those tools that we often use to engage our students in a problem-posing pedagogy. Generative codes are used in the Freirean Problem-Posing Process (Smith-Maddox & Solórzano, 2002; Solórzano, 1989; Solórzano & Yosso, 2001) and are a way of gathering information in order to create a picture (codify) of real situations that real people experience. Working with Freire's concept of generative codes and engaging in pedagogies of race and racism, we perceive them as visual renditions such as pictures, drawings, stories, articles, song lyrics, or films that illustrate significant themes or problems. At the very least, these generative codes can be used to name the problem as part of problem-posing Critical Race dialogue. The photo of Mr. McLaurin is one such example of a generative code. There are many more pictures and other artifacts that we can use to engage our colleagues in a Critical Race problem-posing dialogue that names the injury, analyzes the causes of the injury, and finds solutions to the injury. To that end, one route to address racial microaggressions, institutional racism, and white supremacy might lie in our pedagogy—our critical pedagogies of race and racism.

Second, Derrick Bell's (1992) concept of "racial realism" (i.e., the permanence of racism) argues that we must develop and implement "strategies that can bring fulfillment and even triumph" (p. 374). Although the *McLaurin* case may have brought "fulfillment and even triumph," Bell (1983) reminded us that we must not lose sight of the disease. Bell (1983) cited Robert Carter (NAACP attorney and chief legal architect of the *McLaurin* and *Brown* cases):

> And Carter adds in language that I have quoted many times because, in my view, it represents the penultimate lesson provided by the school desegregation decisions: "It was not until *Brown I* was decided that blacks were able to understand that the fundamental vice was not legally enforced racial segregation itself; that this was a mere by-product, a symptom of the greater and more pernicious disease—white supremacy." (p. 295)

Bell has taught us that in the journey to "fulfillment and even triumph," we can't lose sight of the disease of white supremacy. Not acknowledging the disease of white supremacy and continuing to focus on such symptoms as racial segregation reinforces the permanence of racism. These have been the lessons learned from Professor Bell as I continue this journey to use the tools of Critical Race Theory to understand the importance of *McLaurin v. Oklahoma* as well as more contemporary cases of institutional racism and white supremacy.

NOTES

1. I use the term "McLaurin's Seat" in reference to Margaret Russell's 2002 article, "McLaurin's Seat: The Need for Racial Inclusion in Legal Education."
2. These are Professor Bell's 6th and last *Casebook* and *Teacher's Manual* before his death in 2011. I used the 4th edition (Bell, 2000).
3. By the time the case was initiated in 1948, Mr. McLaurin had been a professor for 33 years at Langston University in Langston, Oklahoma—An Historically Black College.
4. Opinion in *Shuette v. Coalition to Defend Affirmative Action* was released on April 14, 2014; opinion in *Fisher v. University of Texas et al.* (2016) was released on June 23, 2016.
5. In 2004, I used a hard copy of the NAACP Finding Aid to locate and organize the documents related to the case. Today, you can use the *National Association for the Advancement of Colored People:*

A Finding Aid to the Collection in the Library of Congress (revised April 2010), which is available online at: http://lcweb2.loc.gov/service/mss/eadxmlmss/eadpdfmss/2008/ms008007.pdf

6. *McLaurin v. Oklahoma* was the only pre *Brown v. Board* case that focused on segregation in colleges or graduate schools of education. This fact motivated my interest in the case.

7. Here I recognize Chester Pierce (1970, 1988, 1995) whose seminal work on racial microaggressions serves as the basis for all subsequent work on microaggressions—specifically mine. In other works we define one form of everyday racism as racial microaggressions (see Kohli & Solórzano, 2012; Ledesma & Solórzano, 2013; Pérez Huber & Solórzano, 2015a; Pérez Huber & Solórzano, 2015b; Solórzano, 1998; Solórzano, Ceja, & Yosso, 2000; Solórzano & Pérez Huber, 2012; Yosso, Ceja, Smith, & Solórzano, 2009).

8. It should be noted that Robert Carter argued the *McLaurin* and *Brown* cases before the U.S. Supreme Court. Indeed, during his career with the NAACP, Mr. Carter argued 23 cases before the Supreme Court and won 22 of them.

9. Robert Carter actually makes a similar argument in a 1968 law review article (see Carter, 1968).

10. See *McLaurin v. Oklahoma State Regents for Higher Education, et al.* (1948).

11. There were two other Jim Crow statutes that regulated racial separation in educational institutions in Oklahoma. Oklahoma Statute, Title 70, Section 456 stated: It is a misdemeanor, punishable by a fine of not less than $10 nor more than $50, for *any instructor to teach* "in any school, college or institution where members of the white race and colored race are received as pupils for instruction." Oklahoma Statute, Title 70, Section 457 stated: It is misdemeanor, punishable by a fine of not less than $5 nor more than $20 for "any white person *to attend any school, college or institution*, where colored persons are received as pupils for instruction."

12. Mr. McLaurin was not allowed to check books out of the Bizzell Library.

13. The *Mendez* case in California ruled that segregated Mexican schools were unconstitutional. Also, the NAACP submitted an amicus curiae (friend of the court) brief supporting the *Mendez* plaintiffs.

14. In 1950 the Supreme Court did not record or keep a written transcript of oral arguments (see Barrett, 2002, footnote 25). For a review and synopsis of the cases presented before the Court that week see: *United States Law Week*, "Arguments Before the Court: Racial Segregation Attacked" (1950), *18*(39). Retrieved from (http://www.houseofrussell.com/legalhistory/sweatt/uslw/uslw41150.html

15. The Chief Justice of the Supreme Court at the time of the decision was Fred Vinson. The Associate Justices were Hugo Black, Harold Burton, Tom Clark, William Douglas, Felix Frankfurter, Robert Jackson, Sherman Minton, and Stanley Reed.

16. The full case materials for *McLaurin v. Oklahoma* can be found at: *U.S. Supreme Court Briefs and Records*, October Term 1949, Volume 339, 619–637, Roll 8.

17. For additional history of the McLaurin Case see: Bittle, 1959; Cross, 1975; Hubbell, 1972, 1973; Kluger, 2004; Marshall, 1952; Moon, 1958; Palmer, 1989; Tushnet, 1987; Tushnet, 1994; Weaver & Page, 1982.

18. For examples of late-19th-and early-20th-century Jim Crow laws see: http://americanhistory.si.edu/brown/history/1-segregated/jim-crow.html

19. In September of 2014, I attended the Ford Foundation Conference of Fellows. Over the last 50 years, this Fellowship has been very successful in the supporting, training, and promoting of faculty of color in all disciplines. As a 1987 Postdoctoral Fellow in Sociology, I have attended many of the annual Ford Conferences. Unfortunately, one story hasn't changed over the last 29 years: many colleagues of color lament the fact that they are often the only one in their departments as either faculty or doctoral students.

REFERENCES

Banks, J. (1993, June/July). The canon debate, knowledge construction, and multicultural education. *Educational Researcher, 22*, 4–14.

Barrett, J. (2002). Teacher, student, ticket: John Frank, Leon Higginbotham, and one afternoon at the Supreme Court—Not a trifling thing. *Yale Law & Policy Review, 20*, 311–323.

Bell, D. (1983). Time for the teachers: Putting educators back into the *Brown* remedy. *Journal of Negro Education, 52*, 290–301.

Bell, D. (1992). *Faces at the bottom of the well: The permanence of racism.* New York, NY: Basic Books.

Bell, D. (1993). The racism is permanent thesis: Courageous revelation or unconscious denial of racial genocide. *Capital University Law Review, 22*, 571–587.

Bell, D. (2000). *Race, racism and American law* (4th ed.). New York, NY: Aspen Law and Business.

Bell, D. (2008). *Race, racism and American law* (6th ed.). Austin, TX: Aspen.

Bell, D., & Radice, J. (2008). *Teacher's manual: Race, racism, and American law* (6th ed.). Austin, TX: Aspen.

Bittle, W. (1959). The desegregated all-White institution ... The University of Oklahoma. *Journal of Educational Sociology, 32*, 275–282.

Calmore, J. (1997). Exploring Michael Omi's "messy" real world of race. *Law and Inequality, 15*, 25–82.

Carter, R. (1968). The Warren Court and desegregation. *Michigan Law Review, 67*, 237–248.

Carter, R. (1988). 1988 survey of books relating to the law: The NAACP's legal strategy against legal segregation, 1925–1950. By Mark Tushnet. *Michigan Law Review, 86*, 1083–1095.

Cross, G. (1975). *Blacks in White colleges: Oklahoma's landmark cases.* Norman, OK: University of Oklahoma Press.

Fields, B., & Fields, K. (2012). *Racecraft: The soul of inequality in American life.* New York, NY: Verso.

Freire, P. (1970a). *Cultural action for freedom.* Cambridge, MA: Harvard Educational Review Monographs.

Freire, P. (1970b). *Pedagogy of the oppressed.* New York, NY: Continuum.

Goldberg, D. (1993). *Racist culture: Philosophy and the politics of meaning.* Cambridge, MA: Blackwell.

Gomez, L. (2012). Looking for race in all the wrong places. *Law and Society Review, 46*, 221–245.

Hubbell, J. (1972). The desegregation of the University of Oklahoma, 1946–1950. *Journal of Negro History, 57*, 370–384.

Hubbell, J. (1973). Some reactions to the desegregation of the University of Oklahoma, 1946–1950. *Phylon, 34*, 187–196.

Kluger, R. (2004). *Simple justice: The history of* Brown v. Board of Education *and Black America's struggle for equality.* New York, NY: Vantage Books.

Kohli, R., & Solórzano, D. (2012). Teachers, please learn our names!: Racial microaggressions and the K–12 classroom. *Race, Ethnicity, and Education, 15*, 441–462.

Ladson-Billings, G., & Tate, W. (1995). Toward a Critical Race Theory of education. *Teachers College Record, 97*, 47–68.

Ledesma, M., & Solórzano, D. (2013). Naming their pain: How everyday microaggressions impact students and teachers. In D. Carter Andrews & F. Tuitt (Eds.), *Contesting the myth of a "post racial" era: The continued significance of race in U.S. education* (pp. 112–127). New York, NY: Peter Lang.

Lorde, A. (1992). Age, race, class, and sex: Women redefining difference. In M. Andersen & P. Hill Collins (Eds.), *Race, class, and gender: An anthology* (pp. 495–502). Belmont, CA: Wadsworth.

Marable, M. (1992). *Black America*. Westfield, NJ: Open Media.

Marshall, T. (1952). An evaluation of recent efforts to achieve racial integration in education through resort to the courts. *Journal of Negro Education, 21*, 316–327.

McLaurin v. Oklahoma State Regents for Higher Education, 87 F. Supp. 526 (D. Oklahoma 1948).

McLaurin v. Oklahoma State Regents for Higher Education, U.S. Supreme Court Records & Briefs, Case No. 34, October Term 1949, Volume 339, 619–637, Roll 8.

Moon, F. (1958). Higher education and desegregation in Oklahoma. *Journal of Negro Education, 27*, 300–310.

National Association for the Advancement of Colored People. (2008). *National Association for the Advancement of Colored People: A register of its records in the Library of Congress*. Washington, DC: Library of Congress.

Palmer, J. (1989). *The Vinson Court era: The Supreme Court's conference votes: Data and analysis*. New York, NY: AMS Press.

Parker, L., Deyhle, D., & Villenas, S. (Eds.). (1999). *Race is … race isn't: Critical Race Theory and qualitative studies in education*. Boulder, CO: Westview Press.

Pérez Huber, L., & Cueva, B. (2012). Chicana/Latina *testimonios* on effects and responses to microaggressions. *Equity & Excellence in Education, 45*, 392–410.

Pérez Huber, L., & Solórzano, D. (2015a). Visualizing everyday racism: Critical Race Theory, visual microaggressions, and the historical image of Mexican banditry. *Qualitative Inquiry, 21*, 223–238.

Pérez Huber, L., & Solórzano, D. (2015b). Racial microaggressions as a tool for Critical Race Research. *Race, Ethnicity, and Education, 18*, 297–320.

Pierce, C. (1970). Offensive mechanisms. In F. Barbour (Ed.), *The Black seventies* (pp. 265–282). Boston, MA: Porter Sargent.

Pierce, C. (1988). Stress in the workplace. In A. Coner-Edwards & J. Spurlock (Eds.), *Black families in crisis: The middle class* (pp. 27–34). New York, NY: Brunner/Mazel.

Pierce, C. (1995). Stress analogs of racism and sexism: Terrorism, torture, and disaster. In C. Willie, P. Rieker, B. Kramer, & B. Brown (Eds.), *Mental health, racism, and sexism* (pp. 277–293). Pittsburgh, PA: University of Pittsburgh Press.

Russell, M. (2002). McLaurin's seat: The need for racial inclusion in legal education. *Fordham Law Review, 70*, 1825–1829.

Smith-Maddox, R., & Solórzano, D. (2002). Using Critical Race Theory, Paulo Freire's problem-posing method, and case study research to confront race and racism in education. *Qualitative Inquiry, 8*, 66–84.

Solórzano, D. (1989). Teaching and social change: Reflections on a Freirean approach in a college classroom. *Teaching Sociology, 17*, 218–225.

Solórzano, D. (1997). Images and words that wound: Critical Race Theory, racial stereotyping, and teacher education. *Teacher Education Quarterly, 24*, 5–19.

Solórzano, D. (1998). Critical Race Theory, race and gender microaggressions, and the experiences of Chicana and Chicano scholars. *Qualitative Studies in Education, 11*, 121–136.

Solórzano, D., Ceja, M., & Yosso, T. (2000). Critical Race Theory, racial microaggressions, and campus racial climate: The experiences of African American college students. *Journal of Negro Education, 69*, 60–73.

Solórzano, D., & Pérez Huber, L. (2012). Microaggressions, racial. In J. Banks (Ed.), *Encyclopedia of diversity in education* (pp. 1489–1492). Thousand Oaks, CA: Sage.

Solórzano, D., & Solórzano, R. (1995). The Chicano educational experience: A proposed framework for effective schools in Chicano communities. *Educational Policy, 9*, 293–314.

Solórzano, D., & Yosso, T. (2001). Maintaining social justice hopes within academic realities: A Freirean approach to Critical Race/LatCrit pedagogy. *Denver Law Review, 78*, 595–621.

Tushnet, M. (1987). *The NAACP's legal strategy against segregated education, 1925–1950.* Chapel Hill, NC: University of North Carolina Press.

Tushnet, M. (1994). *Making civil rights law.* New York, NY: Oxford University Press.

Valencia, R. (Ed.). (1997). *The evolution of deficit thinking: Educational thought and practice.* London, England: Falmer Press.

Valencia, R., & Solórzano, D. (1997). Contemporary deficit thinking. In R. Valencia (Ed.), *The evolution of deficit thinking in educational thought and practice* (pp. 160–210). New York, NY: Falmer Press.

Weaver, B., & Page, O. (1982). The Black press and the drive for integrated graduate and professional education. *Phylon, 43*, 15–28.

Yosso, T., Smith, W., Ceja, M., & Solórzano, D. (2009). Critical Race Theory, racial microaggressions and campus racial climate for Latina/o undergraduates. *Harvard Educational Review, 79*, 659–690.

CHAPTER FOUR

The Utility OF "The Space Traders" AND Its Variations AS CRT Teachable Moments

ANA CAROLINA ANTUNES, ROSIE CONNOR, KATHRYN K. COQUEMONT, KEHAULANI FOLAU, ALLISON MARTIN, LAURA TODD, AND LAURENCE PARKER

INTRODUCTION BY LAURENCE PARKER

There has been much historical debate in education research circles surrounding the legitimacy of alternative epistemologies, ways of knowing, and research methodologies emerging from critical race theory (Hylton, 2012; Parker, 2105). For example, there has been criticism leveled by some against Bell (1992a) and his fictional narrative "The Space Traders." In this counterstory, aliens come to earth and offer to solve all of the chronic problems facing the U.S. (environmental contamination, reliance on fossil fuels, the national debt, etc.) if the U.S. agrees to give the aliens all their persons classified as Black. The main character in "The Space Traders" is Professor Golightly, he is an African American moderate Republican who is a member of the president's cabinet. He, among others, voices strong objections to the offer made by the aliens and works with a group of wealthy White capitalist and business leaders to initially lead a campaign against the offer; he does this because he feels that Whites will be capitalist first and racist second and that the financial impact of Blacks being sent to space will hurt the viability of the U.S. economy. But later in the story, Professor Golightly posits that a position of interest convergence is the best one to take to get Whites to vote with Blacks against the offer. He perceives that interest convergence will be in the best interest of Blacks in the U.S. because they will engage in a campaign of saying that the space trader deal is a form of reverse discrimination and that these space traders will treat Blacks so well in terms of equality, civil rights, and economic and political opportunities that Whites will be jealous and want to stop and vote against the offer. In the end, however, the vote to accept the deal overwhelmingly passes and the Blacks are boarded on buses to oceanfront areas and beamed up to the alien spacecrafts in the sky.

When I have used the "Space Traders" story in classes ranging from high school American history classes to undergraduate and graduate school classes on Critical Race Theory and education policy, with predominantly African American and majority White European Americans and/or racially diverse classes (e.g., Asian/Pacific Islanders, Latinos/as and Chicanas/os, tribal nation groups), there have been two (among many) themes that emerge in the class discussion. When asked, could this happen now? (1) the high school students, particularly those who are African American, say "yes, it definitely could." Their responses are that "White people don't want us here anyway so they will be glad to send us off in space"; and (2) the undergraduates, to some extent, and definitely the older/professional Master's and doctoral students, have a different, more mixed, view with some saying that with the U.S. having had its first Black president, and, overall, overt individual racist acts in the U.S. being on the decline, therefore the majority of the population, particularly White European Americans, would vote against the space traders' offer. In the classes, reading the counterstory (and also sometimes watching it on video) has brought up the major tenets of CRT theoretical framework in the fields of law and education that explores the ways in which alleged race-neutral policies, practices, and laws perpetuate racial/ethnic subordination. It emphasizes the importance of viewing policies, practices, and laws within a proper historical and cultural context in order to deconstruct their racialized meanings (Bell, 1995; Crenshaw, Gotanda, Peller, & Thomas, 1995; Ladson-Billings & Tate, 1995). This framework challenges dominant liberal concepts such as colorblindness and meritocracy and shows how these ideas operate to disadvantage people of color while further advantaging Whites (Delgado & Stefancic, 1994). Originally developed by legal scholars of color, CRT is grounded in a "social reality that is defined by our experiences and the collective historical experience of our communities of origin. CRT theorists typically utilize dialogues, stories, chronicles, and personal testimonies as a method in their scholarship because some members of marginalized groups, by virtue of their marginal status, are able to tell different stories from the ones White scholars usually hear and tell (Delgado, 1990). There are at least five defining elements that form the basic assumptions, perspectives, research methods, and pedagogies of CRT (Solórzano & Yosso, 2002).

The Centrality of Race and Racism

CRT acknowledges as its most basic premise that race and racism are defining characteristics of American society. In American higher education, race and racism are imbedded in the structures, discourses, and policies that guide the daily practices of universities. Race and racism are central constructs that intersect with other dimensions of one's identity, such as language, generation status, gender, sexuality, and class (Crenshaw, 1995). For people of color, each of these dimensions of one's identity can potentially elicit multiple forms of subordination, yet each dimension can also be subjected to different forms of oppression.

The Challenge to Dominant Ideology

A CRT in higher education challenges the traditional claims of universities to objectivity, meritocracy, color-blindness, race neutrality, and equal opportunity. This theoretical framework reveals how the dominant ideology of color-blindness and race neutrality acts as a camouflage for the self-interest, power, and privilege of dominant groups in American society (Delgado, 1989; López, 2003).

A Commitment to Social Justice and Praxis

CRT has a fundamental commitment to a social justice agenda that struggles to eliminate all forms of racial, gender, language, generation status, and class subordination (Matsuda, 1996). In higher education, these theoretical frameworks are conceived as a social justice project that attempts to link theory with practice, scholarship with teaching, and the academy with the community (Lynn, 1999; Solórzano, 1998).

A Centrality of Experiential Knowledge

CRT recognizes that the experiential knowledge of people of color is legitimate and critical to understanding racial subordination. The application of a CRT framework in an analysis of research and practice in the field of higher education requires that the experiential knowledge of people of color be centered and viewed as a resource stemming directly from their lived experiences. The experiential knowledge can come from storytelling, family history, biographies, scenarios, parables, *cuentos*, chronicles, and narratives (Delgado, 1989; Delgado Bernal, 2002).

A Historical Context and Interdisciplinary Perspective

CRT challenges ahistoricism and the unidisciplinary focus of most analyses in law and educational research. In the field of higher education research and practice, these frameworks analyze race and racism in both a historical and contemporary context using interdisciplinary methods (Delgado, 1989; Lynn & Dixson, 2013).

In addition, other new trends have emerged as part of the discussions about "The Space Traders" and its connection to new trends in CRT, such as those posited by Bonilla-Silva (2015), which include: (1) the epistemology of race, (2) the origins of race analysis in geo-special sectors and organizations, (3) intermediate racial categories, (4) refinement and changing analysis of intersectionality, (5) an interrogation as to how deep-whiteness is salient, (6) the racialization of immigrants, (7) racial socialization, and (8) interracial relationships. To this end, I have collected "Space Trader" spin-off counterstories that my doctoral students developed in my CRT class at the University of Utah (spring 2015) that add depth to Bell's original intent with the story but also bring up new issues for discussion as we use his work in our field as we move into using race and naming racism while questioning these categories themselves in research and theory; while still acknowledging their racial realist saliency in these times of violence against youth of color and tribal nation youth and the materialist conditions of poverty linked to structural racism (Bell, 1992b; Harris & Liberman, 2015; Leonardo, 2013).

THE SPACE TRADERS RETURN: THE STORY OF SOUTHEAST ASIAN AMERICANS BY KATHRYN K. COQUEMONT

On the 25th anniversary of the Space Traders' first contact with the United States, they returned to the beaches of New Jersey. Like the last time, their arrival had been broadcast for weeks through radio messages, and millions of people woke up early to crowd the Jersey shore, turn on their television, or watch on their phones, tablets, or computers. As New Jersey one of the states with the largest Asian American population, it was of no surprise that while the majority of those standing on the beach were White, a sizeable number were also Asian American, mostly East Asian American.

The weeks leading up to the Space Traders' return had been filled with excitement for a large portion of the American public. White Americans remembered the benefits of the last exchange, when the aliens left extraordinary amounts of gold to remove the national debt, chemicals to remove pollution, and a nuclear engine and fuel to replace depleted fossil fuels.

Unfortunately, the U.S. government had not wisely used these gifts to make better financial choices, but instead used the lack of debt as a reason to spend at higher rates, particularly in areas of defense and space exploration. Additionally, the exemption of local, state, and federal taxes for a year after the Space Traders' original exchange led to pressure on Congress to lower taxes to a much smaller rate than the pre-Space-Trader era. Republicans, desperate to stay in power, acquiesced to the public's demands. Together, these decisions led federal, state, and local governments to again fall into deep debt.

Additionally, the chemicals that removed pollutants from the environment ran out after 20 years and could not be duplicated in laboratories. Instead of using these 2 decades of clean air, land, and water to create more sustainable ways of living and commuting, American businesses used them as a reason to suspend investments into hybrid and electric transportation and began selling more extravagant vehicles that made Hummers one of the most fuel efficient options of the modern era. The last 5 years without the Space Traders' chemicals made it apparent that the U.S. was heading back towards high toxicity levels in the air in most urban areas.

Because excess had been a way of life for the 25 years after the Space Traders' visit, it was difficult for Americans to change their expectations to make better use of their fiscal and environmental resources. Polls showed that the majority of White Americans felt excited about the Space Traders' return, because they hoped the U.S. would receive more gold, chemicals, and aid for their current problems.

However, for American citizens of color, the Space Traders' return was highly alarming. With the removal of 20 million Black Americans, U.S. racial dynamics had changed dramatically. Although those over 70 and those with serious disabilities and illnesses had been exempt, most of these Black Americans had passed away or been institutionalized in the last 25 years. Additionally, the 1,000 Black detainees had been reduced to only a few hundred due to violent crimes and inhumane treatment that allowed White Americans and the U.S. government to eventually take over the vast property and possessions over which the detainees had been named as trustees. Because of their suspended citizenship, the Black detainees were moved to live in government housing in a specially zoned area, similar to Nazi ghettos and American Indian reservations. Like European Jews and American Indians before them, the detainees did not have access to the health care, education, or rights that were inalienable to other Americans. Disease, violence, and poverty were all now a way of life for the surviving Black Americans. Most Americans under the age of 30 could not remember ever having direct contact with a Black person, and most historical representations in movies and television were now through African-filmed productions or non-Black actors wearing Blackface.

Without Black Americans existing in U.S. society, more racism and hostile scrutiny had been directed at the Latino/Latina Americans, Asian Americans, Pacific Islander Americans, Middle Eastern Americans, Native Americans, and Jewish Americans. Some affluent Middle Eastern Americans and Jewish Americans moved to Canada and Europe, and a small minority of these populations connected with their ethnic roots by moving to Israel and the Middle East. Many Middle Eastern American and Jewish Americans who could pass as White, non-Jewish Americans changed their names to escape hostility directed at their ethnic groups. Jewish Americans in particular were held in contempt as they were still seen as American traitors for having allied themselves with Black Americans during the original Space Trader offer. Jewish jokes were acceptable in mainstream society, and more and more Jews chose to live in neighborhoods with other Jewish families. Predominantly Jewish public schools were often underfunded by local governments. Although public sentiment indicated that Jewish Americans were seen as untrustworthy, they were not seen as violent criminals like Latino/Latina Americans, Pacific Islander Americans, and Southeast Asian Americans were now widely believed to be.

Latino/Latina Americans, Pacific Islander Americans, and Southeast Asian Americans were now even more widely targeted by institutional and systemic racism in ways similar to how Black Americans had been treated previously. Because these communities often went to Black schools before the Space Traders' visit and had similar social disadvantages and discrimination leveraged against them, it was not surprising that public sentiment now held these populations in the same disparagement given previously to Black Americans. In surveys and polls it was shown that White Americans believed many current social issues such as crime, economic waste, and negative race relations were due to Latino/Latina Americans, Pacific Islander Americans, and Southeast Asian Americans.

East and South Asian Americans continued to be labeled as model minorities by which other racial and ethnic groups were measured. Despite the blatant racism of the American government in the Space Traders' exchange, East and South Asian Americans were still the proof to many White Americans that the U.S. was a meritocracy and that racial minorities could find success if they tried hard enough and stopped being lazy and violent. Because of the government's recent lack of focus on Black Americans, the U.S. now had more time to disaggregate data about the Asian American community. Due to this, it was now widely understood that a wide achievement gap existed between East and South Asian Americans and Southeast Asian Americans. While White America acknowledged the success of many East and South Asian Americans (though not the systemic and oppressive barriers through which they had to persist), White America categorized Southeast Asian Americans as likely to be in gangs, hostile to others, lazy, and unable or unwilling to assimilate to mainstream culture, particularly in education and the job market. Despite these negative stereotypes and racist actions taken against them, Southeast Asian Americans did not consider leaving the U.S. since their migration was often by refugee status due to unsafe past living conditions.

As the sun rose on the New Jersey shore, many Southeast Asian Americans watched from home as the Space Traders greeted the U.S. delegation awaiting them. Again, the aliens acknowledged that their spaceships held enormous amounts of gold and special chemicals to keep the environment unpolluted. This time, they also offered the formula so that laboratories could replicate the chemicals when they were depleted. In return, the visitors asked for another group of

Americans that they could take back to their home star. Although there was no specific type of American for whom the Space Traders asked, they did ask that there be at least 2 million Americans who would board their ships in one week's time in exchange for the gold, chemicals, and formula. Again, the visitors' leader acknowledged that the proposed trade would be voluntary and not forced on the U.S., but what would happen to those potentially traded would not be addressed.

When the visitors departed again in their ships, the president of the United States who had been watching the exchange from his bunker in the White House breathed a sigh of relief. This time, his Cabinet knew to be ready and waiting for a meeting. All members of the Cabinet and the president identified as White and most as men.

Although the Space Traders never mentioned race in their current offer, the Cabinet already had packets of information about each marginalized race of Americans. Thus, the conversation started with the assumption that one of these groups would be offered to the Space Traders. It was immediately noticed that Pacific Islander Americans, Native Americans, and Middle Eastern Americans on their own would not fulfill the quota, but that Latino/Latina Americans, East Asian Americans, South Asian Americans, and Southeast Asian Americans would all more than compensate for the 2 million. Although Latino/Latina Americans and East Asian Americans numbered far more than the amount for which the Space Traders asked, Southeast Asian Americans were counted under 3 million in total population. As one Cabinet member immediately noted, exempting those over 70 and those with serious disabilities and illnesses would still allow for a little over 2 million Southeast Asians to be counted. The secretary of homeland security responded, "It is much safer for a group to have almost its entire population removed than to leave a large number of healthy, young, and angry members behind. If we considered other groups, we would needlessly either give more than 2 million people to the Space Traders or else deal with riots across the U.S. from the remaining population. It is logical and safer to pick the group that most closely represents the number demanded."

"It's a good group to consider, because they aren't actually Americans. I mean, a lot of them aren't even willing to learn our language, much less contribute to the American economy in a meaningful way," added the secretary of labor. "Their kids don't care to try in school, and so most of them become thugs or blue collar workers that won't be overly missed."

"Latinos not only make up a much larger portion of the workforce, they are almost all the agricultural workers of our nation. If we choose them, it would have an enormous impact on our food production," said the secretary of labor.

"And East Asian Americans are connected to much more powerful countries than some of the other groups. I worry that if we selected them, we may have a war on our hands," commented the secretary of defense.

"East Asian Americans and South Asian Americans are also tied to countries where we have significant economic relations that should be protected," added the secretary of commerce.

"Looking at the statistics, Southeast Asian Americans have a history of low income and high use of government handouts. Trading them would not only bring in gold but also remove the need to pay for welfare, healthcare, and other social services," said the secretary of health and human services.

"They also are not achieving in K–12 education. They cost more money to educate since they often require special education. We also provide many of them free school breakfasts and lunches since they often live in poverty, though few go on to college so will probably never pay the states back with much tax money as high income earners," stated the secretary of education.

"Should we consider Jewish Americans? Or asking for volunteers?" asked the White House chief of staff.

"Not only would Israel have issues with that, but so would most of Europe given the history," said the ambassador to the United Nations.

"I don't think we could find and organize 2 million volunteers in the next 6 days," commented the president. "It sounds like the most favorable option would be to select the Southeast Asian community for this honor of serving our country. It also sounds like we are in agreement that we should not pass up this highly valuable offer to fix our economic and environmental struggles. Attorney General, can you please draft proposed legislation? I will call a special session of Congress so that we can get something passed as soon as possible. Thank you for your time and ideas. Meeting adjourned."

AN EXAMINATION OF BLACK FEMALE PHYSICIAN FACULTY USING A CRITICAL RACE THEORY LENS BY ROSIE CONNOR

This is a fictional account of a conversation I had with a White colleague, who we will call Robert. Robert is founder and president of a medical device company in southern California. He is well connected with many well-known physicians and within the healthcare industry.

Robert: "So what's your dissertation topic?"
Me: "I'm planning to do a critical examination of the Black female physician faculty pipeline."
Robert: "That should be interesting."
Me: "Well, there's hardly any published research on this group. I became interested in this group of doctors when I worked at the medical school. I worked with these awesome women who were not well represented

	in the school's leadership and not very well represented in the scholarly literature either."
Robert:	"What kind of study will it be?"
Me:	"Well it started out as a qualitative study, but once I started looking at the numbers I realized that the numbers also tell a story all by themselves."
Robert:	"Why's that? How many Black female physicians are there in the country?"
Me:	"Well, there are a little more than 18,000 Black female physicians. That's only about 2 percent of the physician population. The numbers are even worse for medical school faculty members where there are only about 2,000 Black female physician faculty members in the nation."
Robert:	"18,000! I'm surprised it's that high!"
Me:	"What?"
Robert:	"What's the Black population in the U.S.?"
Me:	"It's about 13.5 percent."
Robert:	"The Black population is about 13 percent and 2 percent of the doctors in the country are Black women. That's freaking amazing! I mean just think about all the shit that Black women have to go through. That's why I'm surprised the number is that high."
Me:	"Well, I agree with that, but …"
Robert:	"Hey, most of them don't even know who their fathers are."
Me:	"Did you really just say that? That's such stereotypical crap! I grew up in a home with my father. So did most of my friends. And, yes we were poor and in the hood. So, please don't …"
Robert:	"Okay, okay, okay. So that point is debatable. But it's still true that you guys have unbelievable obstacles. The fact that 2 percent made it through medical school is f*ing amazing! I work with these White guys. I know what happens there."
Me:	"That's exactly why I need to do this research. It's not because of the 2 percent who make it. It's all about all the others who don't and all the reasons why they don't."
Robert:	"That's true, but I think having the women tell their stories would make an unbelievable dissertation. Just one woman's story would be incredible."
Me:	"You're right. One woman's story would be amazing, but I think this story with the data needs to be told first. The numbers will tell a story that's a little harder to deny."

There are points to like and loathe about Robert's point of view: the fact that Robert acknowledges that Black women face unique challenges in America; and his "insider" perspective on "what goes on" in medical education. But his stereotypical characterization of Black family life was problematic (which was more completely expressed later in a conversation). More troubling than Robert's misguided stereotypical viewpoint was his perspective that 2 percent was good, actually not just good but "f*ing amazing." This kind of perspective, which is not rare, contributes to the denial or lack of awareness of the problem and supports the maintenance of the status quo.

SPACE TRADERS IN THE WEALTHY ROCKIES
BY LAURA TODD

In a small Rocky Mountain resort town, privilege and White elitism runs deep. Five-star hotels and restaurants, award-winning ski resorts, and a climate conducive for year-round outdoor activities has created a niche lifestyle and drawn a cadre of ski and mountain biking enthusiasts who *choose* to live here. They visit during a ski vacation and realize the endless trails, open space, and choice schools—along with globalized markets that can be "virtually" run anywhere, make it viable to get out of the crowded suburbs of Los Angeles and the exorbitantly priced boroughs of New York City. And so they come. For people used to diversity in their neighborhoods, this resort mountain town initially feels like an episode of *The Twilight Zone*. An abundance of Whiteness, with little-to-no color in the demographic landscape, save for the Latin@s serving the White families—cleaning their homes, hotels rooms, and vacation rentals. In the schools, there is a deep divide between the two groups of students. The Lululemon-wearing, Range-Rover driving moms sidle up to the school for morning drop-off and make their way into the school for PTO meetings, Academic League, Dual-Language parent meetings, and a session with the school counselors to confirm that their child will be missing the next 2 weeks because they will be competing at Fill-in-the Blank Nationals, or their family cruise to St. Bart's cannot possibly be wrapped up in one measly week over spring break, or Tommy's lacrosse camp at Duke will be extended to include a sail around Martha's Vineyard. All this with the assurance that said son or daughter will be completing all work on the school-issued Pear Book Pro computer with built-in Wi-fi hotspot.

One day during pick up—not regular pick up, but the *Early Release pick up*, where the skiers, ski jumpers, Nordic skiers, lugers, aerialists, snowboard free-stylists, hockey players, equestrians, mountain bike racers, and ice skaters leave to train for aforementioned Nationals (basically the majority of the White population), the school intercom reverberates with a high-pitched static. The kids start moaning and covering their ears. The teachers are not surprised—they are used to the droning on over the speakers at all times of day. This time it is not the principal or the front-office secretaries, it is Standardized Alien. Standardized Alien commences by stating its faction of deficit-loving aliens will taking over Mount Excellence Middle School and transporting all students to Neoliberalimville unless *all* students are proficient on the end-of-year state test. The pod of moms in the pickup lane is privy to the demands and becomes indignant, whereby they convene at their makeshift Central-Command—the local Suckyourbucks Coffee—to map out a logistics plan of attack:

"Well, this does not include our kids, our children score well above proficiency."

"Why don't they just take the non-proficient students? We'd all be better off without their scores bringing down our school grade. We might make an "A" instead of a "B+.""

"How can they expect we bear the burden for the Low Latin@s (LLs)? It is unjust the way the school enables them."

"We do not have the advantages they do—we have to do it all on our own by paying for private tutors and ski coaches, summer camps, and travel to broaden their horizons, yet they have Latinos in Action."

"What programs does the school sponsor for *our* children?"

"We should have CIA. (Caucasians in Action) to equalize the playing field. Latinos in Action gives them a leg up when they apply to college. The Ivies look favorably upon these programs. Our kids deserve the same."

"The district has opened up the dual-language classes for native speakers. How is this fair? They already speak a foreign language."

"Now we are going to have to go to a lottery system for our younger kids. They might not get a seat in the classes, and we already have our tickets booked for Spain next summer."

"I am over how Mt. Excellence under-educates our children as it is and Standardized Aliens are threatening to take over the schools because of *their* scores?!"

"What more can we do? I email all Bobby's teachers every week. I volunteer in the library shelving books so the librarians can take a break, and I do not see any LL parents at the school helping, yet we are expected to suffer because they are not prepared and proficient? I think not."

"What are our options?"

"Why don't we start a charter school?"

"Yeah, we can be the board and make sure only 'qualified' applicants are accepted to the school."

"Our charter will start with no standardized testing, dual-language classes will only be offered for students who do not speak any other languages."

"We will have a mandatory summer study abroad program in Chile or Spain."

"Instead of shelving books, we will create a Cyber Café with e-books and espresso machines."

After all, they are more than your average moms; they are committed to White Smother Mothering because their children's lives depend on it.

SPACE TRADERS IN THE U.S. ON TV IN BRAZIL
BY ANA CAROLINA ANTUNES

The news first broke out in the U.S., but in the era of the blink-and-you-miss-it news cycle it did not take long for the story to make its way to Brazilian television. The channel's logo took over the screen, interrupting the afternoon re-run of high-school-set American drama. Janaína wasn't much of a news enthusiast, so she lazily reached for the remote on top of her belly to change the channel. Her TV set was not new, in fact, she thought, it was as old as old can be, like pre-flat-screen old. Janaína didn't even have to wait for the image to form, in her old TV set the sound would come in first to a black screen, the image would form in a few seconds, but for the girl that was enough time to know that the report had taken over all of the channels in her basic cable package. After circling through all the channels once, she finally settled on one.

"It is still not known," the perfectly coiffed reporter announced, "what the aliens intend to do with the population offered up as trade or if the offer will be extended to other countries, but the Brazilian president has already called a meeting with civil and religious leaders in order to be prepared for future contact."

Janaína looked around, trying to take in the moment and the news. Aliens. People. As. Trade. But for what? She reached for her canvas backpack on the foot of her bed. Trying to be economical in her movements, she got up from her bed just enough to touch the opened front pocket, and, with the tips of her fingers, she grabbed her phone.

While the TV and other appliances in the house may not have been top of the line, Janaína had told her mother that she could not, "I mean literally, could not," in her exact words, go to school without the newest, coolest smartphone. Her mother, Maristella, had conceded in this case. For most of their lives, it had been just the two of them, and Janaína had had to live without a lot of the luxuries that some of her schoolmates have. No trips to Disneyworld, no private English lessons, no dance class, and no fancy birthday party when she turned 15. So Maristella had put the fancy phone on the credit card and hoped for the best.

In the next few minutes, Janaína read all the posts on Facebook, Tumblr, Twitter, and Instagram, trying to piece together what was happening. Not an easy task, the threads, posts, and tweets were faster than she could follow, but the key points of the situation were becoming clear: an alien ship had appeared above Washington, DC and the … the people—Janaína wasn't sure how to refer to aliens, people didn't seem right but what else was there?—had proposed some sort of trade, all of the Black Americans for a sort of fix-all ticket. At that moment, Janaína thought about the TV infomercials, with their tacky voiceovers and their promises of solving all of the viewers' problems. She could see the "wait, but there is more" part coming soon. That is why the Brazilian government was calling for an emergency meeting. "We are the free bonus," she thought, "the two for the price of one."

She sat up on her bed, and looked at the clock on the nightstand. "I want to remember the exact time," she thought. Janaína had been too young to remember 9/11, but she had heard her older cousins talking about the exact moment they learned what had happened. "This is one of those moments, a moment I'll remember for the rest of my life." She wasn't sure how this moment would affect her, but she knew deep in her gut that it would be in a big way.

As the afternoon progressed, more information started to arrive on TV, status updates, and the hashtags. Janaína followed closely as reports of meetings between political, religious, and civil rights leaders happened in the United States. "How can there be so much discussion? Nobody would say yes to this." Janaína got so caught up in the never-ending reports that she forgot it was her turn to make dinner. It was only when she heard the key entering the lock that she realized how late it was. She tried to rush out of her bedroom and into the kitchen, but her mother was already in the house by the time she made it past the hallway.

Maristella shook her head as she set her purse on the table by the door. She knew her daughter too well. Without saying anything the woman entered the kitchen, turned the stove on and grabbed a frozen lasagna from the freezer. Janaína tried to muster an explanation: "I'm sorry ... I ... have you been watching the news? It is crazy!" Maristella worked as secretary at a small firm, and while she worked in front of a computer all day, she hardly had time to do anything else other than work. She was the scheduler, accountant, human resource, and courier. "I heard about it but have not gotten a lot of information about it. ... Something about aliens? Now, I did not think I would live to see something like that!" "It's all over the news," said Janaína. "I mean, it is the ONLY thing on TV." Janaína turned the TV on and set on the couch. In the rush to get to the kitchen before her mother came in, the girl had left the TV in her bedroom on, and the same transmission could be heard from the living room, with a slight delay. Normally, nothing would have bugged Maristella more than two TVs on at the same time, but today was a different day. She sat by her daughter and took off her shoes.

"And reports are just in that the American government has just decided to accept the aliens' proposal! This is incredible! Despite the protests that have sparked all over the world, the American government has announced that the benefits that the trade would bring to the overall population outweigh the human loss," said the international correspondent straight from New York City. The image of the reporter gave way to footage of Black Americans reacting differently to the news: hugging their families, crying hysterically, looting stores on the street, trying to flee to Canada and to Mexico. The women sat in silence as the news played through the night. The images of people reacting to the news became images of people being escorted to the place assigned for pick up.

As she sat next to her mother, holding hands together, Janaína started to think about the possibility of the proposal being extended outside of American borders. In Brazil, she had always been called "morena" "café com leite" or "escurinha," but as she watched the people being taken to the trade-off spot she noticed people who were a lot lighter than she was. What would happen if the deal got extended to other countries? Would each country determine what it means to be Black? Would American standards be extended to all? Janaína held her mother's hand a little tighter, and then an even scarier thought came to her mind. She looked at her mother's hand again; juxtaposing both of their skins she could see how much darker her mother was. She had never really noticed it until now. "What if," she tried to push the idea away from her mind, "no, that wouldn't happen. … What if … what if mom was considered Black but I wasn't." She thought about her life without her mother. Who would take care of her? She knew she couldn't count on her dad, and if her mother was traded, her grandmother would be too, definitely. Suddenly a sense of guilt came over her; she remembered all of the times her grandmother came to pick her up from school and her friends thought she was the nanny. "I never corrected them," she thought, "I should have told them she was my grandma, but I didn't." Despite their limited means, Maristella always put Janaína's education first, and for the last couple of years they had counted on the help of Janaína's grandmother to pay for the girl's school. The weight of the old woman's sacrifice was even heavier now.

The night turned into day as the sun rose up through their window. The alarms rang in the bedrooms, first in Maristella's and then in Janaína's, adding to the TV echoing in the back. The cacophony played on, but nothing disturbed the women. They were lost so deep in their thoughts, hoping that their fate would be different than the people on TV.

They couldn't be sure what time it was, but when the sun was already high in the sky a reporter came on live from Brasília. "We just received the information that the president will make an announcement shortly confirming a trade with the United States. We've been hearing rumors all night that the American government was offered to have its fresh water and renewable energy supply doubled if it could double the number of people traded with the aliens. The previous deal promised to solve all current problems but did not guarantee they would not arise again; with the second offer the country would most likely never have issues again. In order to fulfill the deal, The United States has offered free-trade agreements to the nations that are willing to help the Americans fulfill the second quota." The reporter turns her back to the camera, "it seems that the president is walking out as we speak." The camera moves away from the reporter and zooms in on the podium.

Maristella and Janaína look motionless at the screen, their hearts racing for what is about to come.

THE SPACE TRADERS COME TO TAKE A "PROBLEM" OFF A SCHOOL'S HANDS BY ALLISON MARTIN

Mr. Johnson hung up the phone and laid his head on his desk. It was after 6 p.m. and he was still in his office. To say today had been long would be an understatement. It began, as the past 4 days had begun, with news crews lining the entrance to Park Hills High, the school where Mr. Johnson had been principal for the past 11 years. When Mr. Johnson had started, Park Hills was considered one of the best high schools in the state. The students attending this large suburban school were mostly wealthy and White. The combination resulted in high test scores and graduation rates and a trophy case full of academic and athletic awards. But in the last few years, the school had been in something of a decline. As the economy shifted and White families moved out of Park Hills neighborhoods, the school's racial composition shifted. At first, Mr. Johnson and his staff were happy with the changes. Diversity was something the school always struggled with and now they were finally getting some students they could point to when criticized for being an "all-White" school. And Mr. Johnson was proud of the way his teachers kept all their curriculum and pedagogy the same despite the school's shifting demographics. That showed they believed all students were the same, regardless of race, right? Mr. Johnson wished someone would explain that to Mrs. Boston, the nosy board member who keeps publically criticizing the school and its teaching staff for not providing a quality education to its African American students.

At the thought of Mrs. Boston, Mr. Johnson lifted his head from his desk and looked around. Was she right? Sure, test scores had gone down recently but that was nothing compared with the controversy currently facing the school. Miles Jensen, the school's star quarterback, was accused of wearing a KKK hood during the school's "White-out" pep assembly last week and taunting other, mostly Black, students with it. Reports of other instances of racial discrimination kept coming in as well. Other football team members stood accused of drawing a swastika on the locker of a teammate who was African American. Teachers were accused of not intervening when they heard students use the n-word in the hallway. Even Mr. Johnson was accused of racism for not more harshly punishing a student who called another student the n-word during a fight that ended with the African American student in the hospital. That one really got to him. After all, school policy was very clear. Both students were fighting so both were punished equally. Mr. Johnson couldn't let one off easy just because he lost the fight or was called a mean name. What kind of leadership would that be?

Try telling that to the news cameras lined up outside. Mr. Johnson audibly snorted. All the media seemed interested in reporting was how Park Hills High was racist. Headlines such as "KKK football player not punished" and "Racist incident at Park Hills" had run each day since the controversy made the news. Meanwhile, Mrs. Boston used the attention to further criticize Mr. Johnson and his staff for failing to meet the needs of their African American students. It was all too much; Mr. Johnson put his head back on his desk. What was he to do now?

Just then a bright light and loud beeping noise interrupted the silence. Mr. Johnson looked up just in time to see a video seemingly projected in mid air above his desk. On the screen, a White, middle-aged man appeared. "Mr. Johnson, I represent a consortium of powerful individuals who are interested in helping you out. We can solve your school's PR problem, raise student test scores, and ensure the School Board views you and your school positively. As an added bonus we can guarantee you the state football championship as well as scholarships to top-tier schools for all your graduates. All we ask in return is all of your African American students."

Mr. Johnson was stunned. "What do you mean all African American students?" he asked.

"We simply ask for access to every African American enrolled in your school. They will be removed and no longer your concern. In return, you, your all-White teaching staff, and remaining students will benefit from everything we have offered you. High test scores, a positive reputation, support and praise from the School Board, a football championship, and scholarships for all graduates."

"What will happen to the African American students?" Mr. Johnson asked.

The man in the video replied simply, "Do not worry about that, this is our offer. You have 24 hours to accept."

The next morning Mr. Johnson called an emergency meeting with his two assistant principals. As the three were sitting down in the conference room, Mrs. Boston and the district superintendent walked in insisting they be heard. As it turned out everyone in the room had received the same message and were eager to discuss their options.

"This could be a great benefit to the school and the remaining students," Superintendent Calhoon began. "We wouldn't have a problem with racism if we didn't have Black students and the school could certainly use higher test scores. Not to mention how happy parents will be with the scholarships."

The two White, male assistant principals nodded in agreement. Mr. Johnson then looked to Mrs. Boston. Certainly she would have an opinion on this.

Mrs. Boston looked like an average White, middle-aged, suburban mom. She was elected by a slim margin and seemed to gain the favor of her constituents by criticizing the school and arguing for reforms. She had a talent for persuasion and frequently pushed the school to adopt policies and practices aimed at "evidence-based" changes that would help the school's "low performers rise to the top."

Mrs. Boston scanned the room before she spoke. "I was elected to serve the families of Park Hills High and intend to do what is best for them. ALL of them." At this she paused and looked directly at the superintendent, "Of course, students who no longer attend Park Hills High are not our concern …"

The superintendent nodded knowingly, "Yes, Mrs. Boston, if we accept this offer, our African American students will no longer be our students and therefore not our concern. We have to consider the needs of the students we serve."

"Research shows that when students attend schools with high achievement, they also achieve more. There are plenty of students who will be left and will benefit from such a trade being made." Mrs. Boston added.

Mr. Johnson leaned forward in his chair, "But how will we remove these students without drawing attention to the trade? I don't know about you, but I don't need any more negative media attention for this school or our students."

"I don't think that will be a problem," Superintendent Calhoon quickly replied. "Part of the deal was positive PR and I think the trade-makers could handle that. For all we know, they're sending these students to a special charter school better suited for teaching Black students. These kids are probably going to get a far better education someplace like that anyway."

At this point, Mr. Wilson, one of the two assistant principals, spoke up, "But it sure will hurt our athletics. I mean, I know they promised us a state football championship but I don't see how that happens without Black players, and, of course, we have to consider basketball as well."

"Wilson brings up a good point," conceded Superintendent Calhoon.

"We have to stop worrying so much about sports!" Mrs. Boston exclaimed. "It's test scores that determine whether or not students will be successful in life! We cannot allow other concerns to trump that. Now, I went ahead and looked at the data for this school. Without the African American students, test scores will get a small boost automatically but this trade gives us a guaranteed 100% proficiency score. That is amazing and will really show that our students are ready for those college scholarships. How can we turn this down?"

"It looks like we're agreed then." Mr. Johnson said quietly. "I wonder how we go about letting the traders know."

Just then the video screen reappeared. "That won't be a problem, Mr. Johnson. We'll take it from here …"

POETIC COUNTERSTORIES: SPOKEN-WORD POETRY AS A FORM OF TALKING BACK BY KEHAULANI FOLAU

Note to reader: This section cannot be read from page to page. I present two different stories side-by-side: the majoritarian and the counterstory. When you have read one side of the story, you must go back to read its counterstory.

Majoritarian Story	Counterstory
Ten Reasons to Make English the Official Language of the United States	**My Rant To Public Schooling's View on Language**
History has blessed [the U.S.] with all the freedom and advantages of multiculturalism. But it has also blessed us, because of the accident of our origins, with a linguistic unity that brings a critically needed cohesion to a nation as diverse, multiracial and multiethnic as America.	*I'm getting sick of you telling me* *That my multilingual tongue* *Presents a problem against your* *Bias educational system.* *You tell me that my language* *Is the barrier* *But let's be real here,* *Since supposedly your educators* *Do not tell lies, where the real barrier lays.*
1. To **stipulate** that although government may use other languages, to be legally binding and authoritative, e.g., "official," it must act or communicate in the English language.	*The barrier is your solution in this institution* *that calls my English broken* *While everyone else is* *being objectified, commoditized, and exploited.*
2. To **clarify** that whenever there is a conflict in meaning between government laws, regulations, or pronouncements issued in more than one language, the English version is the authoritative one.	*You call your language an art,* *Requiring me to take it every year* *I'm in your system,* *And by the time I'm out* *Your institution has given birth* *to a perfect little assimilated me.*
3. To **clarify** that unless government decides to provide it, no one has an entitlement or right to government services or documents in a language other than English.	*Answering my mom in English* *when she asks pwopwo, iahirehmwi?* *Answering my dad in English* *when he asks fefeako?* *Answering my Papa in English*
4. To **recognize** thes historical fact that the United States has been an overwhelmingly English-speaking nation since it was created and that its constitution and foundational documents are in English.	*when he asks fefe hake?* *Recognizing for the first time that* *anga' fakatonga and faka'apa'apa* *Sounds like I'm saying something* *totally different … in English.* *Language is not the barrier.*
5. To **recognize** that while the people of United States value and respect diversity, they want to preserve English as their common language and therefore immigrants have the responsibility to learn English.	*Language is not the barrier.* *But the melting persists.* *Because the only way I'll have an opportunity* *to get an opportunity,* *Is through your system.* *But I'm forgetting.*
6. To **conform** to the majority of the states (**31**) that have already made English their official language.	*I'm forgetting what I do not speak,* *Do not hear,* *Do not see written.*

7. To **respond** to the will of the American people, **87 percent** of whom believe English should be our official language, according to a May 2010 Rasmussen Reports survey.	*I'm forgetting that favor on my tongue* *Only to find myself getting* *tongue-tied from the lost words,* *Remembering that I have an opportunity* *to get an opportunity.*
8. To **conform** to the rest of the world: Eighty-five percent of the United Nations' member nations have official languages. Fifty-three (53) of those nations have adopted English as their official language.	*Language is not the barrier.* *So let's be real here,* *Since supposedly your educators* *did not tell lies,* *Where the real barrier lays.* *The barrier is your system.*
9. To **avoid** the costs, burdens, and conflicts that arise in nations like Canada or international organizations like the European Union that attempt to conduct business in more than one official language.	*The barrier is this bias institution.* *The barrier is your hegemonic discursive* * ideology* *Language is not the barrier.* *Language is a tree.*
10. To **bring** the federal government into conformity with national institutions like the U.S. Army and the federal court system, who for practical reasons have decided to operate in English. ("Ten Reasons to Make English the Official Language of the United States," n.d.)	*With roots deeply embedded in its ancestry,* *Branching out to its inheritance.* *Leaving words of truths,* *Stories of the past, passed down* *to the fruits of their labor.* *You have created a struggle of remembering.* *Trying to hook us into your* *culture of the assimilated* *But even Captain Hook would have* *no hold on hooks words* *When she writes,* *"Language is also a place of struggle.* *We are wedded in language,* *have our being in words."* *So now that I know* *I choose to resist and speak.* **Kehaulani Folau**

MY COUNTERSTORY

As a multilingual student, I struggled as a child academically. During elementary, I was taken out of class to attend English as a Second Language and speech therapy courses to push my speech towards the "standard language." I recall when I was 6 years old I came home and when my dad asked me how school was in his native language, Tonga, I answered, *"Tuku lea faka-Tonga.* I'm gonna speak English only." My parents migrated from the Pacific Islands for a better future for my siblings and me. So without much thought, they agreed with me and started speaking English at home. Now, reflecting on my schooling experience, I regret that moment telling my dad I only wanted to speak English.

I find strength in spoken word poetry and the spoken word poems of these modern-day orators. I also find decolonization to be a hard and long process, but being aware, I find myself in the margins that have become a space of openness and site of resistance against internalizing oppression. Spoken word poetry is the platform to express my emotions, insights, and frustrations. "My Letter/Rant to Public Schooling" was a way I found to cope with the stresses of being marginalized by a system I am trying to navigate as well as a way I talk back to the oppressive schooling system.

REFERENCES

Bell, D. (1992a). *Faces at the bottom of the well: The permanence of racism*. New York, NY: Basic Books.

Bell, D. (1992b). Racial realism. *Connecticut Law Review, 43*(5), 363–379.

Bell, D. (1995). Who's afraid of CRT? *University of Illinois Law Review, 1995*, 893–910.

Bonilla-Silva, E. (2015). More than prejudice: Restatement, reflections, and new directions in critical race theory. *Sociology of Race & Ethnicity 1*(1), 75–89.

Crenshaw, K. W. (1995). Mapping the margins: Intersectionality, identity politics, and violence against women of color. In K. W. Crenshaw, N. Gotanda, G. Peller, & K. Thomas (Eds.), *CRT: The key writings that formed the movement* (pp. 357–383). New York, NY: The New Press.

Crenshaw, K. W., Gotanda, N., Peller, G., & Thomas, K. (Eds.), (1995). *CRT: The key writings that formed the movement*. New York, NY: The New Press.

Delgado, R. (1989). Storytelling for oppositionists and others: A plea for narrative. *Michigan Law Review, 87*(8), 2411–2441.

Delgado, R. (1990). When a story is just a story: Does voice really matter? *Virginia Law Review, 76*(1), 95–111.

Delgado, R., & Stefancic, J. (1994). CRT: An annotated bibliography 1993, a year of transition. *University of Colorado Law Review, 66*, 159–193.

Delgado Bernal, D. (2002). Critical Race Theory, Latino critical theory, and critical raced-gendered epistemologies: Recognizing students of color as holders and creators of knowledge. *Qualitative Inquiry, 8*(1), 105–126.

Harris, F. C., & Liberman, R. C. (2015). Racial inequality after racism. *Foreign Affairs, 94*(2).

Hylton, K. (2012). Talk the talk, walk the walk: Defining critical race theory in research. *Race Ethnicity and Education, 15*(1), 23–41.

Ladson-Billings, G., & Tate, W. F. (1995). Toward a CRT of education. *Teachers College Record, 97*(1), 47–68.

Leonardo, Z. (2013). *Racial categories*. New York, NY: Teachers College Press.

López, G. R. (2003). The racially neutral politics of education: A Critical Race Theory perspective. *Educational Administration Quarterly, 39*(1), 68–94.

Lynn, M. (1999). Toward a Critical Race pedagogy: A research note. *Urban Education, 33*(5), 606–627.

Lynn, M., & Dixson, A. D. (Eds.). (2013). *Handbook of Critical Race Theory in education*. New York, NY: Routledge.

Matsuda, M. J. (1996). *Where is your body? And other essays on race, gender and the law.* Boston, MA: Beacon Press.

Parker, L. (2015). Critical race theory in education & Qualitative Inquiry: What each has to offer the other now. *Qualitative Inquiry, 21*(3), 199–205.

Solórzano, D. G. (1998). CRT, race and gender microagressions, and the experience of Chicana and Chicano scholars. *International Journal of Qualitative Studies in Education, 11*(1), 121–136.

Solórzano, D. G., & Yosso, T. (2002). Critical Race methodology: Counter-storytelling as an analytical framework for educational research. *Qualitative Inquiry, 8*(1), 23–44.

Tate, W. F. IV (1997). Critical Race Theory & education: History, theory, and implications. In M. Apple (Ed.), *Review of research in education* (Vol. 22, pp. 195–247). Washington, DC: American Educational Research Association.

Derrick Bell AND Principles OF Critical Race Theory

Derrick Bell, *Brown*, AND THE Continuing Significance OF THE Interest-Convergence Principle

JAMEL K. DONNOR

... optimism for the future must be tempered by past experience and contemporary facts.
—DERRICK BELL (1976)

DERRICK BELL AND THE INTEREST-CONVERGENCE PRINCIPLE

Partially developed as a scholarly rebuttal to fellow legal scholar Herbert Wechsler's (1959) assertion that the U.S. Supreme Court's rationale in *Brown v. Board of Education* in 1954 was based neither on "neutral principles" nor on a testable judicial doctrine, such as associational rights, Derrick Bell (1980), through his interest-convergence theory, contended that Wechsler's premise possessed a modicum of truth. According to Bell, "Wechsler's search for a guiding principle in the context of associational rights retains merit ... because it suggests a deeper truth about the subordination of law to interest-group politics with racial configuration" (p. 523).

A former attorney with the U.S. Department of Justice and the NAACP's Legal Defense Fund during its school desegregation campaign, which was also part of the Black Civil Rights Movement of the 20th century, Bell acknowledged that after a quarter century of attempting to racially integrate public schools, the pace of reform had not only stalled but also reversed. Indeed, while "serious racial integration did not occur until the 1970s and was limited outside of the South" (Orfield & Lee, 2007, p. 4), public schools in the United States have been resegregating since the 1980s (Orfield & Eaton, 1996). According to The UCLA Civil

Rights Project (Orfield & Lee, 2007), American schools, which have been gradually resegregating for almost two decades, are "now experiencing accelerating isolation" (p. 3). For example, the "average White student attends schools where 77 percent of the student enrollment is White" (p. 24), while Black and Latino students attend schools where more than half of their peers are Black and Latino despite respectively constituting 16 percent and 24 percent of the total number of students enrolled in public schools (DeMonte & Hanna, 2014; U.S. Department of Education and U.S. Department of Justice, 2014).

For Bell, the *Brown* decision required a critical reappraisal and uncompromising reconceptualization of its "operant ideas" (Orfield & Eaton, 1996, p. xv), which also included the Supreme Court's concomitant rendering of contradictory and obfuscatory verdicts in subsequent school desegregation cases. Specifically highlighting the permanence of racism and the role of exogenous factors such as fortuity and self-interest, Bell (1992) posited that the *Brown* decision could not be "understood without some consideration of the decision's value to whites, not simply those concerned about the immorality of racial inequality, but also the economic and political advances at home and abroad that would follow abandonment of segregation" (p. 524). Stated differently, the U.S. Supreme Court's decision to overturn more than 50 years of judicial precedent whereby state-government-enforced racial segregation (i.e., de jure) was the law of the land required the consideration of the case's implications on the nation's domestic and international political economic interests.

The goal of this chapter is to discuss the continuing significance of Derrick Bell's interest-convergence theory as an analytical tool for explaining contemporary racial inequity in American education. Indeed, Bell's enduring contribution to the proliferation of Critical Race Theory (CRT) remains his departure from traditional legal theory and conventional Civil Rights practices by being the first legal scholar to establish a "scholarly agenda that placed race at the center of intellectual inquiry" in constitutional theory (Crenshaw, 2002, p. 1345). To assist me in my stated goal I examine the Supreme Court's decision in *Parents Involved in Community Schools v. Seattle School District No. 1* (2007) using Bell's convergence of interest theory. Addressing the issues of public school integration and race, this case exemplifies Bell's (2004) foundational premise that civil rights victories, such as equal educational opportunity, are "fleeting even when enunciated in terms of permanence" (p. 4). For instance, in *Parents Involved in Community Schools v. Seattle School District No. 1* the Supreme Court determined that the Seattle School District's voluntary public school integration program was unconstitutional, because it unfairly forced White students to "compete for seats at certain high schools that use race as a deciding factor in many of its admissions decisions" (*Parents v. Seattle School District No.1*, 2007, Section II, p. 10, ¶ 2). More important, the high Court's decision to strike down voluntary school integration is illustrative of Bell's

(1980) second theoretical presupposition that posits that public policies and laws established to foster racial equality are permissible until it "threatens the superior societal status of middle and upper class whites" (p. 523).

CHAPTER OUTLINE

This chapter consists of three sections. The first section presents a synopsis of Derrick Bell's interest-convergence principle. The second section summarizes the Supreme Court's decision in *Parents Involved in Community Schools v. Seattle School District No.1*, while the third section analyzes the aforementioned and explains the continuing significance of Derrick Bell's convergence of interest thesis in understanding contemporary racial inequity in American education.

THE GENESIS OF THE INTEREST-CONVERGENCE THESIS

Rather than myopically cling to the narrow focus of measuring societal and racial progress according to the rate of interracial contact in public schools initially championed by *Brown's* supporters, Derrick Bell sought a wider and more nuanced understanding of the landmark decision's limited impact and subsequent retrenchment. According to Bell (2004), "I continued to view *Brown* as basically a positive decision, but as the years passed, my understanding of the complexity of race in America and our efforts to remedy its injustices raised new doubts" (p. 4). Utilizing a multifocal approach consisting of "political history as legal precedent" (Bell, 1980, p. 523), and a positivistic frame (i.e., realism), Bell concluded that the "interest of blacks in achieving racial equality will only be accommodated only when it converges with the interests of whites" (p. 523)—hence the convergence of interest principle. For Bell (1992),

> history is an aid in identifying the continuing problems of race. History has thus far given little hope that any lasting solutions will be found soon. It is not that the white majority is rigidly opposed to enjoyment by blacks of rights and opportunities that whites accept as a matter of course; it is rather that for a complex[ity] of racial reasons, whites are not willing to alter traditional policies and conduct that effectively deprive blacks of these rights and opportunities. (p. 7)

Accordingly, in viewing the American judicial system as an "instrument for preserving the status quo and only periodically and unpredictably serving as a refuge of oppressed people" (Bell, 1995, p. 302), one is better positioned to understand, critique, and respond to the fluidity of White racism, and the multiplicity of racial inequity.

The Problem With *Brown*

As previously mentioned, *Brown* was a unique case (Dudziak, 2004). Meaning, not only did the decision "depart from the normal rule in American law that where a right has been violated, there is a remedy" (p. 39), it iconoclastically revealed "how government and political institutions influence and interact with each other, and how features of politics and institutional structure influence the creation and development of constitutional doctrine" (Balkin, 2004, p. 1537). According to historian James T. Patterson (2001),

> [t]he [*Brown*] decision cut through a tissue of lies that white Southerners and others had woven to maintain the subservient status of black people. It offered the possibility of a long-awaited change that other political institutions—the Congress, state legislatures— seemed wholly incapable of producing. And it suggested that the Court ... would henceforth interpret the Constitution in light of changing circumstances, not a fixed document whose meaning had always to be found in the intent of the Founding Fathers. (p. 69)

In summary, the *Brown* decision not only expanded American jurisprudence by highlighting the doctrinal limitations of normative constitutional theory (Dudziak, 1987; Balkin, 2004), it also heightened the political and societal significance of the U.S. Supreme Court (Klarman, 2004).

Moreover, public schools were selected as the site for abolishing state-supported racial segregation because of their symbolic value internationally, and its purported preparatory role domestically. Internationally, *Brown* was central to the Unites States' war against Communism (Bell, 1980; Dudziak, 1988, 2004; Gaines, 2004; Klarman, 2004). According to Dudziak (2004), U.S. State Department files from the period reveal that segregation provided "grist for the Communism propaganda mills, and raise[d] doubts even among friendly nations as to the intensity of our devotion to the democratic faith" (p. 34). In particular, public school racial segregation was "singled out for hostile foreign comment" (p. 34). Domestically, public education became further imbued with the American Dream (Hochschild, 1995). For African Americans especially, education has been synonymous with political, economic, and existential freedom (Anderson, 1988). In delivering the unanimous decision, Chief Justice Earl Warren wrote,

> education is perhaps the most important function of state and local governments. Compulsory school attendance laws and the great expenditures for education both demonstrate our recognition of the importance of education to our democratic society. It is required in the performance of our most basic public responsibilities. ... It is the very foundation of good citizenship. Today it is a principal instrument in awakening the child to cultural values, in preparing him for later professional training, and helping him to adjust normally to his environment. In these days, it is doubtful that any child may reasonably be expected to succeed in life if he is denied the opportunity of education. Such an opportunity, where the

state has undertaken to provide it, is a right which must be made available to all on equal terms. (*Brown v. Board of Education of Topeka*, 1954)

Ironically, the Supreme Court's edict did not call for immediate school desegregation. In fact, the high Court's ensuing decision on implementation in *Brown v. Board of Education* 1955 (i.e., *Brown II*) was vague and gradualist. More important, the *Brown* decisions radicalized and emboldened Whites to develop a set of reactionary ideas and oppositional tactics that persist in the 21ˢᵗ century.

Parents v. Seattle School District No. 1

Decided by the narrowest of margins, five to four, the U.S. Supreme Court in *Parents Involved in Community Schools v. Seattle School District No.1* (2007) determined that the district's voluntary integration policy, which considered race among a myriad of factors for assigning students to oversubscribed and top-performing high schools, was unconstitutional. Citing the plaintiffs' injury claim of "not being forced to compete for seats in certain high schools" (*Parents Involved in Community Schools v. Seattle School District No.1*, 2007, Section II, p. 10, ¶ 2), the Court's majority determined that the integration policy did not employ race as part of an "expansive project to achieve exposure to widely diverse people, cultures, ideas, and viewpoints" (Section III, Subsection A, ¶ 4), but rather as a "determinative standing alone for some students" (Section III, Subsection A, ¶ 4). Because the city of Seattle has never operated a racially de jure segregated public school system, the Supreme Court viewed the district's good faith effort to offset the pernicious effects of housing segregation as "fatally flawed" (Syllabus, Subsection 1, p. 4). Writing for the Court's majority, Chief Justice John Roberts remarked,

> dividing people by race is inherently suspect because such classifications promote notions of racial inferiority and lead to a politics of racial hostility, reinforce the belief, held by too many for too much of our history, that individuals should be judged by the color of their skin, and endorse race-based reasoning and the conception of a Nation divided into racial blocs, thus contributing to an escalation of racial hostility and conflict. (Section 2, p. 4)

For the affirming justices (Roberts, Scalia, Thomas, Alito, and Kennedy), upholding the Seattle school district's integration policy was "reminiscent of that advocated by the segregationists in *Brown v. Board of Education*, 1954" (Section II, p. 25, ¶ 1). As noted by the Chief Justice,

> [b]efore *Brown*, schoolchildren were told where they could and could not go to school based on the color of their skin. … For schools that never segregated on the basis of race, such as Seattle, … the way to achieve a system of determining admission to the public school on a nonracial basis is to stop assigning students on a racial basis. The way to stop discrimination on the basis of race is to stop discriminating on the basis of race. (Syllabus, p. 24, ¶ 2)

Viewing itself as the arbiter for defining racial equality in the United States, the Supreme Court not only declared the utilization of colorblind practices in pupil placement assignments as the solution for racial inequality in public education, more significantly, it also framed the practice of using race as a tool for promoting racial equity in education as inimical.

THE CONTINUING SIGNIFICANCE OF INTEREST-CONVERGENCE THEORY

As previously discussed, the problems with the *Brown* decision(s) were manifold. In addition to its obfuscation and emphasis on incrementalism, *Brown* also provided White people with the liminal entry point necessary to limit its impact and justify its abolishment (Donnor, 2011a, 2011b; Klarman, 1994). According to Bell (2004),

> [w]hen the *Brown* decision was followed by civil rights laws, mostly motivated by black activism that highlighted the continuing racism that undermined our Cold War battles with the Soviet Union, policymakers and much of white society easily reached the premature conclusion that America was now fair and neutral. With implementation of the moderate civil rights laws [and *Brown*], the trumpets of "reverse discrimination" began sounding the alarm. (p. 186)

Indeed, since the mid-1970s, as federal courts started enforcing school desegregation orders, White people also started winning racial equal protection lawsuits in public education, which, in conjunction with initial evasion tactics such as interposition and freedom-of-choice plans, led to *Brown's* demise (Bonastia, 2012; Kairys, 2004, 2006; Klarman, 1994, 2004; Patterson, 2001; Orfield & Lee, 2007).

A reason for Whites people's success in the aforementioned is due to their simultaneous anastrophe of *Brown's* spirit and appropriation of the Black Civil Rights Movement's narrative (Hall, 2005). According to Hall,

> the [White] conservative movement reinvented itself in the 1970s, first by incorporating neoconservatives who eschewed old-fashioned racism and then by embracing an ideal of formal equality ... positioning itself as the true inheritor of the civil rights legacy. Reworking the civil rights movement narrative for their own purposes, these new "color-blind conservatives" ignored the complexity and dynamism of the movement. (p. 1237)

A vital rhetorical construct of the Black Civil Rights Movement's narrative, color-blindness was central to defeating public policies and social practices that distributed societal opportunities and resources according to an overtly expressed

White supremacist doctrine. Ironically, colorblindness has metastasized into a political tool for liberals, social conservatives, and members of the far right to repeal landmark legislation such as *Brown* (Brown et al., 2003; Cokorinos, 2003; Higginbotham, 2013; Lopez, 2014).

In addition to framing authoritarian policies that promote racial inclusion and attempt to remediate the legacy effects of racism as unfair, colorblindness constructs Whites as the expressed victims of the aforementioned. For example, the parent organization in *Parents Involved in Community Schools v. Seattle School District No.1* (2007) contended that the Seattle school district's voluntary integration program caused undue harm and was injurious because it limited student and parental choice of school. In the program's only year of operation, "80.3%" (*Parents Involved in Community Schools v. Seattle School District No. 1, Brief for Respondents*, 2006, p. 9) of the total number of ninth graders were assigned their first choice of school, compared to "80.4%" (p. 9) when the program was abolished. In other words, the Seattle School District's voluntary integration plan did not interfere with a student's choice of preferred school (p. 9). Furthermore, disaffected families could have pupil placement assignments overridden for "psychological" and medical reasons (*Parents Involved in Community Schools v. Seattle School District No. 1*, 2007). Finally, the policy arguments advocating the abolishment of the Seattle School District's voluntary integration program are not novel, but rather part of an anti-desegregation movement in Seattle dating back to the 1970s (Donnor, 2011a, 2011b; *Parents Involved in Community Schools v. Seattle School District No. 1, Brief for Respondents*, 2006).

As the policy platform upon which interest-convergence theory remains central for understanding contemporary racial inequity in education, colorblindness not only serves as the signpost illuminating defenders of the status quo of race neutrality, it also represents the strategic tool of choice for absolving the beneficiaries of systemic racism. Because political history allows for a comprehensive understanding of the continuities and discontinuities of racial inequity, interest-convergence theory is not only a viable framework for measuring "racial progress," it is also useful for conceptualizing new pathways for racial justice. In moving beyond "racial fortuity" *Brown* and interest-convergence theory teaches its adherents that the pursuit of abstract principles (e.g., equality) is not only vulnerable to cooptation from defenders of the status quo, but is also limited in scope. According to Bell (2004),

> Just as the *Brown* decision's major contribution to the freedom struggle was the nation's response to the violent resistance of its opponents, so we who were its intended beneficiaries can learn from the myriad [of] ways in which the relief we deserved was withheld. *Brown* in retrospect, was a serious disappointment, but if we can learn the lessons it did not intend to teach, it will not go down as a defeat. (p. 193)[1]

NOTE

1. Thank you, Derrick Bell.

REFERENCES

Anderson, J. D. (1988). *The education of Blacks in the South, 1860–1935*. Chapel Hill, NC: University of North Carolina Press.

Balkin, J. M. (2004). What "*Brown*" teaches us about constitutional theory. *Virginia Law Review, 90*(6), 1537–1577.

Bell, D. (1976). Serving two masters: Integration ideals and client interest in school desegregation litigation. *The Yale Law Review, 85*(4), 470–516.

Bell, D. (1980). *Brown v. Board of Education* and the interest-convergence dilemma. *Harvard Law Review, 93*, 518–533.

Bell, D. (1992). *Race, racism and American law* (3rd ed.). Boston, MA: Little, Brown.

Bell, D. (1995). Racial realism. In K. Crenshaw, N. Gotanda, G. Peller, & K. Thomas (Eds.). *Critical race theory: The key writings that formed the movement* (pp. 302–312). New York, NY: The New Press.

Bell, D. (2004). *Silent covenants:* Brown v. Board of Education *and the unfulfilled hopes for racial reform*. New York, NY: Oxford University Press.

Bonastia, C. (2012). *Southern stalemate: Five years without public education in Prince Edward County, Virginia*. Chicago, IL: University of Chicago Press.

Brown v. Board of Education of Topeka, 347 U.S. 483 (1954).

Brown, M. K., Carnoy, M., Currie, E., Duster, T., Oppenheimer, D. B., Shultz, M. M., & Wellman, D. (2003). *Whitewashing race: The myth of a color-blind society*. Berkeley, CA: University of California Press.

Cokorinos, L. (2003). *The assault on diversity: An organized challenge to racial and gender justice*. Lanham, MD: Rowman & Littlefield.

Crenshaw, K. W. (2002). The first decade: Critical reflections, or "a foot in the closing door." *UCLA Law Review, 49*(5), 1343–1372.

DeMonte, J., & Hanna, R. (2014, April 11). *Looking at the best teachers and who they teach*. Retrieved from the Center for American Progress website: https://www.americanprogress.org/wp-content/uploads/2014/04/TeacherDistributionBrief1.pdf

Donnor, J. K. (2011a). Whose compelling interest:? The ending of desegregation and the affirming of racial inequality in education. *Education and Urban Society, 44*(5), 535–552.

Donnor, J. K. (2011b). Moving beyond *Brown*: Race in education after *Parents v. Seattle School District No. 1. Teachers College Record, 113*(1), 735–754.

Dudziak, M. L. (1987). The limits of good faith: Desegregation in Topeka, Kansas, 1950–1956. *Law and History Review, 5*(2), 351–391.

Dudziak, M. L. (1988). Desegregation as a Cold War imperative. *Stanford Law Review, 61*–120.

Dudziak, M. L. (2004). *Brown* as a Cold War case. *The Journal of American History, 91*(1), 32–42.

Gaines, K. (2004). Whose integration was it? An introduction. *The Journal of American History, 91*(1), 19–25.

Hall, J. D. (2005). The long civil rights movement and the political use of the past. *The Journal of American History, 91*(4), 1233–1263.

Higginbotham, F. M. (2013). *Ghosts of Jim Crow: Ending racism in post-racial America*. New York, NY: New York University Press.

Hochschild, J. L. (1995). *Facing up to the American dream: Race, class, and the soul of the nation*. Princeton, NJ: Princeton University Press.

Kairys, D. (2004). More or less equal. *Temple Political and Civil Rights Law Review, 13*, 675– 689.

Kairys, D. (2006). A brief history of race and the Supreme Court. *Temple Law Review, 79*, 751–772.

Klarman, M. J. (1994). How *Brown* changed race relations: The backlash thesis. *The Journal of American History, 81*(1), 81–118.

Klarman, M. J. (2004). *From Jim Crow to civil rights: The Supreme Court and the struggle for racial equality*. New York, NY: Oxford University Press.

Lopez, I. H. (2014). *Dog whistle politics: How coded racial appeals have reinvented racism and wrecked the middle class*. New York, NY: Oxford University Press.

Orfield, G., & Eaton, S. E. (1996). *Dismantling desegregation: The quiet reversal of* Brown v. Board of Education. New York, NY: The New Press.

Orfield, G., & Lee, C. (2007, August). *Historic reversals, accelerating resegregation, and the need for new integration strategies*. Retrieved from The Civil Rights Project website: http://civilrightsproject. ucla.edu/research/k-12-education/integration-and-diversity/historic-reversals-accelerating-resegregation-and-the-need-for-new-integration-strategies-1/orfield-historic-reversals-accelerating.pdf

Parents Involved in Community Schools v. Seattle School District No. 1, Brief for Respondents, No. 05–908 (2006).

Parents Involved in Community Schools v. Seattle School District No. 1, 2007, 127 S. Ct. 2738.

Patterson, J. T. (2001). Brown v. Board of Education: *A civil rights milestone and troubled legacy*. Oxford, England: Oxford University Press.

Stephens, O. H. (2002). Equal protection. In D. S. Clark, J. W. Ely, J. Grossman, & N. E. H. Hull (Eds.), *The Oxford guide to American law* (pp. 265–268). New York, NY: Oxford University Press.

U.S. Department of Education and U.S. Department of Justice. (2014). *Notice of language assistance. Dear colleague letter on the nondiscriminatory administration of school discipline*. Retrieved from http://www.justice.gov/crt/about/edu/documents/dcl.pdf

Wechsler, H. (1959). Toward neutral principles of constitutional law. *Harvard Law Review*, 1–35.

The Rules OF Racial Standing

Critical Race Theory for Analysis, Activism, and Pedagogy

DAVID GILLBORN

INTRODUCTION: *RACISM LIVES*

My chapter focuses on "The Rules of Racial Standing" (hereafter "The Rules"),
Chapter 6 of Derrick Bell's remarkable book *Faces at the Bottom of the Well: The
Permanence of Racism* (1992, pp. 109–126), which achieved such widespread appeal
as to briefly appear in *The New York Times* bestseller list (Delgado & Stefancic,
2005, p. 10). I will explore some of the key insights of the piece and its usefulness
as an analytic tool, an aid to activism, and a key pedagogic device—not a bad range
of uses for a chapter of fewer than 20 pages.

"The Rules" is usually one of the first pieces that I share with people as a
way of introducing them to Critical Race Theory (CRT), and the effect is often
profound. A good way of describing the piece's impact is to liken it to a science
fiction film of the 1980s, John Carpenter's (1988) *They Live*. The metaphor is
apt because Bell used science fiction a great deal in his CRT chronicles, and,
as Colette Cann (2014) has noted, science fiction can be an especially powerful
medium for antiracists that "provides the space to imagine a future that holds revolutionary potential for racial equality, justice, retribution and reparations" (p. 11),
such that "science fiction offers an alternative where that which deviates from the
norm is the norm" (Mosely, 2007, cited in Cann, 2014, p. 12). Carpenter's movie
includes a striking scene where a man discovers that the world is run through
mind control and that behind the everyday facade of normality lies a society
built on oppression and manipulation. The resistance movement has developed a

special compound that blocks the mind control and reveals the true nature of the world. Unsuspectingly, the film's hero puts on a pair of sunglasses made from the revolutionary compound and for the first time in his life sees through the fake superficial gloss of everyday life; in horror he realizes that newspapers, billboards, and shop signs conceal deep-rooted commands such as "Stay Asleep," "Do Not Question Authority," and "Obey." In class I sometimes show this scene to students as a way of introducing "The Rules." Like the sunglasses in *They Live*, at first "The Rules" appear straightforward and fairly mundane: a short chapter in a book that includes more celebrated pieces, including the author's most famous work "The Space Traders" (Bell, 1992, pp. 158–194). But the impact of "The Rules" is extraordinary: unmasking hidden oppressions of tremendous power that are made all the more shocking by their hidden operation as part of the unquestioned fabric of society.

Bell's five rules, and the accompanying discussion, add up to a powerful analysis of how mainstream debate about race and racism (which appears to be open and democratic) is actually shaped by hidden assumptions and judgements that determine *who* is allowed to speak with authority about race and racism, and *what* they are permitted to say. Bell (1992) showed how racism lies at the very heart of debate, rendering truly "free speech" impossible. He showed how people are judged in relation to a combination of two factors:

- their own racialized identity; and
- whether they are supporting the racist status quo or seeking to overthrow it.

"The Rules" offer a laser-sharp analysis of the operation of power in a society dominated by the interests and desires of White people. Bell's chapter shows how we are all captured by the operation of racism regardless of our intended and/or professed aims and motivations. For those prepared to question "common sense" and the received wisdoms of longer established approaches, the central concepts and ideas within CRT in general, and "The Rules" in particular, arm us with a penetrating and troubling 20:20 vision that, over time, helps to unmask the central and violently oppressive nature of racism in contemporary society. For many students (regardless of their own ethnicity), reading "The Rules" is very much like putting on those x-ray sunglasses; news broadcasts, movies, and their favourite TV shows are revealed as part of the racist oppression that shapes society. It can be a profoundly disturbing experience but also an energizing one that prompts them to get involved in activist work through unions and/or community-based groups. The following statements, for example, are taken from students' evaluative feedback on a "race and education" course that I taught to practicing teachers in London (the respondents are of many different ethnic backgrounds and aged anywhere between their mid-20s to 60s):

... After every session my understanding of the world was questioned which is exciting and scary!

... The module has profoundly altered my world view and led me to challenging much of my personal and professional practice.

... It opened up avenues that I have previously never looked into.

... Every session challenged my thinking and made me more aware of how to take action.

In the rest of this chapter I examine some of the many applications of "The Rules"; I consider some of its analytical uses in Critical Race theorizing, its potential as a spur to activist engagement and strategizing, and its role as a model in Critical Race pedagogy. The chapter ends with a brief reflection on the significance of "The Rules" for this author and other White-identified people seeking to aid the destruction of White Supremacy.

ANALYSIS AND CRITIQUE: "THE RULES" IN ACTION

Bell's chapter "The Rules of Racial Standing" features his two most famous literary creations: the unnamed narrator (a Black law professor engaged in civil rights activism) and Geneva Crenshaw, a Black woman who appears in several of Bell's works, often displaying supernatural abilities and described by law professor Cheryl Harris as an "otherworldly Chiara" (quoted on the back cover of Bell, 1998). The chapter opens with the narrator describing a dream whereby his life's work and struggles are analysed by an invisible supernatural force that distils them down to five essential insights:

> YOU HAVE BEEN GRANTED TO KNOW THE RULES OF RACIAL STANDING. TAKE THE PAGES WITH YOU. THE ESSENCE OF YOUR WORK IS NOW TRANSFORMED INTO A DESCRIPTION OF YOUR GIFT. USE IT WISELY. GUARD IT WELL. AND REMEMBER, NO GIFT COMES WITHOUT A PRICE. (Bell, 1992, p. 110)

The narrator then describes finding the rules printed and bound in his desk drawer, a gift from Geneva. The rest of Bell's chapter describes the two friends considering the rules, how they presently operate, and their consequences for revolutionary race activism.

Black Voices and White Racism

The first rule notes that: "*Black people ... are denied ... legitimacy ... when they discuss their negative experiences with racism. ... No matter their experience or expertise, blacks' statements involving race are deemed 'special pleading' and thus not entitled to serious consideration*" (Bell, 1992, p. 111).

The theme of whose voices are heard loudest is continued in a later rule:

> *The usual exception [is] ... the black person who publicly disparages or criticizes other blacks who are speaking or acting in ways that upset whites. Instantly, such statements are granted "enhanced standing" even when the speaker has no special expertise or experience in the subject he or she is criticizing.* (from the Third Rule, p. 114)

These rules offer a lens on public debates and institutional practices; they show how and why so-called "free speech" and "open debate" are actually slanted in favour of White supremacy. As Leonardo & Porter (2010) have argued in relation to the idea that "safe spaces" can be created to help White and minoritized peoples come together to discuss and address racism:

> the term "safety" acts as a misnomer because it often means that white individuals can be made to feel safe. Thus, a space of safety is circumvented, and instead a space of oppressive color-blindness is established. ... If we are truly interested in racial pedagogy, then we must become comfortable with the idea that for marginalized and oppressed minorities, *there is no safe space.* As implied above, mainstream race dialogue in education is arguably already hostile and unsafe for many students of color whose perspectives and experiences are consistently minimized. *Violence is already there.* (pp. 147 & 149)

Hence, when racially minoritized people try to address White racism they often meet with scoffing derision that condemns their words as self-serving and disingenuous: "playing the race card" or asking for "special treatment." In contrast, any possible criticism of people of colour by a speaker who shares their minoritized status is likely to be seized upon and amplified. These processes operate across continents. In 2008, for example, Barack Obama marked Father's Day with a speech that included a rebuke to "missing" African American fathers:

> missing from too many lives and too many homes. They have abandoned their responsibilities, acting like boys instead of men. And the foundations of our families are weaker because of it. You and I know how true this is in the African-American community. We know that more than half of all black children live in single-parent households, a number that has doubled—doubled—since we were children. (Obama, 2008)

On the other side of the Atlantic, David Cameron, the White male leader of the Conservative Party, seized on Obama's words and recycled them to attack Black British men in a familiar cycle of deficit stereotyping that scapegoats Black males as a cause of racist inequity and ignores research showing that non-resident Black fathers are active participants in their children's lives (Reynolds, 2009). It is difficult to overestimate the significance of Obama's speech as a means of enabling Cameron to revisit a familiar racist stereotype, but to do so under the cover of a Black voice, thereby laying claim to a non-racist motivation. In a similar vein, Cameron also invoked un-named "black church leaders" to offer further raced support for his view: "They are very concerned about family breakdown and social breakdown and want to see what I call a responsibility revolution take place" (quoted in Andrews, 2008). The resulting newspaper headlines that greeted Cameron's statement clearly display this blending of a racist stereotype (absent Black fathers) and the licence granted by being able to quote Obama (a Black voice):

> "Cameron: absent black fathers must meet responsibilities: Tory leader backs Barack Obama on race and family breakdown"—*The Guardian* (Wintour, Watt, & Topping, 2008).

> "Cameron echoes Obama by calling on absent black fathers to take more responsibility"—*Daily Mail* (Andrews, 2008).

> "Cameron backs Obama over absentee fathers."—*The Independent* (2008).

The Politics of Authenticity and Somersaulting Conservatives

The politics of race and voice is especially important in view of the rise of Black conservative figures in both the US and the UK. Bell (1992) directly addressed this issue and noted that it is possible for Black figures to gain "national celebrity as experts on race" based not on their scholarship or achievements, but because of "their willingness to minimize the effect of racism on the lowly status of blacks" (p. 115). When Bell wrote "The Rules" this was mostly a US phenomenon, as Paul Warmington (2014) noted in his history of Black British intellectuals and education: "In Britain there is no real archetype of the black conservative public intellectual. Being a black British public thinker has, almost by definition, meant being located somewhere on the liberal-left spectrum" (p. 143). This has changed dramatically over the last decade. Several minoritized figures have now risen to prominence on the conservative side of debates about race, class, and education. As Warmington highlighted, these figures not only gain enhanced standing because they are Black voices in defence of White racism, they also go a stage further, by claiming a special kind of *authenticity* based on their racialized standing as minoritized *and* conservative. This is a stark perversion of one of the central tenets of Critical Race Theory: whereas CRT seeks to respect and honor the experiential knowledge of people of color in the service of social justice (see Tate, 1997), here, people of color who testify to the violence of White racism are derided on the basis that these conservative critics are minoritized and if *they* say that racism is not a key factor, then *their* insight takes precedence.

Munira Mirza (2006), for example, has been a forthright critic of what she terms the "race relations industry," claiming that "racial thinking leads to the simplistic explanation that the 'white male establishment' is full of bigots" which in turn "leads to positive discrimination schemes that put ethnicity before talent."

Introducing a special issue of *Prospect* magazine dedicated to attacking multiculturalism, she stated:

> The following articles are by people who want to change the way in which racism and diversity are discussed in Britain and question the assumptions of some "official anti-racism." None of them is white and therefore cannot easily be dismissed as ignorant, naïve or unwittingly prejudiced. (Mirza, 2010, p. 31)

As Warmington (2015) noted, this is a perfect example of the intellectual somersaults performed by the minoritized voices on the political right in Britain; they claim authenticity on the basis of their racialized identity, just as they dismiss the antiracist claims of Black students, parents, and communities as necessarily self-serving and inauthentic: "Their black 'authenticity' is derived from positioning themselves in opposition to white liberal educators, as well as blacks who speak out of turn. That positioning is the feint that draws attention away from their disparaging of other blacks" (p. 1166).

Further manoeuvres are performed routinely and expertly. Tony Sewell (2009, 2010), for example, condemned Black communities for adopting a mentality of victimhood while simultaneously saying that they *are* victims—though victims of White liberal sentimentality not White racist power structures. Similarly, Katharine Birbalsingh (2011) leapt to the defence of hard-working teachers who she said are outrageously accused of racism by antiracist critics, but then she condemned those same teachers for their complicity in a system of low expectations, poor performance, and political correctness that fails Black students (see Warmington, 2015, p. 1163).

The Cowardice of Racism: From "Spineless" to "Courageous" in a Single Political Leap

Derrick Bell's (1992) reflections on the superstar standing that can be achieved by minoritized critics of minoritized communities remain as vital today as when they were first published. While making clear that many, possibly all, such critics may genuinely believe what they say (p. 117), Bell rightly called attention to the pride that can be taken from the fact that, despite the praise and rewards on offer, such people remain relatively rare:

> I think it's cause for wonder and more than a little credit to our integrity that more black scholars don't maim one another in a wild scramble to gain for ourselves the acclaim, adulation, and accompanying profit almost guaranteed to those of us willing to condemn our own. (p. 116)

In a simple, yet powerful, rhetorical manoeuvre, the dominant forces that reproduce and normalize racism in society act to celebrate the supposed courage needed to defend racism against minoritized people seeking justice. In this 180-degree spin, the dominant trope of news media and mainstream politics presents antiracists and other social justice campaigners as somehow having all the cards, while a voice speaking out in defence of the status quo is reimagined as a brave lone voice of reason and lauded as *by definition* demonstrating moral valour. This aspect of "The Rules" can be seen most graphically when someone changes sides; in the UK the most notable example is Trevor Phillips.

The son of parents who migrated to Britain from then-British Guiana (now Guyana), Trevor Phillips has been one of the most prominent Black people in British politics for more than two decades. A broadcaster, political activist, and campaigner, Phillips has also held formal positions leading the state bodies charged with safeguarding and advancing race equality under UK legislation, i.e., the Commission for Racial Equality (CRE) (between 2003 and 2006) and its successor, the Equality and Human Rights Commission (EHRC) (between 2007 and 2012). His treatment at the hands of the right-wing British press demonstrates "The Rules" in action with shocking clarity and simplicity. For the sake of brevity we can examine how Phillips appeared in just one newspaper, *The Daily Mail*, a title that occupies a particularly important place in UK publishing. *The Mail*, as it is known, has the largest circulation, is known for its right-wing politics, and is by far the most politically influential of the national newspapers in the UK.[1] *The Mail's* style and influence was noted by ex-prime minister Tony Blair (2010), "If a paper like *the Daily Mail* decides to do it [i.e., make a personal attack on a public figure], others soon join in, not wanting to be left out of the pack." In 2003, while still heading the CRE, Phillips was described as spineless by *Mail* columnist Melanie Phillips (White, no relation) (2003) when he cautioned that government ministers should be careful not to appear to treat all Muslims as potentially part of a terrorist threat. A few months later Andrew Alexander (2004), another White *Mail* columnist, referred to him as: "Trevor Phillips, Obersturmbannfuehrer for the Gestapo and thought-police at the Commission for Racial Equality—or more correctly the Commission for Racial Enmity—and thus a national leader in political correctness." The following year, however, Phillips began to warn that certain South Asian communities were self-segregating and that "multiculturalism" was causing problems. *The Mail's* judgement changed with lightning speed:

> this former lefty and New Labour luvvie should be congratulated for his bravery in saying what has been unsayable. The first stage on what is going to be a difficult path for this country is to recognise that multi-culturalism is literally a divisive creed. Britain cannot be a happy and successful multi-cultural society. No such society has ever existed, or ever will. ("Ghetto Britain," 2005)

Just a year after Alexander's blistering attack, therefore, the "national leader in political correctness" had transformed into a brave voice daring to say the "unsayable."

Phillips has continued this move to the right and enjoyed growing support. In 2008 the paper described him as "a distinguished and courageous figure. Rather than mouthing the conformist platitudes of the race relations industry, he has spoken out against its wilder advocates" ("When Children Suffer," 2008). A year later *Mail* columnist Richard Littlejohn (White) complimented Phillips as being "courageous" for saying that the concept of "institutional racism" was no longer useful. Indeed, Littlejohn's (2009) article began with an anecdote that perfectly captures Bell's rules and the enhanced standing that awaits minoritized people willing to add to the rhetoric of White supremacy and denigrate minoritized communities:

> When I asked Trevor Phillips why he'd turned his back on a successful career in television and taken his last job as head of the race relations commission, he replied: "Because I can say things *you* can't." Not that it's ever stopped me, but I took his point. As a black man on the inside track, he could tell the truth without being accused of "racism."

Littlejohn's remarks are significant; they explain the symbolic and rhetorical importance of minoritized voices that defend White racism: as members of minoritzed groups, these speakers' enhanced standing reflects their racialized claims to authenticity and their political usefulness as alternative truth-tellers. In the upside-down world of conservative politics, to denigrate minoritized people and justify race inequity is to display courage and bravery, while those who oppose racism are described as merely "mouthing … conformist platitudes" ("When Children Suffer," 2008). Although they frequently profess a desire for a colorblind world, the terrible irony is that these minoritized speakers owe their enhanced standing to their racialized identity and their actions in defence of White interests.

Double Standards, "Decent" People, and White Martyrdom

> *When a black person or group makes a statement or takes an action that the white community or vocal components thereof deem "outrageous," the latter will actively recruit blacks willing to refute the statement or condemn the action. Blacks who respond to the call for condemnation will receive superstanding status. Those blacks who refuse to be recruited will be interpreted as endorsing the statements and action and may suffer political or economic reprisals.* (The Fourth Rule, Bell, 1992, p. 118)

I and many others have written elsewhere about the fact that when White people commit a crime (real or imagined, and regardless of its severity) they are viewed in the mainstream as an individual and in no way as representative of their racial group. They may be a horrific figure but their crime is not viewed as anything for which other White people *as a group* bear responsibility (e.g., see Delgado, 2003; Gillborn, 2006, 2009; McIntosh, 1992). Minoritized groups do not share the same privilege, and this, of course, underlies wider processes of stereotyping and ethnic profiling. In the UK, racial profiling of South Asian people (especially those of Pakistani and Bangladeshi ethnic heritage) has become commonplace since 9/11, and, in particular, the London bombings of 2005. This is often justified under the banner of "intelligence-led" policing, i.e., the authorities claim to have information ("intelligence") that suggests heightened activity among terrorist groups, some of which identify as Islamic, and so increased stop-and-search of South Asian people, who are more likely to be Muslim, is judged a rational response. If such profiling is challenged as humiliating, disproportionate, and racist, the response is typically that any *reasonable* person would not object. In the words of ex-secretary of state Hazel Blears: "That's absolutely the right thing for the police to do ... I think most ordinary decent people will entirely accept that in terms of their own safety and security" ("Searches to target ethnic groups," 2005)

In this way, racial profiling was officially condoned and anyone objecting was, by definition, not an "ordinary, decent" person. A similar process of putting White perceptions at the centre and denigrating anyone who objects is at stake in Bell's (1992) fourth rule, where entire minoritized communities are placed under suspicion and required to publicly distance themselves from the words or deeds of particular minoritized individuals who have given offence to White people. Bell gave a series of examples drawn from late-1980s US politics, but the rule is alive and well in twenty-first-century England. Indeed, a particularly vicious double-standard is currently at work where White racism goes unchecked while Muslim communities are required to repeatedly denounce beliefs that, despite being legal, the state finds unpalatable. Worse still, at the same time that White people as a group escape censure, they are given the status of race martyrs, victims of multiculturalism who (media and politicians tell us) are unfairly held accountable to a higher standard than minorities:

> when a white person holds objectionable views, racist views for instance, we rightly condemn them. But when equally unacceptable views or practices come from someone who isn't white, we've been too cautious frankly—frankly, even fearful—to stand up to them. (Cameron, 2011)

In a neat rhetorical trick (similar to that performed by Black conservative voices—see above) Cameron positioned himself as courageous by arguing that "we" (politicians? White people?) have been too "fearful" to take the position that he now advocated. His assertion that White people are the victims of an unfair double-standard is part of the routine backdrop to contemporary race politics in England, where, for example, statistics are routinely misrepresented (by government and media) to present White "working class" students as the lowest achieving ethnic group (e.g., Clark, 2009; Paton, 2008; "Racism fear held back White working class pupils", 2014), and White people are told that their interests have been sacrificed to minoritized groups and political correctness (Gillborn, 2010a).

And yet the evidence clearly contradicts this image. *On the same day* that Cameron made this speech, the town of Luton (30 miles north of London) was brought to a total standstill by a demonstration by the English Defence League (EDL), a high-profile anti-Muslim hate group ("EDL and UAF Stage Rival Protests," 2011) Despite Cameron's assurance that "we rightly condemn" racist Whites, and despite the fact that the march had been planned for many weeks, the prime minister made no reference to the EDL in his speech. Responding to the subsequent accusation that the leader of the country had boosted the EDL's message, one of the most senior members of the government, said: "This is a prime minister giving a speech about the future of our country. That doesn't have to be rescheduled because some people have chosen to march down a street that particular day" (Foreign Secretary William Hague, quoted in Dunt, 2011).

And so, a town closed down by racist Whites is simply "some people" marching down a street. There is no public condemnation, let alone any suggestion that all White people should bear some responsibility and apologize on behalf of such outrageous behaviour, nor that "moderate" Whites should take the lead in fighting their racist peers. And yet, as Bell (1992) noted, these are *exactly* the demands made of minoritized people when the roles are reversed.

To this point I have concentrated on the many analytic uses of Bell's (1992) "Rules." In the following section I move on to their utility as a basis for antiracist activism and strategizing.

ACTIVISM, PROPHECY, AND CONSPIRACY: USING "THE RULES"

> *True awareness requires an understanding of the Rules of Racial Standing. As an individual's understanding of these rules increases, there will be more and more instances where one can discern their workings. Using this knowledge, one gains the gift of prophecy about racism, its essence, its goals, even its remedies. The price of this knowledge is the frustration that follows recognition that no amount of public prophecy, no matter its accuracy, can either repeal the Rules of Racial Standing or prevent their operation.* (The Fifth Rule, Bell, 1992, p. 125)

Derrick Bell's (1992) final rule touches on his thesis that racism is permanent, though *not* fixed and unchanging. Bell's belief that racism will never be fully removed from US society has been the topic of much debate and misunderstanding. Bell never argued that racism was unchanging or that protest was useless; indeed, his own professional life (as well as his writings) is testament to a profound belief that change is possible and belief in the need for political action as an essential part of a life well lived (see Bell, 2002; Tate, 1997). I have written about hope and Bell's CRT elsewhere (Gillborn, 2011a); in this chapter I wish to focus on the fifth rule's notion of prophecy, as a basis for informing critical antiracist activism.

Bell's (1992) fifth rule is vitally important because it makes the move from *analysis* (understanding how racism works) to *activism* (opposing and disrupting racism). This is an essential part of CRT, where, for many writers, an orientation towards protest and change in the service of social justice is an essential tenet of the approach (see also Crenshaw, Gotanda, Peller & Thomas, 1995, p. xiii; Delgado & Stefancic, 2000; Solórzano & Yosso, 2002, p. 26). Put simply, Bell's argument is that the better you understand the rules by which racism operates, the better placed you are to (a) predict how racism might work in the future, and (b) identify weaknesses that can be exploited to advance social justice. I made this argument the core of a book where I argued that racism in education can be understood—and opposed—as a form of *conspiracy* in the service of White power elites (Gillborn, 2008).

The idea of racism as a form of conspiracy is not new (see Turner, 1993). Huey Newton (co-founder of the Black Panther Party in the 1960s) is often credited with saying, "It's not paranoia if they're really out to get you." It is sobering to realize how many beliefs about racism that were once denigrated as wild fantasies and dangerous "conspiracy theories," have subsequently been shown to be true; e.g., in the US, official involvement in murderous action against civil rights activists, including the assassination of Dr. Martin Luther King, Jr. (see "Assassination Conspiracy Trial," n.d.; Churchill & Vander Wall, 1990). Similarly, in the UK, few race activists were entirely surprised when it emerged that undercover police had infiltrated anti-racist organisations for years with the express intention of finding material that could be used to smear the campaigning family of Stephen Lawrence—a Black teenager murdered by White racists (Evans & Lewis, 2013; Symonds, 2013).

The idea of conspiracy is not only useful in understanding how racism has operated in the past; it can also help to build in resilience, and, in Bell's (1992) terms, "the gift of prophecy" about the future of attempted reforms. Knowing that antiracist work will almost certainly be marginalized, cut back, and contested at every stage helps the activist to build in safeguards and strategize from the outset (Delgado, 1998; Gillborn, 2010b). It also alerts us to be sensitive to the racist potential in *every* policy move, regardless of its professed good intentions and the colorblind nature of the accompanying official discourse. For example, changes in assessment procedures and the selected cut-off points above which a student is deemed an "academic success" are often discussed in politics and the media as if they were technical questions, entirely separate from wider issues of equity and social justice. Nevertheless, experience in the UK clearly demonstrates that whenever politicians act to "raise standards" by changing the form of assessment that is used, or modifying pass/fail criteria, there is *always* the potential for racist impacts. Hence, in the mid-2000s, the English government (formed by the left-of-centre

Labour Party) changed the way in which children were assessed when they started mainstream school. The system increased the significance of teachers' assessments of student "ability," and, virtually overnight, Black children (with family heritage in Africa and/or the Caribbean) fell from being one of the highest-ranked groups at age 5 to being one of the lowest attaining groups (Bradbury, 2013; Gillborn, 2008, Chapter 5). The following decade another English government (this time led by a majority of Conservative right-of-centre members) established a new benchmark for attainment at the end of compulsory schooling, which they named the *English Baccalaureate*. The "E.Bacc" (as it is known) requires higher-grade passes in a defined range of high-status subjects that Black students have a reduced chance of even being allowed to enter (let alone pass). Consequently, the achievement gap between White students and their Black Caribbean peers grew wider simply because "success" had been redefined in a manner that inherently disadvantaged Black students: eight out of ten Black Caribbean students who had succeeded under the previous measure were deemed to have failed in terms of the E.Bacc; the figure for White students was around seven in every 10 (Gillborn, 2014, pp. 34–35). Hence, two different governments led by different political parties around a decade apart changed the assessment applied at the start and end of compulsory schooling; the only similarity is that both moves disadvantaged Black students relative to their White peers. The lesson is clear: whenever policy reforms are enacted, antiracists must scrutinize their likely racist impacts early and often because the likelihood is that change will be for the worse.

CRITICAL RACE PEDAGOGY: TEACHING AND RE/WRITING "THE RULES"

The apparent simplicity of "The Rules" is a key part of its success. Many students that I have worked with report a growing realization of their power as the weeks pass; what seemed "interesting" at first gradually becomes profound, even life-changing; to quote from a diverse range of students' comments once again:

> *… For some students the course clearly opened up a whole new world. For me, it gave me fresh perspectives/increased reflexivity on my own conduct and interactions.*

> *… It helped realize things that were there but I couldn't see them.*

> *… The course has completely changed the way I look at official and unofficial policies in my school. At times I felt very uncomfortable, worried and angry. I realised that it was due to the way CRT destabilised everything I thought was concrete, "true" and "earnest"! It was the first time I became aware of my position within dominant ideology and my part in reproducing it and maintaining the privileges I benefit from.*

Towards the end of one course that I led with teachers in London, I invited the group to write some *new* rules of racial standing. The idea was not to replace Bell's (1992) rules but to add to them, perhaps refine them—most of all, to find additional examples of the routine, predictable, mundane, and yet devastating operation of racism within the fabric of everyday life. For example, one of the new rules that the class generated was as follows:

> *A person of color who names racism will generally be viewed by White power-holders as at best "crude," at worst insulting, even racist!*

Anyone who explicitly calls attention to White racism as a central driver of inequity (e.g., in schools, in the economy, in the workplace) will be positioned by the mainstream as at best simplistic and misguided. At worst they will be condemned as racist for having recklessly deployed such an inflammatory and hurtful insult. If the accuser is a person of color, their motives will be assumed to be self-serving and negative; the White accused will feel empowered to display their sensitivity and good nature by being offended, upset, even outraged.

Likely responses include:

- *"But what about class?" [or gender, or sexuality, or disability or anything other than race]*
- *"… it's not as simple as that. … It's more complicated than that. …"*
- *"You're not seeing the bigger picture."*
- *"You're being racist against White people."*
- *"Only a racist sees race."*
- *"Calling people names won't help."*

Examples of this rule in practice are legion. One of the most disgusting and high-profile cases concerns Derrick Bell himself and the posthumous attack launched on him in March 2012, when 21-year-old video footage of Bell and (the then student) Barack Obama embracing at a student rally was paraded in the US media in a shallow attempt to smear the president by association. Initially broadcast by the right-wing "news" website *Breitbart.com* (Adams, 2012), the story was rapidly relayed by *Fox News* (see Martel, 2012) and picked up internationally, for example, by Britain's *Daily Mail* (Keneally & Gye, 2012). The blogosphere echoed to entries such as "Records Show Racist Bigot Derrick Bell Twice Visited White House in 2010" (KGS, 2012), while *Fox News* featured Bill O'Reilly describing Bell as "anti-White" and Sarah Palin calling him a "radical college *racist* professor."[2] Bell's crime, of course, was to go on record speaking against White racism and the benefits that White people derive from living in a racist society.

Having students engage in their own rule-writing can be a shocking, moving, and enlightening process. Most importantly, it shows another dimension to Bell's genius: the ability to construct such an important analysis in such an accessible, useful, and inspiring manner.

TOWARDS A CONCLUSION

The power of Derrick Bell's legacy does not lie only in his laser-sharp insights nor in the eloquence of his prose, it also stems from the simplicity and clarity of his voice. Bell speaks directly to the reader, whoever and wherever they are. Unlike countless "grand theorists," from old-style Marxists to sometimes impenetrable post-structuralists, Derrick Bell does not ask us to admire his intellect: he simply wants us to be involved in his analysis and to see new ways of moving forward. Derrick Bell was a scholar and an activist. He not only wrote about social justice, he tried to make it a reality. The Rules of Racial Standing are everywhere, and once you see through the veneer of normality and recognize the racist patterning that shapes "business as usual" (Delgado & Stefancic, 2000, p. xvi), the better placed you are to resist "The Rules" and your part in their reiteration and reification.

EPILOGUE: *ARE YOU WHITE?*

In this chapter I have explored the analytic, revolutionary, and pedagogic potential of Bell's (1992) "Rules of Racial Standing": I cannot end without saying something, albeit briefly, about my own autobiographical positioning in and by "The Rules." As a White-identified antiracist scholar I know that, regardless of my own politics and best efforts, I benefit from Whiteness. Bell's second rule addresses this directly:

> *Not only are blacks' complaints discounted, but black victims of racism are less effective witnesses than are whites, who are members of the oppressor class. This phenomenon reflects a widespread assumption that blacks, unlike whites, cannot be objective on racial issues.* (from the Second Rule, p. 113)

Bell noted that Black writers tend to receive much less acclaim and reward than White scholars covering similar ground, and quoted Gloria Joseph (as quoted by bell hooks, 1984, p. 51) reflecting that "it takes whiteness to give even Blackness validity" (p. 113). This is a hard reality that White antiracists must acknowledge: your efforts *may* be crucial to achieving greater racial justice, but, despite your best efforts and regardless of your motives, White antiracists *do* benefit from Whiteness and White Supremacy, in the academy and in society at large. I have written elsewhere about these contradictions, and some of the strategies that I adopt in my attempts to be a conscious Critical Race scholar and ally (Gillborn, 2008, pp. 197–203; Gillborn, 2011b). I take these problems seriously but rarely address them in print, not least because of the ever-present danger that even well-intentioned reflections on Whiteness can easily slip into self-serving, pretentious tracts that re-centre White voices and interests. As Michael Apple (1998) warned so prophetically when the Whiteness Studies movement began to build momentum, such writing can "become one more excuse to recenter dominant voices" by subverting a critical analysis and substituting an argument along the lines of "but enough about you, let me tell you about me" (p. xi).

In my work with racially minoritized scholars, community-based campaigns, teacher unions and others engaged in the struggle for racial justice, I try to *use Whiteness against itself.* That is, I try to be critically aware of how my identification as a White person might best serve wider antiracist aims; e.g., by gathering data when included in otherwise "private" race talk between White teachers or as an academic whose critique of the biased and misleading use of statistics by government and right-wing commentators gains added value through the Rules of Racial Standing (because as a member of the oppressor group my analysis cannot be instantly dismissed as "special pleading"). But even Whiteness is limited by the overriding authority of racism. For example, I have previously (Gillborn, 2008) quoted an incident where I was approached by a White female student following a lecture where I had focused on institutional racism as a driver of the Black/White achievement gap:

> [the student] asked if they could ask me "a personal question?" Their hesitant demeanour suggested that the question was of an extremely sensitive and possibly intrusive nature. I said they could ask but I might choose not to answer. They looked around nervously and then said in a quiet voice, *"Are you White?"* I said something about my family coming from varied backgrounds in England, Scotland and Eire but yes, I was pretty sure that everyone in my family would describe themselves as White. She said, "Oh, I wasn't sure." The student (who looked White to me) was clearly uncomfortable, she smiled and moved away. (p. 200)

The crowd of people who wanted to carry on talking with me after the lecture meant that I felt unable to pursue the student in order to ask why my own racialized identity had such significance for her? Reflecting on the incident now I am struck by the fact that *whatever* I had replied, the "Rules of Racial Standing" point to ways in which my arguments could easily have been dismissed, not on the basis of counter-evidence, but simply because of my own racialized identity and the antiracist analysis that I expounded. For example, as a White scholar I can be dismissed as having no personal experience as a victim of White racism—*"you don't know what you're talking about."* Alternatively, if I had answered that I *am* minoritized, say as a person of mixed-ethnic heritage, then (à la Bell's First Rule) my career can be dismissed as elaborate "special pleading." *When it comes to playing the race card, racism always has the better hand.*

The "Rules of Racial Standing" have immense power, and Bell's analysis of their operation adds hugely to our resources as antiracists. However, as Derrick Bell (1992) noted with some sadness, there is a cost to gaining such clear vision: "The Rules" can be opposed, debunked, exposed, and sometimes subverted, but they should never be ignored, and complete freedom from their operation may prove impossible: "*The price of this knowledge is the frustration that follows recognition that no amount of public prophecy, no matter its accuracy, can either repeal the Rules of Racial Standing or prevent their operation*" (p. 125).

NOTES

1. In 2010 the *Daily Mail* was given an award, by the Political Studies Association, for "consistently leading public opinion" ("The Daily Mail," 2010), and in 2014 *Mail* titles became the most read newspapers in the UK (Ponsford, 2014).
2. These are verbatim quotations from excerpts included in a feature where Professor Bell's widow answered the claims (see Taintor, 2012).

REFERENCES

Adams, J. C. (2012). Obama's beloved law professor: Derrick Bell. *Breitbart.com*. Retrieved from http://www.breitbart.com/Big-Government/2012/03/08/obamas-beloved-law-professor-derrick-bell

Alexander, A. (2004). So who's speaking now for England? *Daily Mail*. Retrieved from http://www.dailymail.co.uk/debate/columnists/article-229346/So-whos-speaking-England.html#ixzz1jvrV8mwz

Andrews, E. (2008). Cameron echoes Obama by calling on absent black fathers to take more responsibility. *Daily Mail*. Retrieved from http://www.dailymail.co.uk/news/article-1035520/Cameron-echoes-Obama-calling-absent-black-fathers-responsibility.html

Apple, M. W. (1998). Foreword. In J. L. Kincheloe, S. R. Steinberg, N. M. Rodriguez, & R. E. Chennault (Eds.), *White reign: Deploying whiteness in America* (pp. ix–xiii). New York, NY: St. Martin's Press.

Assassination conspiracy trial. (n.d.). Retrieved from The King Center website: http://www.thekingcenter.org/assassination-conspiracy-trial

Bell, D. (1992). *Faces at the bottom of the well: The permanence of racism*. New York, NY: Basic Books.

Bell, D. (1998). *Afrolantica legacies*. Chicago, IL: Third World Press.

Bell, D. (2002). *Ethical ambition: Living a life of meaning and worth*. London, England: Bloomsbury.

Birbalsingh, K. (2011). *To Miss with love*. London, England: Viking.

Blair, T. (2010). *A journey* [Kindle version]. London, England: Random House.

Bradbury, A. (2013). *Understanding early years inequality: Policy, assessment and young children's identities*. London, England: Routledge.

Cameron backs Obama over absentee fathers. (2008). *The Independent*. Retrieved from http://www.independent.co.uk/news/uk/politics/cameron-backs-obama-over-absentee-fathers-869026.html

Cameron, D. (2011). PM's speech at Munich Security Conference. Retrieved from *Gov.UK* website: https://www.gov.uk/government/speeches/pms-speech-at-munich-security-conference

Cann, C. (2014). *Reckoning with Whiteness: A reboot of Derrick Bell's "space traders."* Unpublished manuscript.

Carpenter, J. (Director). (1988). *They live* [Motion picture]. United States: Alive Films & Larry Franco Productions.

Churchill, W., & Vander Wall, J. (1990). *The Cointelpro papers: Documents from the FBI's secret wars against dissent in the United States* (2nd ed.). Cambridge, MA: South End Press.

Clark, L. (2009). White working class boys are schools' worst performing ethnic group by age of 11. *Daily Mail*. Retrieved from http://www.dailymail.co.uk/news/article-1163212/White-working-class-boys-worst-performing-ethnic-group-schools-age-11.html#ixzz3iiJq90pS

Crenshaw, K., Gotanda, N., Peller, G., & Thomas, K. (1995). Introduction. In K. Crenshaw, N. Gotanda, G. Peller, & K. Thomas (Eds.). *Critical Race Theory: The key writings that formed the movement* (pp. xiii–xxxii). New York, NY: New Press.

The Daily Mail, the most influential paper in Britain. (2010). *Daily Mail*. Retrieved from http://www.dailymail.co.uk/news/article-1334894/The-Daily-Mail-influential-paper-Britain.html#ixzz3igdyrM1c

Delgado, R. (1998). Rodrigo's committee assignment: A skeptical look at judicial independence. *Southern California Law Review, 72*, 425–454.

Delgado, R. (2003). *Justice at war: Civil liberties and civil rights during times of crisis*. New York, NY: New York University Press.

Delgado, R., & Stefancic, J. (2000). Introduction. In R. Delgado & J. Stefancic (Eds.), *Critical Race Theory: The cutting edge* (2nd ed., pp. xv–xix). Philadelphia, PA: Temple University Press.

Delgado, R., & Stefancic, J. (2005). *The Derrick Bell reader*. New York, NY: New York University Press.

Dunt, I. (2011). Cameron's multicultural speech sparks fury. *Politics.co.uk*. Retrieved from http://www.politics.co.uk/news/2011/2/6/cameron-s-multicultural-speech-sparks-fury

EDL and UAF stage rival protests in Luton. (2011). *BBC News Online*. Retrieved from http://www.bbc.co.uk/news/uk-england-beds-bucks-herts-12372713

Evans, R., & Lewis, P. (2013) *Undercover: The true story of Britain's secret police*. London, England: Faber and Faber.

Ghetto Britain and a brave, if surprising, voice. (2005). *Daily Mail*. Retrieved from http://www.dailymail.co.uk/debate/columnists/article-362922/Ghetto-Britain-brave-surprising-voice.html#ixzz1jvmMJF3n

Gillborn, D. (2006). Rethinking White supremacy: Who counts in "Whiteworld." *Ethnicities, 6*(3), 318–340.

Gillborn, D. (2008). *Racism and education: Coincidence or conspiracy?* London, England: Routledge.

Gillborn, D. (2009). Risk-free racism: Whiteness and so-called "free speech." *Wake Forest Law Review, 44*(2), 535–555.

Gillborn, D. (2010a). The White working class, racism and respectability: Victims, degenerates and interest-convergence. *British Journal of Educational Studies, 58*(1), 2–25. Retrieved from http://dx.doi.org/10.1080/00071000903516361

Gillborn, D. (2010b) "Just the right amount of racism": The cultural politics of race and reform. In Z. Leonardo (Ed.), *Handbook of cultural politics and education* (pp. 383–401). Rotterdam, The Netherlands: Sense.

Gillborn, D. (2011a). Once upon a time in the UK: Race, class, hope and Whiteness in the academy (personal reflections on the birth of "BritCrit"). In K. Hylton, A. Pilkington, P. Warmington, & S. Housee (Eds.), *Atlantic crossings: International dialogues on Critical Race Theory* (pp. 21–38). Retrieved from http://www.academia.edu/1473600/Atlantic_Crossings_International_Dialogues_on_Critical_Race_Theory_free_PDF_

Gillborn, D. (2011b). The fight against racism and classism. In P. W. Orelus (Ed.), *Rethinking race, class, language, and gender: A dialogue with Noam Chomsky and other leading scholars* (pp. 17–30). Boulder, CO: Rowman & Littlefield.

Gillborn, D. (2014). Racism as policy: A Critical Race analysis of education reforms in the United States and England. *The Educational Forum, 78*(1), 26–41.

hooks, b. (1984). *Feminist theory: From margin to center*. Cambridge, MA: South End Press.

Keneally, M., & Gye, H. (2012). "We hid this during the election": Obama ally confesses he covered up "race" video Andrew Breitbart threatened to release before his death. *Daily Mail*. Retrieved from http://www.dailymail.co.uk/news/article-2111679/Andrew-Breitbart-Obama-race-video-Charles-Ogletree-hid-Derrick-Bell-support-speech-2008-election.html

KGS. (2012). Records show racist bigot Derrick Bell twice visited White House in 2010. *Tundra Tabloids*. Retrieved from http://tundratabloids.com/2012/03/records-show-racist-bigot-derrick-bell-twice-visited-white-house-in-2010/

Leonardo, Z., & Porter, R. K. (2010). Pedagogy of fear: Toward a Fanonian theory of "safety" in race dialogue. *Race Ethnicity and Education, 13*(2), 139–157. doi: 10.1080/13613324.2010.482898

Littlejohn, R. (2009). Getting up the noses of the "guilt-tripping white folks." *Daily Mail*. Retrieved from http://www.dailymail.co.uk/debate/article-1123124/LITTLEJOHN-Getting-noses-guilt-tripping-white-folks.html#ixzz3iEwDMsIT

Martel, F. (2012). Hannity debuts Breitbart Obama college video reveals "controversial" hug with embattled professor. *Mediaite*. Retrieved from http://www.mediaite.com/tv/hannity-debuts-breitbart-obama-college-video-media-hid-video-of-obama-hugging-professor/

McIntosh, P. (1992). White privilege and male privilege: A personal account of coming to see correspondences through work in Women's Studies. In R. Delgado & J. Stefancic (Eds.), *Critical White studies: Looking behind the mirror* (pp. 291–999). Philadelphia, PA: Temple University Press.

Mirza, M. (2006). Diversity is divisive. *The Guardian*. Retrieved from http://www.theguardian.com/commentisfree/2006/nov/21/diversityhasbecomedivisive

Mirza, M. (2010). Rethinking race. *Prospect, 175*, 31–32.

Mosely, W. (2007). Black to the future. *The Liberator Magazine*. Retrieved from http://weblog.liberatormagazine.com/2007/12/walter-mosley-black-to-future.html

Obama, B. (2008). Text of Obama's fatherhood speech. *Politico.com*. Retrieved from http://www.politico.com/news/stories/0608/11094.html

Paton, G. (2008). White working-class boys "worst performers at school." *Daily Telegraph*. Retrieved from http://www.telegraph.co.uk/education/3708770/White-working-class-boys-worst-performers-at-school.html

Phillips, M. (2003). Spinelessness that makes us all sitting ducks. *Daily Mail*. Retrieved from http://www.dailymail.co.uk/columnists/article-229951/Spinelessness-makes-sitting-ducks.html#ixzz3iEiQQbba

Ponsford, D. (2014). *Mail* titles overtake *Sun* to become most read UK newspaper brand according to NRS. *Press Gazette*. Retrieved from http://www.pressgazette.co.uk/mail-titles-overtake-sun-become-most-read-national-newspaper-brand-according-nrs

Racism fear held back white working class pupils—Ofsted inspector. (2014). *BBC News Online*. Retrieved from http://www.bbc.co.uk/news/uk-politics-25743035

Reynolds, T. (2009). Exploring the absent/present dilemma: Black fathers, family relationships, and social capital in Britain. *The ANNALS of the American Academy of Political and Social Science*, *624*(1), 12–28. doi: 10.1177/0002716209334440

Searches to target ethnic groups. (2005). *BBC News Online*. Retrieved from http://news.bbc.co.uk/1/hi/england/london/4732465.stm

Sewell, T. (2009). *Generating genius: Black boys in love, ritual and schooling*. Stoke on Trent, England: Trentham.

Sewell, T. (2010). Master class in victimhood. *Prospect*, *175*, 33–34.

Solórzano, D. G., & Yosso, T. J. (2002). Critical Race methodology: Counter-storytelling as an analytical framework for education research. *Qualitative Inquiry*, *8*, 23–44.

Symonds, T. (2013, June 24). Police "spied on" Stephen Lawrence family, says *Guardian* newspaper. *BBC News Online*. Retrieved from http://www.bbc.co.uk/news/uk-23022634

Taintor, D. (2012, March 13). Derrick Bell's widow speaks about "outrage" against her late husband. *TPM*. Retrieved from http://tpmmuckraker.talkingpointsmemo.com/2012/03/derrick_bells_widow_speaks_about_outrage_against_h.php

Tate, W. F. (1997). Critical Race Theory and education: History, theory, and implications. In M. W. Apple (Ed.), *Review of research in education, Vol. 22* (pp. 195–247). Washington, DC: American Educational Research Association.

Turner, P. A. (1993). *I heard it through the grapevine—Rumor in African American culture*. London, England: University of California Press.

Warmington, P. (2014). *Black British intellectuals and education: Multiculturalism's hidden history*. Abingdon, England: Routledge.

Warmington, P. (2015). The emergence of black British social conservatism. *Ethnic and Racial Studies*, *38*(7), 1152–1168. doi: 10.1080/01419870.2014.987792

When children suffer to satisfy Labour dogma. (2008). *Daily Mail*. Retrieved from http://www.dailymail.co.uk/news/article-1024936/When-children-suffer-satisfy-Labour-dogma.html#ixzz1jvmzkqCO

White working-class pupils "unseen" & underperforming: White working-class pupils perform worse in their GCSEs than any other ethnic group. (2014). *Channel 4 News*. Retrieved from http://www.channel4.com/news/white-working-class-poor-school-worst

Wintour, P., Watt, N., & Topping, A. (2008). Cameron: Absent black fathers must meet responsibilities: Tory leader backs Barack Obama on race and family breakdown. *The Guardian*. Retrieved from http://www.guardian.co.uk/politics/2008/jul/16/davidcameron.conservatives1

CHAPTER SEVEN

Letter TO My Unborn Daughter

My Career in the Academy—Reasons for My Mental Breakdown

NICOLA ROLLOCK

Derrick Bell's (1992) *Faces at the Bottom of the Well: the Permanence of Racism* is one of those books that seem to reach deep into me and speak directly to the essence of my being. It *speaks* my experiences. Like *The Autobiography of Malcolm X*, bell hooks's *Yearning*, Ralph Ellison's *Invisible Man*, to name but a few, *Faces at the Bottom of the Well* forged in me a sense of affirmation and heightened perspicuity. The whispered conversations in toilets with the (few) other faculty and support staff of color; the telephone calls with pained Black colleagues or friends working in other sectors; the dinner party conversations; the yelling at the radio or television at the superficial engagement with race all became repositioned within a frame of normality and visibility.

I was not mad.

Chapter Six of the book sets out five rules—The Rules of Racial Standing—which speak to the underlying assumptions and norms that dictate how race is played out and normalized, and racism kept intact within structural processes that serve to benefit Whites. However, it is not merely the profundity of these rules that resonates. I was, and remain, captivated by the powerful allegorical stories, which Bell (1992) deployed to drive home his arguments and which, while seemingly innocuous in rhythm and script, in fact act as powerful, disturbing conduits through which to distil the harsh realities of racism and White Supremacy. As Linda Greenhouse (1992) of *The New York Times Book Review* writes in her review of *Faces at the Bottom of the Well*: "The stories challenge old assumptions and then linger in a way that a more conventionally scholarly treatment of the same themes would be unlikely to do." It is precisely this, the creative use of stories—counter-narratives—that has stayed with me from Bell's work and that has served both as a liberatory, medicinal necessity in my own scholarship (e.g., Rollock, 2012a, 2012b), and as an accessible means through which to engage with communities of color beyond the academy (Lynn, Jennings, & Hughes, 2013).

CRITICAL STORY-TELLING FOR ACTIVISTS

Counternarrative is one of the tools of Critical Race Theory (CRT), a body of scholarship steeped in radical activism that seeks to explore and challenge the prevalence of racial inequality in society. CRT foregrounds the experiential knowledge of people of color in helping to comprehend, deconstruct, and challenge racism by working to subvert the status quo and centre traditionally marginalized voices (Delgado, 2000; Delgado & Stefancic, 2001; Solórzano & Yosso, 2002).

Counternarrative or counterstories can be semi-autobiographical or fictional in nature and often comprise composite characters; that is, actors and snapshot or amalgamated accounts sourced from a range of real experiences. There is often a strong reliance on footnotes to lend contextual literature and explanation to the matters set out in the allegory. As a tool, counternarratives lend "important contextual contours to the seeming 'objectivity' of positivist perspectives" (Ladson-Billings, 2009, p. 22) and thus have the potential to act as a persuasive and transformative tool to challenge liberal racist ideology.

My own engagement with counternarrative stems from this very investment in the racial justice project (Stovall, 2006), as well, as I intimated earlier, from its ability to act as a humanizing device. More precisely, it reflects my commitment to shed light on the hegemonic processes within the academy that serve to retain the now well-documented track record of poor representation and progression of faculty of color (about which I say more below), and the equally poor experience and degree classification of students from this same demographic. Specifically, I am interested in how decisions get made, policies drawn up, actions taken; in how these normalized and normalizing "structured relations" (Grenfell & James, 1998, p. 24) serve in explicit, and frequently implicit, ways to disadvantage already marginalized groups and protect the boundaried positions of those in power. My point is that there remains a gap between policy promises of diversity and equality and the reality of how policy is actually interpreted and enacted. As Apple (2004: viii) reminds us: "Academic boundaries are themselves culturally produced and are often the results of complex 'policing' actions on the part of those who have the power to enforce them" (p. viii).

Bourdieu's notion of *misrecognition* (i.e., tacit recognition) is clearly relevant here: "Misrecognition relates to the ways these underlying processes and generating structures of fields are not consciously acknowledged in terms of the social differentiation they perpetuate, often in the name of democracy and equality" (Grenfell & James, 1998, p. 23). Bourdieu (1986) defines a field as a structured system or network of social relations that operate at micro and macro levels. These relations work to produce and reproduce various forms of social activity; it is this that marks them out from other fields or sites. Therefore, higher education is a field and universities can be seen as subfields within the overarching system. Of course, each university comprises inner worlds—faculties, schools, departments— each of which subscribe (are subject) to the dominant norms of the institution and are simultaneously shaped by their own cultural practices, internal rules, and ways of being. These practices and rules are not neutral, as evidenced in profile statistics on recruitment and retention; presence on committee boards; degree outcomes. Educational institutions act as sites of "cultural preservation and distribution" (Apple, 2004, p. 2), determining who is included, who is excluded, who has access to power, which forms of knowledge (Delgado Bernal & Villalpando, 2002) are deemed to have legitimacy:

> The common image of the professions ... takes into account not only the nature of the job and the income but those secondary characteristics which are often the basis of their social value ... and *which though absent from the official job description, function as tacit requirements,* [emphasis added] such as age, sex, social or ethnic origin, *overtly or implicitly guiding co-option choices, from entry into the profession and right through a career, so that members of the corps who lack these traits are excluded or marginalized* [emphasis added]. (Bourdieu, 1986, p. 102)

It is precisely the "tacit" that interests me; that which conventionally remains unspoken, uninterrogated, taken as "normal," yet which has violent, damaging consequences for under-represented groups. Counternarrative has the enlightening potential to serve as a clever, complex, and creative means through which to "render visible these invisible operations as a way of making available the possibility at least of democratizing the product and processes of the field" (Grenfell & James, 1998, p. 22).

Setting the Context

In the counternarrative that follows, I set out the emotional entanglement, contradiction, and insecurity that can result from occupying a space in the margins and from trying to navigate the tacit. And yet I hope to do more than this. This is not *merely* an account of life at the margins, but, I hope, a distillation of the pained recollections from those positioned thus and how they (we) have struggled and fought to gain recognition (both formal and informal) within our professions. While I have previously explored the possible advantages of being located at the margins (Rollock, 2012b), reflecting on arguments advanced by Wynter (1992) and Ladson-Billings and Donnor (2008), I argue here that being positioned thus can be problematic, difficult, and perhaps all the more so when such location is resisted and you refuse to "know your subjugated place."

The setting is the academy, although, as stated, the narrative draws together experiences from beyond this sector. I have already set out an argument for the academy as a site of "cultural preservation and distribution" (Apple, 2004, p. 2). The statistics detailing the career experiences of faculty of color provide damning evidence of the consequences of these processes. In the UK, for example, just 4% of home domiciled[1] Black academics are professors compared to 10.7% of home domiciled White academics who hold positions at this level. In short, you are almost three times as likely to be a professor if you are White. However, sometimes the percentages mask the sheer direness of the situation. Looking to the raw numbers, this equates to 60 UK Black professors across the whole of the UK compared with 12,445 UK White professors (Equality Challenge Unit, 2014). Of all ethnic groups, Black academics are least likely to occupy this senior role. These figures take on an intersectional starkness when gender is also brought into the equation. Just 5% (3,365) of all[2] White female academics are professors. This compares with 3% (270) of female academics of color who hold posts at this level[3] and only 17 of these are Black. The small body of research documenting the experiences of UK faculty of color reports that their experience and status are often called into question, they are undermined and ignored, and the value of their work is seldom recognised (Hey et al., 2011). With this in mind, it is hardly surprising that UK faculty of color are more likely than their White counterparts to consider leaving the country to work overseas (Bhopal, Brown, & Jackson, 2015). The US is one of the countries at the top of their list; however, the research on the experiences of US faculty of color offers little optimism. As Altbach, Lomotey, and Rivers (2002) pointed out in their critique of race in US higher education, "the professorate is overwhelmingly White, male and middle class" (p. 30), a fact routinely evidenced in data published by the US National Center for Education Statistics (US Department of Education, NCES, 2014). For example, Latina/o and Black faculty continue to be under-represented at the level of full professor, making up a mere 3% and 4% of the professoriate respectively compared with White professors, who make up 84% of this population. As Misra and Lundquist (2015) reported in their commentary on the NCES data:

> most groups [of color] have barely increased their representation among full professors. Asian men's gains at the full level have recently slowed, despite their steady increase among associate faculty. Native American men and women, black men and women, and Latinos also have stalled.

Jackson (2004) reveal some of the issues affecting African Americans in high level administrative higher education and postsecondary posts, noting that they experience racism, sexism, and are often presumed to lack relevant knowledge or experience for their role. Similar issues are detailed in *Presumed Incompetent*, an edited collection of essays, that documents the career experiences—the negation of identity; presumption of incompetence; accounts of microaggressions; the rules, challenges, and contradictions of the academia—of female faculty of color (Gutiérrez y Muhs, Flores Niemann, González, & Harris, 2012). Being subjected to these processes, and working to constantly navigate and survive them, takes its toll in real, physical terms. While scant literature exists in the UK on racial microaggressions and racial battle fatigue, this remains an important area of examination in the US (e.g., Smith, Hung, & Franklin, 2011; Solórzano & Yosso, 2000; Sue, Capodilupo, & Holder, 2008). Giles and Hughes (2009) describe, for example, the pressures for faculty of color working in mainly White academic institutions as giving rise to fatigue in the form of high blood pressure, stuttering, sweaty palms, and incidents where, as the result of being constantly undermined and presumed incompetent, they begin to second-guess their own intellectual capabilities. As Smith et al. (2011) portend there is an "emotional, physiological, and psychological cost of gendered racism" which "social, educational and professional institutions" (p. 64) must recognize.

It is in this context, that the following counternarrative is written.

LETTER TO MY UNBORN DAUGHTER

[Note to reader: To be read slowly, carefully. The character is upset and has been crying.]

I am sorry, my love, I am sorry.

I am so deeply sorry. I tried to be strong but they broke me.

I write this so that maybe you will understand why I am not there for you, why they are coming to take me away. I want you to know that I tried. I really did. I tried to protect myself. I took solace in reading. And oh my God, I read! Malcolm X, Maya Angelou, Zora Neale Hurston, Alex Haley, Okri, Achebe, Ayi Kwei Armah, Chimamanda Ngozi Adichie … I could go on, darling. And not just the Black classics either. Their own books tell you about how things are done, about the craziness of this society, this world. Read the classics, darling, read them. Make them your cultural Bible to understand this world.

I'm not really sure where to begin. I used to be—not long before I learnt about you, my love—I used to work on issues to do with equality … race, really. I was interested in how we might improve our lot in this country; have a better life. It was hard but it could be so rewarding. I used to write about the kind of things that bothered us. When I say us, I suppose I mean Black people here in the UK, those of us who have somehow managed to remain proud of our identity, our culture, and history despite the racism, despite the constant negativity they keep throwing at us. I used to do research too. Research is amazing—you pull together ideas to understand society better. And I did some truly amazing things … oh, I'm not sure they'll make sense to you now but at the time it was really important stuff. My work was debated in Parliament. I was so very humbled when I learned that. I was called in to give evidence to one of the political parties of our day about how to improve the experiences of children … of our children in their schools. I designed and delivered teacher training on race equality and cultural diversity to teachers across the UK. Even the Ministry of Defence—they're a government agency, sweetheart—they commissioned me to train their teachers working at their bases in Europe. Me! It was all so thrilling, that sense of shaping change. It was all so very exciting but. … [she pauses, her mind cloudy with distant memories] … well that was a long time ago now, darling. That was a time when they spoke, albeit with little understanding, about racism. And that only happened because a young Black man called Stephen Lawrence[4] was murdered in a racist attack in south-east London. He was a teenager really. You need to Google him, darling. It is so important you know who he was. And darling, just before those days when I stopped getting out of bed because it all became too much, too hard, I started to receive so many invitations to speak at really prestigious universities around the world. I was so humbled, so excited at the possibilities: Europe; South Africa; Australia; America. It's not any better in any of those places, my love, especially in the US—the endless accounts of innocent African American men being shot or murdered are heart-wrenching.[5] It happens here too,[6] but more quietly, as though framed by a polite civility, which means we don't really discuss it or give it the attention it deserves. At least when I went to the US I could talk, I could talk about racism, about being Black, about Whiteness, without the defensive anger and blank denial I received in the UK.[7] I suppose what I am saying, my love, is that I tried. I did really try to make things better for you.

[She feels the baby move and take up an awkward position on her bladder. She shifts, trying to compensate and redistribute the heaviness. Her heart is heavy as though large boulders are dragging it southward and swollen tears quiver unsteadily at the edge of her already blurred eyes. A deep sigh—a deep deep sigh—rises from within her and fills the silent room].

[She dabs at the tears with the edge of a frayed sleeve].

The way they do things is so difficult to understand.

She wonders where best to begin.

They undermine you constantly.

The disrespect is constant.

[New tears replace the old ones, and, with gradual determination, make their way down already damp cheeks].

My love, I could almost, I think, cope with all of that but it is the contradictions that drove me crazy, that kept me awake at night, that left me sobbing endlessly into my pillow.

Darling, they write mission statements, statements of intent, strategic plans. They scream bold commitments of what they call "diversity" or engaging "community populations."[8] Darling, part of your challenge will be to work out which of these terms relate to you, to people who look like you. They demand that you fill in forms about how much work you have done and will do that bear no semblance to reality. There are boxes to fill in on that form, and if the work that you do doesn't fit into any of those boxes, well then, darling, as far as they are concerned it simply doesn't exist. It doesn't matter if you say, oh I don't know, that one of your students came on six separate occasions with weeping and with panic attacks about their grades and took up 15 hours of your time in one term even though the form says they should only have 6 hours.[9] It doesn't matter. The extra 9 hours is magicked away into insignificance. It doesn't matter that because your profile has grown and you are, writing regularly for mainstream newspapers (they love that—gets the university's name in the press) that you are dealing with more public enquiries as a result. And it doesn't matter that one of those enquiries was actually from some crazy-a*** White supremacist who curses you for existing and tells you to go back to where the **** you came from. There is no box on the workload form for that, you see, so the fact that it happened becomes, is *made* to become, insignificant even though it takes me a while to get over the brute force of the language in his e-mail and I'm unable to concentrate on my work. But *they* love the fact that you are bringing the university such a great profile. And all the while they keep going on about wanting to make a difference, about wanting to improve diversity, about wanting to address equality in the workplace. What I am doing does that but it does not fit into their pro forma.

Darling, I promise you I tried.

PROMOTION

I applied for promotion. This must be about two years ago ... before you.

She smiles a weak but fond smile and touches her stomach absent-mindedly.

I filled in their forms. I counted the pages of articles, I tried to make sense of journal citation figures (which no one ever teaches you about, by the way) and cite these in my application. I tried to work out the percentage of time I contributed to each of the modules I taught. I wrote that down. I found ISBN numbers. I went back through old memory sticks and files and paperwork to find out when I actually first joined some association or society or the other. (This matters, apparently.) And I read *every single* university guidance document or policy I could find that set out the vision for the place. I read this *in addition to* the promotion material and I used the same words they used: "strategic plan"; "vision"; "international agenda"; "public engagement"; "impact" to demonstrate explicitly how my achievements complemented what they were seeking to do. Darling, I even read the criteria for the level *above* the one I was actually applying for, and, seeing that many of my achievements ticked boxes at that level, I stated this, I pointed this out, I highlighted this. I told them. I did! Darling, I didn't simply tell them *I spoke* at certain events, I also told them *where* the event took place, how many people were there, *who* was there (but only if they were high-profile, darling, because apparently that's all that matters). Darling, I *really* tried. I did.

My love, they asked on that promotions form about gaps in employment or if your career pathway had been unusual in any way. I wrote it all down. And darling … my love, as I wrote down the fact that my early career was characterized by short-term research contracts, I know, my love, I know that this is not unusual for women or for Black academics.[10] Darling, I know because this is my area of expertise. Darling, I know too that some poor soul (a Black woman) at another university has had her short-term research contract renewed and renewed again and again over a course of 20 years! I thought that was illegal.[11] And darling, I know this because we all speak to each other. I know this, darling, when they look me in the eye and tell me, unflinchingly, that they are committed to equality.

So, when they told me that they weren't even going to consider my application for promotion I was stunned, despite knowing how they tend to operate. I was so angry. My application was excellent. It was damn excellent. I wanted to jump up and start cursing, screaming at them for their lies, the ridiculousness of it all. [She laughs]. Can you imagine! [The laugh quickly fades]. However, I tried to work out how I could make the best of the situation. You know, be strategic. I tried to remind myself of what I knew; what I knew about the empirical evidence, about them and these damn processes. I tried darling, I really did, try to think strategically but …

[She struggles both with the tears that are now streaming relentlessly down her face and with sheer effort as she tries to ensure that her writing retains some degree of legibility].

… I was just so angry. They told me that one of the reasons my application wasn't being considered was because I hadn't seen any doctoral students through to completion. I remember staring angrily back at him—the bearer of this news. Doctoral students? I asked what weighting had been given to the fact of the short-term contracts at the start of my career. (I somehow was lucid enough to ask this question.) That question probably makes little sense. OK, darling, let me explain. Being on a short-term research contract affects the likelihood of taking on doctoral students who will generally be registered for between 3 and 6 years. I'd done some supervision but my record wasn't strong precisely because of my career profile. So what consideration *had* been paid to my career profile, given that they asked a question about this at the end of the form? None, I was told. None. No consideration.

The bearer does not blink when disclosing this information. There is no hesitant pause. There is no awareness that the question holds any significance whatsoever. Why is it asked then? Why is there a question on the form about breaks in career, if it has no impact on how they assess my application?

I am given options.

I am told I can appeal, or I can apply again next year.

Those are my options.

That's what they said when I applied the first time—4 years ago. "You're young," they said. "Apply next year," they said. And I try not to think of the poor Black woman at the other university who had her contract renewed again and again over 20 years.

She just left in the end. No one knows what happened to her.[12]

I remember studying the bearer angrily. I tell him that I am unimpressed and deeply disappointed and leave the room. I take refuge in my office (thank God for individual offices!), lock the door, and pace the floor angrily.

It must have been mere days later, darling, when I heard a woman, an academic at another university, on *Woman's Hour* (a flagship BBC radio programme aimed at women) who had taken her institution to court over a very similar issue. I wondered fleetingly whether I should do the same. However, I have no inclination, no strength to engage in more of their "processes" only to be spat out, a shadow of my former self, some 2, 3 years later. I am tired of constantly fighting, of demonstrating to them, of speaking out and seeing so very little change. I am so very tired of the contradictions and lies, but most of all, I am angry at the nonchalance with which injustice is handed out.

WHITE FEMALE FACULTY

Whenever I try to raise these issues with my mentor (some scheme they introduced at work)—her name is Jilly Huntington—she starts talking about herself and about gender. It makes me so angry, my love. She tells me endless stories of how she was disadvantaged at some time or the other because of her gender as if to somehow demonstrate her understanding of my situation. But each time she opens her mouth it is as if she is taking one of those thick whiteboard pens that I carry around in my handbag and scribbling it across my face, my body, my identity, my experience, my history. I want her to shut up. No matter how many polite, firm words I conjure up to tell her that it is *not* the same, she keeps telling me about her White female experience. By doing this she is shutting me down, sweetheart. She is shutting out my experiences. And those rare times I do decide to tell her about some prestigious writing invitation or speaking engagement she coos "congratulations" at me in the awed, breathless, excited tones reserved for congratulating a toddler who has taken its first, fumbling steps. And, you know, she keeps telling me that I can come to speak to her if anything is bothering me: "just drop me a line. Call me! You are amazing. I will do whatever I can to support you."

And you will have to be mindful of this, darling. White women think they get it because they too have experienced discrimination because of their gender but they always fail to acknowledge that they are White and that being White brings them a privilege that we do not have. Black men are pathologised. Black women are simply invisible.[13] When she speaks I try to pause my knowledge that there are 2735 White female professors in the UK and a paltry 180 from (what they call) minority ethnic backgrounds.[14] As I listen to her tell me the story (yet again) of some job she went for years back where the White man got it, and she didn't even though she was qualified, I really want to scream at her: "shut the f** up! You are *already* a professor!" I, however, am not. And darling, I don't know how much things will have changed by the time you grow up, but now there are all manner of initiatives, schemes, charters for women, but darling, know that they are never for us. They never speak race. If they mean more White women in post without some of them being from what they call BME backgrounds (and sometimes, horrifically, BAME[15] backgrounds), no one will bat an eyelid or call the programme unsuccessful. They will pat each other on the back and say how well they've done on gender.

My love, I did try.

I had lunch with a friend who works in the private sector a few weeks ago. It was just after one of my episodes of what I call lowness, but I now know was just the lead up to where I am now and why they are coming to take me away. She told me that she had been promoted at work. I smiled with heartfelt joy and congratulated her, missing the deadpan flatness in her voice, in her eyes. "It is long overdue," she said, looking at me but not expanding on the comment. She knows I know. My smile fades. I simply nod, "I understand," I said. "I understand."

And they keep telling us they are committed to equality.

THE RISKS OF SPEAKING OUT

I have learnt that to be brave means learning to accept you will be bullied. In recent years, I have dared to speak up, only to be shouted down and humiliated by White men. Once, the man in question had been invited to our Race Equality Forum (a group where Black staff can find solace and seek advice from one another about race equality matters). This man had been assigned a role to address race equality by the VC of the university even though he admitted to us, without flinching embarrassment, that he knew absolutely nothing about race. I would have laughed, we all would have, if these issues were not so fundamental to our careers, to our very existence. You could not make it up. He somehow produced a report without consulting the whole group and which did not mention the words race or racism once. I mentioned this. He sat with us at one of our meetings. It was just us—Black members of staff—and this man, talking about this report. He shouted at me, accusing me of trying to downplay the importance of the report, and he shouted at me, in front of everyone, in the one space that I thought was safe from such abuse.

More recently, my love, I was shouted at by a very senior White man during a meeting about promotions. You see, I asked a question about citizenship,[16] which is something they assess us on. The woman from HR who was there told me that the definition was "fuzzy" (she actually used this word) and that the people who would be assessing the promotion applications would basically know in their own minds what they were looking for. As you can imagine, my love, this concerned me. I couldn't understand how this amounted to a transparent and equitable process. I intimated as such and was shouted down (put in my place, if you will) by this man who told me that I should stop lecturing him and listen to what he was saying. The woman from HR said nothing. No one in that room of 20, 30 people said anything. He was allowed to shout at me, to humiliate me as though I was something he had wiped off his shoe. What do you do in such situations? Shout back? Tell them they have no right to speak to you like that? If the woman from HR says nothing, if the other senior staff say nothing, then it becomes quietly sanctioned as acceptable behaviour.

And you read their policies stating their commitment to equality.

[She stops. She places the pen carefully on the table, at a slight angle so it doesn't roll away, and glances up at the clock on the wall. She needs to take her second dose of Diazepam. She had always been against medication. It had once seemed somehow as though taking it meant she was admitting defeat, becoming another statistic, another of the many Black people with mental health issues in the UK. Heading to the kitchen, she recalls the Black man who used to beg for change at the traffic lights not far from her home. She recalls another who used to simply repeat, hand outstretched, "20 pence please, 20 pence please, 20 pence please," while walking back and forth outside the nearby train station. The recollection pains her.[17] She feels she has failed them. She has failed herself but most of all, she feels she has failed the unborn child weighing down her stomach. She turns on the tap and allows the water to run for a moment before filling a glass, throwing the tablet into her mouth and swallowing. The tears seem unable to stop today but then some days are just like that.

She returns, glass in hand, to the letter].

RACIAL GESTURE POLITICS

Hello darling, I'm back. I just had to pop to the kitchen for something. Where was I? Ah yes, the contradictions. We had a staff meeting just the other day, actually. There was a document that set out our mission and vision. And there, in unashamed print in the final bullet point was the statement "Ensuring the needs of our diverse staff and student groups are met and that their overall experience is enhanced wherever possible." Again, it is as if someone is standing at the sidelines poking, jeering, laughing at me because in a department of 35 staff, there is only one other academic who looks like me and he is elsewhere on that day. "Ensuring our needs … are met?" This is something written by the Equality Lead (also a White woman) who interrupts me in meetings and pretends not to hear my ideas but yet makes the same suggestion seconds later, to enthused nods. This is the same person with whom I tried to speak discreetly about the promotion fiasco, who tilted her head with a sympathetic frown and suggested that perhaps it *was* best if I applied next year. I was incensed when I read that statement. I asked whether there were particular initiatives or outputs that we might be working towards that would serve as a benchmark to our knowing we were meeting the needs of such staff and students. She tells me that at this stage it is a "statement of intent" and that it is "so very important" to have a statement that "reflects our working practice." I try to resist snorting in derision. "An action plan might be something to work on next," she says in that feigned academic way that I know means she has not given the practicalities of the statement any real thought whatsoever. I lower my eyes and try to stop the words spoken by Jack Straw from going around and around in my mind.[18]

You see, my love, for us to exist in those spaces we have to tell ourselves a lie. We lie to ourselves that if we work hard, tick boxes, go to ridiculous Christmas lunches and drinks—show we're a good sport, then we will succeed even when there is very little evidence to suggest this is the case. I've already told you the number of racially minoritised female professors in the academy. Don't think it's limited to just there. Media is the same, law, journalism; all the professions, in fact.[19]

And they keep telling us they are committed to equality.

Their policies, rules, guidance documents are not implemented in a way that will benefit you. The earlier you understand that the better. We silly older ones thought that through our success we might be able to chip away at those structures, but they are too embedded, my love, they are far too embedded, and besides, they believe they resolved these issues back in 2009.[20] Be careful also of false gestures or meaningless acts that *look* like change. They invited me to sit on endless steering groups but never to act as co-PI with them. (PI means Principal Investigator; it's the person who develops, writes, and leads on the proposal and subsequent project management.) Being on a steering group means relatively little for your CV and there is no box for it on their workload form and it is not asked about when you go for promotion. They will wheel you out for photo opportunities so that your beautiful brown skin appears on prospectuses[21] or on the front pages of websites as a reflection of how well they are doing at "diversity," but they will continue to undermine you, to shout at you at meetings, to downplay and silence your experiences. But, my love, they will not recognize your scholarship and experience as valid. They will not promote you.

And all the while, they will continue to speak of equality.

I have a few friends, my love, who ask me how I work in these places. They mean mainly White institutions, but there is never a need to spell that out. They ask me how I do it. I don't know, is what I tell them. "They" are very good at minimizing the importance of race and racism. I struggle every day with the pain of their minimizing. I struggle, my love, which is why …

[She starts sobbing].

… which is why I ended up having a breakdown. They will never, of their own accord, name race or racism or truly engage with the profound ways in which these issues shape our experiences in the workplace. They will pretend to engage. Their strategies for change will always be safe and never ever be implemented with urgency or compulsion. This is why being in a mainly White space was so exhausting, so debilitating, my love.

So, my beautiful, beautiful daughter, I write this letter to you so you know why I am not there for you. I want you to know, from me, what happened. Just because mommy is locked away in a place far from you, you should know that mommy loves you.

I love you so much, my darling.

[She glances over her shoulder at the clock on the wall. There's not much time. She must finish before they arrive].

You will need to think about how you survive. I failed. And I know, locked away from you, I am also failing to protect you, but I promise you, I did try.

Be careful out there. This society is deeply unjust. You may find one or two people in positions of power who you can trust, but these will be few and far between. The rules of the game will keep changing. It will be hard for you to keep up with them. Know that it is not a game meant to benefit you. It has benefitted few of us, and yet foolishly we keep knocking at that door to be let in. But go, my love, fight from this place of knowledge. Go armed with this information into university, into your place of work. I hope that what I have written here, that knowing, will help protect you.

My darling, I must go now. It is time. They will soon be here for me.

I love you, and whether or not they allow you to see me, or, if they do, whether or not I recognize you, know this; I love you.

And I will love you to the end of my days,
Mommy

POSTSCRIPT: A NOTE FROM THE AUTHOR

A colleague who read a draft of this chapter was concerned (understandably so) that I, personally, was in a place of emotional vulnerability. While the issues raised do not sit outside of my experience as a female faculty of color, this letter does not speak to an intention to harm myself. Its purpose is to reveal the accumulative nuances of racial battle fatigue and the way in which it works to quietly erode emotional well-being and professional self-confidence. You may well have reached the end of the letter and desired closure, and, indeed, if this were a traditional academic text, the reviewers would write back to the editor recommending that I include a Conclusion or Discussion. However, there is none. This is real life. Racism is part of the daily reality of faculty of color.

These are the issues with which we must contend.

NOTES

1. Home domiciled refers to UK-based as opposed to international scholars. This distinction is important, as amalgamating the figures (which institutions sometimes do to convey an elevated, though misguided, sense of progress on race) can hide important distinctions in career trajectory and recruitment practices between UK and non-UK academics.
2. That is both home domiciled and international scholars.
3. At time of writing, there are just 17 Black female professors across the whole UK.
4. Stephen Lawrence was murdered by five White youths while waiting for a bus in south London in April 1993. Police incompetence, and their failed handling of the investigation, along with a public condemnation by Nelson Mandela, served as the impetus for then Home Secretary Jack Straw to launch a judge-led inquiry into the circumstances surrounding Stephen's death. The resultant Stephen Lawrence Inquiry report was published in 1999 with 70 recommendations aimed at improving equality across the criminal justice system and placing an imperative on the education system to take a lead in promoting race equality. Two of the White men were eventually convicted in 2012, some 19 years after Stephen was murdered. Reports of police spying and corruption continue to surround the case. It is impossible to understand race and racism within the UK without acknowledging the role that the case has played in the history of British race relations (Macpherson, 1999; Rollock, 2009; BBC, 2014).
5. The Black British *Guardian* journalist Gary Younge (2015) lived in the US for 12 years. In "Farewell to America" he documents his experiences, marred as they were by a backdrop of violent murders of Black men, often, though not exclusively, at the hands of the police.
6. See, for example, work by Inquest (http://www.inquest.org.uk/statistics/bame-deaths-in-police-custody), a campaigning organization that works to highlight and support cases involving

contentious deaths in police custody and immigration detention. A disproportionate number of these deaths are of those from Black and minority ethnic backgrounds.

7. See Rollock (2015) for a discussion of why it is difficult to talk about race in UK universities.

8. Sara Ahmed's (2012) book, *On Being Included: Racism and Diversity in Institutional Life*, powerfully captures the experiences of diversity practitioners as they work to advance equality in higher education. Accounts of resistance are rife, as is the gap between symbolic commitments to diversity and the stark realities for those positioned as "diverse."

9. A study published by the University and College Union (UCU) documented the health and well-being of over 14,000 university employees. It found growing levels of stress levels amongst academics, prompted by "heavy workloads, a long hours culture and conflicting management demands" (Shaw & Ward, 2014). It found that academics experience higher stress than those in the wider population.

10. Equality Challenge Unit (2014).

11. Government guidance on employment legislation actually states: "Any employee on fixed-term contracts for 4 or more years will automatically become a permanent employee, unless the employer can show there is a good business reason not to do so" (https://www.gov.uk/fixed-term-contracts/renewing-or-ending-a-fixedterm-contract, accessed July 1, 2015). Our character in the counternarrative is concerned by the fact that 20 years is a long time to keep renewing a contract while arguing there is no good business case to make the role permanent. It fuels career instability and limits the possibility of pursuing key academic markers of distinction (e.g., bid writing, postgraduate students) that would support career progression. Notably, Black academic staff are more likely to be on these short-term contracts compared with their White counterparts (Equality Challenge Unit, 2014).

12. Hey et al. (2011) reported similar findings in their study examining the career experiences of Black and minority ethnic academics. Their findings, based on survey, focus groups, and interview data, reveal what they describe as "unseen cultural promotional practices" (p. 3) negatively affecting the career progression of racially minoritised staff. One participant comments: "There are blockers here. … Too many people with too many agendas—it's very much the old school—been there for 20 or 30 years. … They were blockers—oh, get this one in—not that one. … It's word of mouth I never got through faculty … [they are] more comfortable with me sweeping the floors than teaching, I'm sure. I see myself as a pro vice-chancellor, while they see me as a toilet cleaner, that's the difference." (p. 3)

13. For wider discussion of these issues in the UK see Dabiri (2013) and Frazer-Carroll (2015).

14. Data relate to UK-domiciled faculty for the period to 2012/13 (Equality Challenge Unit, 2014).

15. Black, Asian, and minority ethnic.

16. US colleagues call this "service."

17. Here, I am drawing upon the sentiment that for many female scholars of color, the pursuit of scholarship is not merely a dichotomized academic one but is deeply implicated with our identities and the need for our work to speak to, and have a positive impact on, the communities of which we remain part (e.g., Hill Collins, 1991; Ladson-Billings, 1997).

18. Speaking in Parliament on the day of the publication of the Stephen Lawrence Inquiry report, Home Secretary Jack Straw (1999) insisted: "Any long-established, White-dominated organisation is liable to have procedures, practices and a culture that tend to exclude or to disadvantage non-White people" (column 391). It was (and still is) unusual for such a high-profile public figure to speak about race, yet alone White privilege and power, so explicitly (Rollock, 2015).

19. A report published by the Commission on Social Mobility & Child Poverty analysed the backgrounds of 4000 leaders in politics, business, the media, and other aspects of public life in the UK. They found these professions to be dominated by those (White, privileged men) who had attended private schools (fee-paying) and elite, high-status universities. They concluded: "Our examination of who gets the top jobs in Britain today found elitism so stark that it could be called 'Social Engineering'" (Milburn, 2014, p. 10).

20. 2009 marked 10 years since the publication of the Stephen Lawrence Inquiry report. In the months leading up to the event, several high-profile figures, including former Home Secretary Jack Straw and the former Chair of the Commission for Racial Equality, distanced themselves from the term "institutional racism," arguing that it no longer had relevance within British society (Rollock, 2015).

21. Ahmed (2015) discusses the superficial ways in which institutions often respond to the diversity imperative. She notes that the reaction of one university to address the charge that they were "white and old-fashioned was to add 'smiling brown faces' to their prospectus." She argues: "The production of happier images of diversity can thus become a technique for not addressing whiteness as an institutional problem; whiteness is treated as an image problem. Those who report racism are thus often treated as threatening this image."

REFERENCES

Ahmed, S. (2012). *On being included: Racism and diversity in institutional life*. Durham, NC; London, England: Duke University Press.

Ahmed, S. (2015). Doing diversity work in higher education, In C. Alexander & J. Arday (Eds.), *Aiming higher: Race, inequality and diversity in the academy*. London, England: Runnymede Trust.

Altbach, P. G., Lomotey, K., & Rivers, S. (2002). Race in higher education. In W. A. Smith, P. G. Altbach, & K. Lomotey (Eds.), *The racial crisis in American higher education: Continuing challenges for the twenty-first century*. New York, NY: State University of New York Press.

Apple, M. (2004). *Ideology and curriculum* (3rd ed.). Abingdon, England; New York, NY: Routledge.

BBC News (2014) Stephen Lawrence murder: A timeline of how the story unfolded. March 6. Retrieved from http://www.bbc.co.uk/news/uk-26465916

Bell, D. (1992). *Faces at the bottom of the well: The permanence of racism*. New York, NY: Basic Books.

Bhopal, K., Brown, H., & Jackson, J. (2015). *Academic flight: How to encourage Black and minority ethnic academics to stay in the UK*. London, England: Equality Challenge Unit.

Bourdieu, P. (1986). *Distinction: A social critique of the judgment of taste*. New York, NY; London, England: Routledge.

Dabiri, E. (2013, November 5). Who stole all the Black women from Britain? *MediaDiversified*. Retrieved from http://mediadiversified.org/2013/11/05/who-stole-all-the-black-women-from-britain/

Delgado, R. (2000). Storytelling for oppositionists and others: A plea for narrative. In R. Delgado & J. Stefancic (Eds.), *Critical Race Theory: The cutting edge* (2nd ed.). Philadelphia, PA: Temple University Press.

Delgado, R., & Stefancic, J. (2001). *Critical Race Theory: An introduction*. New York, NY: New York University Press.

Delgado Bernal, D., & Villalpando, O. (2002). An apartheid of knowledge in academia: The struggle over the "legitimate" knowledge of faculty of color. *Equity & Excellence in Education, 35*(2), 169–180.

Equality Challenge Unit. (2014). *Equality in higher education: Statistical report 2014. Part 1: staff.* London, England: Author.

Frazer-Carroll, M. (2015, June 24). Finding role models in a white-washed world … *Black Ballard.* Retrieved from http://www.blackballad.co.uk/finding-role-models-whitewashed-world/?utm_source=twitter&utm_medium=social&utm_campaign=timeline

Giles, M. S. & Hughes, R. L. (2009) CRiT walking race, place, and space in the academy, *International Journal of Qualitative Studies in Education,* Special Issue: Critical race studies and education, *22*(6), 687–696.

Greenhouse, L. (1992). The end of racism, and other fables [Review of the book *Faces at the bottom of the well: The permanence of racism,* by D. Bell]. *The New York Times Book Review.* Retrieved from http://www.nytimes.com/books/00/06/04/specials/bell-well.html

Grenfell, M., & James, D. (1998). *Bourdieu and education: Acts of practical theory.* Abingdon, England: RoutledgeFalmer.

Gutiérrez y Muhs, G., Flores Niemann, Y., González, C. G., & Harris, A. (2012). (Eds.), *Presumed incompetent: The intersections of race and class for women in academia.* Boulder, CO: The University of Colorado Press.

Hey, V., Dunne, M., Aynsley, S., Kimura, M., Bennion, A., Brennan, J., & Patel, J. (2011). *The experiences of Black and minority ethnic staff in higher education in England.* London, England: Equality Challenge Unit.

Hill Collins, P. (1991). *Black feminist thought: Knowledge, consciousness and the politics of empowerment.* New York, NY: Routledge.

Jackson, J. F. L. (2004). Engaging, retaining and advancing African Americans in executive-level positions: A descriptive and trend analysis of academic administrators in higher and postsecondary education. *Journal of Negro Education: Special issue top line—A status report on African American leadership in higher and postsecondary education, 73*(1), 4–20.

Ladson-Billings, G. (1997). For colored girls who have considered suicide when the academy's not enough: Reflections of an African American woman scholar. In A. Newmann & P. L. Peterson (Eds.), *Learning from our lives: Women, research and autobiography in education.* New York, NY; London, England: Teachers College Press.

Ladson-Billings, G. (2009). Just what is Critical Race Theory and what's it doing in a *nice* field like education? In E. Taylor, D. Gillborn, & G. Ladson-Billings (Eds.), *Foundations of Critical Race Theory in education.* Abingdon, England; New York, NY: Routledge.

Ladson-Billings, G., & Donnor, J. (2008). The moral activist role of Critical Race Theory scholarship. In N. K. Denzin & Y. S. Lincoln (Eds.), *The landscape of qualitative research* (pp. 279–301). Los Angeles, CA: Sage.

Lynn, M., Jennings, M. E., & Hughes, S. (2013). Critical Race pedagogy 2.0: Lessons from Derrick Bell. *Race Ethnicity & Education, Special Issue: The Legacy of Derrick Bell, 16*(4), 603–628.

Macpherson, W. (1999). *The Stephen Lawrence Inquiry.* London, England: Crown Copyright. Retrieved from https://www.gov.uk/government/uploads/system/uploads/attachment_data/file/277111/4262.pdf

Milburn, A. (2014). *Elitist Britain? Report from the Commission on Social Mobility and Child Poverty Commission.* Retrieved from https://www.gov.uk/government/uploads/system/uploads/attachment_data/file/347915/Elitist_Britain_-_Final.pdf

Misra, J., & Lundquist, J. (2015, June 26). Diversity and the ivory ceiling. *Inside Higher Ed.* Retrieved from https://www.insidehighered.com/advice/2015/06/26/essay-diversity-issues-and-midcareer-faculty-members

Rollock, N. (2009). *The Stephen Lawrence Inquiry 10 years on*. London, England: Runnymede Trust.

Rollock, N. (2012a). Unspoken rules of engagement: Navigating racial microaggressions in the academic terrain. *International Journal of Qualitative Studies in Education, 25*(5), 517–532.

Rollock, N. (2012b). The invisibility of race: Intersectional reflections on the liminal space of alterity. *Race Ethnicity & Education*, Special issue on Critical Race Theory in England, 15(1), 65–84.

Rollock, N. (2015, February 9). Why is it so hard to talk about race in UK universities? *The Conversation*. Retrieved from https://theconversation.com/why-is-it-so-hard-to-talk-about-race-in-uk-universities-37299

Shaw, C., & Ward, L. (2014, March 6). Dark thoughts: Why mental illness is on the rise in academia. *The Guardian*. Retrieved from http://www.theguardian.com/higher-education-network/2014/mar/06/mental-health-academics-growing-problem-pressure-university?CMP=share_btn_tw

Smith, W. A., Hung, M., & Franklin, J. D. (2011). Racial battle fatigue and the miseducation of Black men: Racial microaggressions, societal problems and environmental stress. *The Journal of Negro Education, 80*(1), 63–82.

Solórzano, D., & Yosso. T. (2000). Critical Race Theory, racial microaggressions, and campus racial climate: The experiences of African American college students. *Journal of Negro Education, 69*(1–2), 60–73.

Solórzano, D. G., & Yosso, T. J. (2002). Critical Race Methodology: Counter-storytelling as an analytical framework for education research. *Qualitative Inquiry, 8*(1), 23–44.

Stovall, D. (2006). Forging community in race and class: Critical Race Theory and the quest for social justice in education. *Race Ethnicity & Education, 9*(3), 243–259.

Straw, J. (1999) *Stephen Lawrence Inquiry*, Column 391, Available at www.parliament.uk

Sue, D. W., Capodilupo, C. M., & Holder, A. M. B. (2008). Racial microaggressions in the life experience of black Americans. *Professional Psychology: Research and Practice, 39*(3), 329–336.

U.S. Department of Education National Center for Education Statistics. (2014). *The Condition of Education 2014* (NCES 2014-083). Retrieved from https://nces.ed.gov/fastfacts/display.asp?id=61

Wynter, S. (1992). *Do not call us Negros: How "multicultural" textbooks perpetuate racism*. San Francisco, CA: Aspire Books.

Younge, G. (2015, July 1). Farewell to America. *The Guardian*. Retrieved from http://www.theguardian.com/us-news/2015/jul/01/gary-younge-farewell-to-america

Derrick Bell ON Theory

CHAPTER EIGHT

Derrick Bell's Feminism

Profeminism, Intersection, and the Multiple Jeopardy of Race and Gender

ADRIENNE D. DIXSON

Derrick Albert Bell was born on November 6, 1930, in Pittsburgh, Pennsylvania. After 2 years in the Air Force, he attended law school at the University of Pittsburgh. Bell went on to work for the Civil Rights Division of the Department of Justice, NAACP Legal Defense Fund and held several faculty positions in prominent law schools ("Biography of Professor Derrick Bell," 2014).

My scholarship in Critical Race Theory (CRT) and education has been significantly influenced by Bell. I was introduced to Bell and CRT through *Faces at the Bottom of the Well* (1992), a book I read while I was a sixth-grade teacher in New Orleans in the early 1990s. I had heard from people I worked with at a summer program that *Faces* was "controversial" and that Bell's take on race was depressing. Thoroughly enthralled by his writing, I read the book in one weekend. Never had I encountered a "non-fiction" book that captivated me like *Faces*. Like anyone who reads Bell's books and articles, I finished it hungry for more and armed with a new framework for understanding race and racism. This book and this "new" framework would soon become my intellectual home.

As a first year doctoral student at the University of Wisconsin-Madison, I read an earlier book, *And We Are Not Saved* (1989), which preceded *Faces*. What struck me about both *Faces* and *And We Are Not Saved* was the character Geneva Crenshaw. Bell's writing was so elegant and clear that for me, Geneva Crenshaw was not some fictional character but a real person who articulated ideas, especially about gender and Black women's experiences, that I could not only relate to, but had also heard and read in much of the Black feminist literature I was reading as part of my doctoral studies. In many instances, Bell so eloquently captured a Black woman's voice that I nearly forgot that he was actually the sole author of the chronicles and stories in those books. Thus, for me, this notion of CRT and feminism is so intricately connected that I admittedly have not embraced Critical Race Feminism as an additional "gendered" framework for my scholarship in CRT.

The relationship between race and gender (and other identify markers) has been historically contentious. Anna Julia Cooper, a contemporary of W. E. B. Du Bois was one of the most vocal African American women to address the "woman problem" as it related to the "Negro problem" (Lemert & Bahn, 1998). Political philosopher Joy James (1996) noted that although Du Bois is often described as a champion of women's rights, his actions often belied his "theoretical" gender politics. While James described Du Bois as a "profeminist," she argued that his treatment of, and failure to publicly acknowledge, both Anna Julia Cooper and Ida Wells-Barnett illustrates the complicated nature of racial and gender politics and advocacy even for one of our most prolific and important African American scholars. James offered,

> Du Bois's writings champion women's rights, denounce female exploitation, and extol women as heroic strugglers. But while condemning the oppression of African-American women, DuBois veiled the individual achievements of such women as Cooper and Wells-Barnett from the political landscape. In his profeminist politics, he obscured Black women's radical agency and intellectualism. Here *feminist* refers to women's gender-progressive politics, and *profeminists* denotes male advocates of women's equality. In examining the contradictory aspects of Du Bois's profeminism, we should consider his actions on behalf of women's rights, his representations of black women, and the placement of African-American women in his non-fictional essays and political autobiographies. In theory and practice, Du Bois opposed women's subjugation. But his political representations of and relationships with influential female leaders reflect a considerable ambivalence toward Black women's political independence. (p. 37)

Du Bois's support of women's rights is important but his relationship with Cooper and Wells-Barnett (he literally ignored them and refused to respond to their letters) (Lemert & Bahn, 1998) is more than an example of "ambivalence," but illustrates how deeply entrenched patriarchy is even within a progressive racial agenda. This complicated relationship between race and gender within the context of Black social politics has not been lost on CRT.

For CRT scholars, there has never been "ambivalence" toward gender and Black women's political independence. From its inception, women of color, especially Black women, have had a significant role in its development. Scholars in Women's Studies identify Intersectionality, CRT scholar Kimberlé Crenshaw's analytical intervention to examine and understand persistent inequity for women of color, as one of the most important contributions to Women's Studies in the last

20 years (McCall, 2005; Nash, 2008). Thus, calls for a "feminist" analysis within CRT (Wing, 2003) are, for me, curious.

Along with Crenshaw's groundbreaking scholarship on intersectionality (1988; 1989), Derrick Bell had been, in both his scholarship and advocacy, championing gender equity for women of color writ large. In this chapter, I argue that Derrick Bell, as a progressive and prolific race scholar, was also a profeminist; however, unlike Du Bois, Bell not only wrote insightfully about race and gender inequity, he also acted publicly against institutional gender and racial inequity, especially as it impacted women of color.

BLACK FEMINISM WITHIN CRT

Gendered and feminist analyses have been a significant aspect of CRT since its inception. Crenshaw (1988) introduced the concept of intersectionality to illustrate the ways in which race, class, gender, sexual identity, marital status, citizenship status, and other social identities often serve as points of marginality and oppression for Black women. Within the broader history and scholarship of CRT, Black women scholars have offered an expansive view of the relationship between race, gender, class, and marital status (among other identity markers) on the impact of Black women's experiences in the larger U.S. society (Austin, 1989; Crenshaw, 1988; Roberts, 1991; Williams, 1992).

In the social sciences and Women's Studies literature, gendered oppression was analyzed from multiple angles. Sociologist Deborah King's (1989) notable contribution was her "multiple jeopardy" model. Like Crenshaw, King argued that simplistic "race as gender" analyses obfuscate the complex social and political terrain Black women traverse that is distinctively different from that of Black men and White women. Where Crenshaw argued for an intersectional analysis, King explained that Black women are plagued by the multiple jeopardies of not only race and gender, but also class, marital status, and motherhood, among other identities and oppressions. It is worth quoting King at length,

> The legacy of the political economy of slavery under capitalism is the fact that employers, and not black women, still profit the most from black women's labor. And when black women become the primary or sole earners for households, researchers and public analysts interpret this self-sufficiency as pathology, as deviance, as a threat to black family life. Yet, it is black women's well-documented facility to encompass seemingly contradictory role expectations of worker, homemaker, and mother that has contributed to the confusion in understanding black womanhood. These competing demands (each requiring its own set of resistances to multiple forms of oppression) are a primary influence on the black woman's definition of her womanhood, and her relationships to the people around her. To reduce this complex of negotiations to an addition problem (racism + sexism = black women's

experience) is to define the issues, and indeed black womanhood itself, within the structural terms developed by Europeans and especially white males to privilege their race and
their sex unilaterally. Sojourner's declaration, "ain't I a woman?" directly refutes this sort of
conceptualization of womanhood as one dimensional rather than dialectical. (pp. 50–51)

Thus, for King, Black women's oppression exists in, and reflects, a complex dialectical (or what Crenshaw described as intersectional) calculus that extends beyond
simplistic reductions to a function of race or gender. This call to understand the
complexity of analyses of race and racism was also offered by the germinal Black
feminist scholarship of Anna Julia Cooper, Mary Church Terrell, Audre Lorde,
and the Combahee River Collective, to name just a few.

DERRICK BELL'S PROTESTS

Critical race theory measures progress by a yardstick that looks to fundamental
social transformation. The interests of all people of color necessarily require not
just adjustments within the established hierarchies, but a challenge to hierarchies
themselves. This recognition of intersecting forms of subordination requires multiple consciousness and political practices that address the varied ways in which
people experience subordination. (Lawrence, Matsuda, Delgado, & Crenshaw,
1993, p. 7)

A fundamental, yet frequently overlooked, "defining element" of CRT, is social
change. The quote by Lawrence et al. (1993) reminds scholars who engage CRT
that it is more than just a theoretical or analytical framework for scholars to use
when they want to "do" a racial analysis. CRT mandates that scholars agitate for
and demand equity for people of color through a reconstruction of social arrangements and institutions. It is this commitment to social change and the "challenge
to hierarchies themselves" that best describes Bell's activism, as an example of his
"ethical ambition" (Bell, 2002).

After earning his law degree from the University of Pittsburgh Law School,
Bell worked for the Justice Department in the Civil Rights Division. In 1959,
the Department of Justice asked him to give up his membership in the National
Association for the Advancement of Colored People because they saw it as a con-
flict of interest. He refused and instead resigned from the Department of Justice
(Bell, 2002).

As a law professor at Harvard and becoming the first Black professor to earn
tenure, Bell went on to serve as the Dean of University of Oregon Law School
for 5 years. He left the University of Oregon after the faculty refused to hire an
Asian American woman ("Biography of Professor Derrick Bell," 2014). He had
a reputation in Eugene as a great mentor who recruited, supported, and encouraged women of color to enter the law profession. My cousin Elizabeth Branch, a

student at the University of Oregon, spent a considerable amount of time at his home. His wife, Jewel, was very active in the community in the City of Eugene, Oregon, and was a friend of my family. Elizabeth shared stories with me about Bell's involvement with his students and his reputation for his commitment to not only students of color but also gender equity (Personal communication, 2011).

While Professor Bell was interested in increasing the numbers of women of color in law, he was also committed to increasing the presence of all women in the law and often mentored and provided opportunities for White women. He returned to Harvard and soon mounted a 5-day sit-in protesting the Law School's refusal to tenure two women of color ("Biography of Professor Derrick Bell," 2014). Bell's protests were significant because in almost all of the cases, the women he supported were also women he recruited to the institution and mentored. Through these protests, Bell lived his politics and demonstrated his commitment to women of color.

DERRICK BELL'S FEMINISM

Literary critic Michael Awkward (1995) argued that Black men can, "develop political, theoretical and interpretive strategies that help to actualize feminist goals" (p. 43). Awkward quoted literary critic Joseph Boone to illustrate how men can engage in feminist projects:

> In exposing the latent multiplicity and difference in the word "me(n)," we can perhaps open up a space within the discourse in feminism where a male feminist voice can have something to say beyond impossibilities and apologies and unresolved ire. Indeed, if the male feminist can discover a position from which to speak that neither elides the importance of feminism to his work nor ignores the specificity of his gender, his voice may also find that it no longer exists as an abstraction … but that it inhabits a body: its own sexual/textual body. (Boone, cited in Awkward, 1995, p. 43)

Derrick Bell's voice, through both his scholarship and his activism, did not "exist as an abstraction," and indeed inhabited a body, a prolific, textual body. His contribution to the *gendering* of CRT is significant. Bell, as the "father of CRT," though his engagement with the Black feminist voice illustrates that CRT, from its inception, has *always already* been concerned about gender, gender politics, and the subordination of women of color.

In all of his books, *And We Are Not Saved* (1987), *Faces at the Bottom of the Well* (1992), *Gospel Choirs* (1997), Bell created a recurring character, Geneva Crenshaw. In some of his chronicles, he draws on the literary device of magical realism by using a device also used by many women writers of color, along with Geneva Crenshaw's character. The "Celestial Curia," are a mystical chorus of women who appear in Bell's chronicles as a sort of race consciousness that engages Bell (and readers) in thinking about strategies to both challenge racist practices and to disrupt the mainstream American racial narrative. These characters appear frequently in Bell's stories, often as a surprise to him. Readers learn through his discussions with Geneva Crenshaw that the Celestial Curia pushed them to think more complexly about ways to redress racial subordination and inequity. Bell's use of this device demonstrates his understanding of the literary tradition and practices in Black feminist literature and Black women's writing.

Bell created the Geneva Crenshaw character, in part, to give voice to ideas that often ran counter to orthodox legal scholarship, especially orthodox anti-discrimination legal scholarship. Bell credited his understanding of the complexities of both race, gender, and the Black experience through his relationships with the women in his life, i.e., his mother, his first wife Jewel (who preceded him in death), and his second wife (and widow), Janet Dewart Bell ("Derrick A. Bell," n.d.). Bell's work with and through Geneva Crenshaw demonstrates not only his willingness to take up the "plight of the Black woman" but also to engage in a self-critical examination of Black male and female relationships. Through his Geneva Crenshaw character, we see Bell's belief in the insight and intellect of the Black female subject. Bell (1997) described Geneva Crenshaw thusly,

> I am drawn to the poetic, the lyrical. Glowing, magisterial, enigmatic, Geneva is the epitome of a sort of grace, an air I've noticed in other women who understand far more about the world than any mere man. The challenge for us men is to acknowledge (at least to ourselves) this insight and not compete with or question it, and certainly not resent it. (p. 13)

Bell articulated and demonstrated a high regard for women and the need for men to essentially reject patriarchy and male privilege that would restrain, overshadow, and restrict opportunities for women to fully participate and contribute. Through Geneva Crenshaw, we can infer that the "women" Bell referenced are Black women. In this way, Bell's profeminism is highlighted.

THE CHRONICLE OF THE 27-YEAR SYNDROME

In this chronicle Bell (1987) considered the ways in which racism impacts the personal relationships between Black men and women by offering a storyline where unmarried, never-married Black women or those who had never "entertained a *bona fide* offer of marriage to a Black man" (p. 199) regardless of whether they have children, upon their 27th birthday, fall into a sleep that lasts for 4–6 weeks, and they awake with all of their bodily functions intact. The women awake with a form of amnesia that requires them to be retrained in order to return to their careers. The social and emotional costs are quite extensive, and in Bell's rendering, the

DERRICK BELL'S FEMINISM | 137

government shows no interest in sponsoring a cure for the syndrome, but instead crafts a public health mandate that all Black women register with the government by their 26th birthday to "track" their progression before they fall victim to the syndrome. Similarly, the government proposes to advertise the names and ages of women so that Black men who are so inclined to help the women avoid the syndrome will contact them and marry them. Black women who are married to White men are not immune from the syndrome.

The brilliance of the chronicle is in the dialogue between Bell and Geneva Crenshaw. In their exchange we see the complexity and nuance of Bell's understanding of the intersection between patriarchy and race. Bell masterfully weaves in historical, sociological, and psychological explanations for the persistent oppression of Black people writ large but also represents the range of perspectives used to explain Black women's subordination.

Through the story, Bell also engaged in the self-reflection that Awkward (1995) believed is necessary for Black male feminists:

> A Black male feminist self-reflexivity of the type I have in mind necessarily would include examination of both the benefits and the dangers of a situatedness in feminist discourse. The self-interestedness of a Black male feminist would be manifested in part by his concern with exploring a man's place. Clearly if ... speaking *like* a female feminist is not in and of itself an appropriate goal for aspiring male participants, then a male feminism necessarily must explore males' various situations in the contexts and texts of history and the present. (p. 191)

In this chronicle, and indeed in all the chronicles where Geneva Crenshaw appears, Bell is self-reflexive and moves beyond a preoccupation with where Black men "fit" in discussions about gender disparities between Black women and men; Bell also challenged men to think about how they get in the way of women's progress through "interventions" that only serve to perpetuate patriarchy.

CONCLUSION

As "the Father of Critical Race Theory," Derrick Bell is an important example of how CRT can be used to examine subordination and inequity from multiple perspectives. His tremendous scholarly record includes foundational scholarship that could and perhaps should be the primary focus of any graduate-level course in education on race and racism. Moreover, Bell's scholarship nearly always demonstrated the CRT elements of interdisciplinary knowledge and eclecticism (Lawrence et al., 1993). Always one to stand and act on his convictions, he also exemplified the notion of the scholar-activist. His profeminist perspective inspired his protests, quite often in response to racist and gender oppressive practices of liberal academic institutions, and remind us that as CRT scholars we must do more than just theorize and analyze inequity; we must speak out and act out. In his own words, "rather than offering definitive answers, I hope, as a law teacher rather than social seer, mainly to provoke discussion that will provide new insights and prompt more effective strategies" (Bell quoted in Barksdale, 1989, p. 377). Bell's goal was to challenge not only the law, but to also provoke all of us to use our platforms to work toward the end of racial oppression, even though he was skeptical that we would ever be able to do so. Whether we get there or not, Bell's life and scholarly legacy have given us the tools and the mandate to work toward eradicating all forms of oppression.

REFERENCES

Austin, R. (1989). Sapphire bound!, *Wisconsin Law Review*, 539–578.

Awkward, M. (1995). *Negotiating difference: Race, gender, and the politics of positionality (Black literature and culture)*. Chicago, IL: University of Chicago Press.

Barksdale, H. G. (1989). *And we are not saved: The elusive quest for racial justice* by Derrick Bell. *Boston College Third World Law Journal, 9*(2), 363–377.

Bell, D. A. (1987). *And we are not saved: The elusive quest for racial justice*. New York, NY: Basic Books.

Bell, D. A. (1992). *Faces at the bottom of the well: The permanence of racism*. New York, NY: Basic Books.

Bell, D. A. (1997). *Gospel choirs: Psalms of survival in an alien land called home*. New York, NY: Basic Books.

Bell, D. A. (2002). *Ethical ambition: Living a life of meaning and worth*. New York, NY: Bloomsbury.

Biography of Professor Derrick Bell. (2014). Retrieved from http://professorderrickbell.com/about/

Crenshaw, K. (1988). Mapping the margins: Intersectionality, identity politics and violence against women of color. *Stanford Law Review, 43*, 1241–1299.

Crenshaw, K. (1989). Demarginalizing the intersection of race and sex: A Black feminist critique of anti-discrimination doctrine, feminist theory and anti-racist politics. *The University of Chicago Legal Forum, 140*, 139–167.

Derrick A. Bell, Jr., National visionary. (n.d.). Retrieved from the National Visionary Leadership Project website: http://www.visionaryproject.org/bellderrick/#2

James, J. (1996). *Transcending the Talented Tenth: Black leaders and American intellectuals*. New York: Routledge.

King, D. K. (1988). Multiple jeopardy, multiple consciousness: The context of a Black feminist ideology. *Signs, 14*(1), 42–72.

Lawrence, C. R., III, Matsuda, M. J., Delgado, R., Crenshaw, K. W. (1993). Introduction. In M. J. Matsuda, C. R. Lawrence, III, R. Delgado, & K. W. Crenshaw, (Eds.), *Words that wound: Critical Race Theory, assaultive speech and the First Amendment* (pp. 6–7). Pittsburgh, PA: University of Pittsburgh Press.

Lemert, C. & Bahn, E. (Eds). (1998). *The voice of Anna Julia Cooper*. Lanham, MD: Rowman & Littlefield.

McCall, L. (2005). The complexity of intersectionality. *Signs: Journal of Women in Culture and Society 30*(3), 1771–1800.

Nash, J. (2008). Re-thinking intersectionality. *Feminist Review 89*, 1–15.

Roberts, D. E. (1991). Punishing drug addicts who have babies: Women of color, equality, and the right of privacy. *Harvard Law Review, 104*(7), 1419–1482.

Williams, P. J. (1992). *Alchemy of race and rights: The diary of a law professor.* Cambridge, MA: Harvard University Press.

Wing, A. (2003). *Critical Race Feminism, a reader.* New York: New York University Press.

CHAPTER NINE

In Pursuit of Critical Racial Literacy

An (Auto)ethnographic Exploration of Derrick Bell's Three Is

KEFFRELYN BROWN

INTRODUCTION AND GOAL OF THE CHAPTER

We are living in trying racial times. Media accounts of police brutality targeted at Black people flood the airways and virtual ways. The number of Blacks beaten and murdered at the hands of the State and its misguided vigilantes—men, women, transgendered, elderly, youth, and children, too numerous to name—is breathtakingly overwhelming. Overwhelming not for its sheer existence or contemporary novelty, but rather for its steady yet sadly anticipated presence.

Yet I suspect that if we could speak to legal race scholar Derrick Bell (1987, 1992, 1996) now, at the eve of the second term of the Obama presidency, he would likely say that Black people have always experienced trying times in the U.S. Since their arrival to these shores (intended and forced), African Americans have served as a defining marker, an antithesis, to how those that fashioned themselves and fought to become White (Coates, 2015) viewed self and their place in the world. Yet to craft this identity of Whiteness, to place it at the center of life and world required the existence of Black people and Blackness. As counterstory, both of these were punctuated by what it meant to be in, and navigate, a world that has unceasingly affirmed all that is White. At the core of these concerns resides the nagging issue of race.

In this chapter, I explore Derrick Bell's ideas on the cultivation of critical racial literacy, a fundamental element in understanding race as a complex and integral feature of life in the U.S. Bell, a legal scholar and founding theorist of Critical

Race Theory, was concerned with understanding why legal redress in the U.S. consistently failed to produce a more racially just society. Using innovative methodology that combined fictional storytelling and legal and historical analysis, Bell theorized how race and racism serve as defining features in the American social landscape. This is a history indissoluble from the present. It is marked by a paradoxical deep investment in, and radical departure from, the founding ideals of the U.S. nation. The result is an unpalatable legacy of race and racism left for current inhabitants to wrestle with and traverse.

This journey is not easy. It is not for the faint or the weary. This is what Derrick Bell's scholarship tells us. Nevertheless, it is a project that he entreated us all to engage. In this chapter, I pick up his call. Like my fellow travelers—those with me now, along with those that came before and that will come long after I have taken my rest—I make this journey wide-eyed, inspired, and hopeful. Mine is not a naïve hope, rooted in the romantic belief that what I present stands a ghost of a chance of transforming the entrenched indignities wrought by racism. Rather, what I seek to achieve is speaking my truth as an experienced researcher and teacher concerned with how we might more fruitfully engage the topic of race in our work. My truth (admittedly one of many)—laced with insights garnered from Derrick Bell, one of the most cogent, accomplished thinkers on the topic of race and racism in the U.S.—moves from an inspired, yet sober, clear-eyed sense of purpose and resolve.

I begin this task by grounding my autobiographical experiences with Derrick Bell and his ideas on race and racism in the context of my own life history. This history fomented in the educational experiences I had in high school and during my undergraduate years as a K–12 teacher, in graduate school, and finally as a researcher and academic. This chapter draws from the methodologies of (auto) ethnography and critical race testimony. The intent of this work is both narrative and analytical. Hughes, Pennington, and Makris (2012) described (auto)ethnography as a method of inquiry that recognizes the salient role of the researcher in cultural analysis. In reading the experiences of the researcher, one is able to access the larger sociocultural factors that operated in both the site(s) of inquiry and the research itself. In a similar vein, Baszile (2008) referred to the methodology of analytically narrating one's life story around race and racism as critical race testimony. This methodology links the Black prophetic tradition of testimony and Critical Race Theory's counterstorytelling to affirm the lived experiences of race. This work specifically seeks to disrupt dominant White notions of knowledge and reason by calling into question what counts as valid ways of knowing. In this chapter I draw from data embodied in the fleshly remembrances of my everyday experiences of race. Privileging this knowledge, my intention is to show why we need discussions of race that allow one to make a deeper connection between the individual and the structural, the historical and the present.

In rendering my own narratives of race as a valid form of data, I move the reader through social spaces filled with racism, missing knowledges, lack of awareness, unacknowledged Whiteness, anti-Blackness, growing politicization, and theoretical refinement. My experiences teetered between my everyday realities of race as a middle-class, Black female negotiating predominantly White spaces and larger sociopolitical histories that, at the time, I barely understood were fully knotted within them. Through telling these stories I seek to illustrate when, and more importantly, how, race was (not) present in my schooling and interpretive frameworks of racism. In doing this I contextualize Bell's admonishment for a more cogent, incisive analysis of race and racism. I argue that the effects of the presences and absences in my own racial narrative led to my adoption of a partially serviceable kind of racial knowledge that fell short in fully interpreting racism in the way a critical racial literacy approach would advance. It was not until I focused my research squarely on race, in addition to teaching undergraduate and graduate students about the sociocultural knowledge of race, that I had to dissect my understandings of, and methods for talking about, and, ultimately, teaching others about, racism.

Drawing from the foundational ideas theorized by Derrick Bell around the legacy of U.S. racism, legal scholar Lani Guinier (2004) recognized racial literacy as the "capacity to decipher the durable racial grammar that structures racialized hierarchies and frames the narrative of our republic" (p. 100). A foundational insight into this grammar is the permanence of racism in U.S. society; a sobering idea that should lead one to a renewed sense of inspired purpose, struggle, and critical engagement when undertaking race work. Racial literacy insists upon the acquisition of a robust, complex understanding of race and racism. It requires possession of both content knowledge of how these have operated in society and an interpretive framework that enables one to recognize racism by understanding its constituent features and the relationship between these varied expressions (e.g., micro, macro), temporally and spatially. Racism is, but is not solely defined by, what any one, or multiple, persons do to other individuals. Racism is the accumulated ways of thinking, embodied in actions that have divested some bodies of opportunities, resources, and the sanctity (and safety) of their very selves, while concomitantly investing other bodies with benefits, material and symbolic privilege, and unquestioned sanction of choice and access. For Black people this has meant the unquestioned normalization of many deleterious social effects: under-resourced, underwhelming expectations, underachievement, unwarranted death.

I follow this autobiographical discussion by placing my experiences with race in the context of Derrick Bell's theorization of racial knowledge. I consider Bell's perspectives on the permanent nature of racism in U.S. societal relations and its paradoxical role to Whiteness in redressing racial inequality for African Americans (Bell, 1987, 1992, 1996). Bell read racism as endemic to the founding and maintenance of the U.S. nation, with historical precedent pointing to how the civil rights of Blacks are perpetually sacrificed to dominant, White interests. This argument proffers a framework to understand racism in the U.S. that he situated in the context of what he called *the three Is: information, interpretation, and inspiration* (Bell, 1992–1993). I conclude by considering the utility of adapting the three Is to develop a critical race literacy. Here I reflect on my own experiences in relation to employing the three Is when researching and teaching about race.

AN (AUTO)ETHNOGRAPHIC NARRATIVE OF RACE

My experiences with Derrick Bell and his ideas on race began in 1992 during my early undergraduate years in college. I was introduced to him first through his published books, *And We Are Not Saved* and *Faces at the Bottom of the Well*, and a subsequent symposium he participated in that I attended. I was a psychology major and had recently picked up a double major in political science. I had an interest in understanding the experiences of African Americans in the U.S. My plan was to pursue doctoral studies in political psychology with a focus on examining the psychological effects of political repression on African Americans. The idea of power—how people and state governments accessed and wielded it—captivated me. Adding to my missing sociocultural knowledge was an understanding of how state power operated within and outside of nations that were democratic. I was deeply troubled by the underbelly of state power; all of its unsavory, yet generally semi-invisible stealth hidden from everyday life. This was the early 1990s. It was well before the post-911 era demonstrations (and justifications) for excessive, overt state power that generally go unquestioned in the present. As I learned during these years, the U.S. has a long history of enacting repressive political state power; a power that has paradoxically existed alongside the ideals of U.S. democracy. That I did not learn of this history until I was midway through my undergraduate degree shocked and disappointed me. It was indicative of the problems of curriculum and formal schooling.

My growing awareness of the construct of power as a key component in the political maintenance of the nation-state came on the heels of my deepening critical consciousness of self and the world. My explorations of personal identity were linked to forays into unexplored terrains of knowledge I increasingly realized I did not possess. This body of knowledge was expansive. It covered a wide swath of fields (e.g., political, historical, sociological, cultural, spiritual), reflecting the null curriculum—or the curriculum that is not taught (Eisner, 1979). Like many other students of color, I underwent a personal transformation during my undergraduate years in college. Wanting to increase my sociocultural knowledge of self and the world around me, I pursued courses affiliated with the African American Studies

Program at my university. The Associate Director of the program shared with me his excitement for Professor Bell's published books. He was particularly keen on his then newly published book, *Faces at the Bottom of the Well*. He also suggested I attend a symposium where Professor Bell was to speak.

I was intrigued by the idea of race that Bell discussed at the symposium, and in the little I gathered from his writings. Yet, I found difficulty in the latter, making connections between his dialogue and race chronicles with his partner and main character, Geneva Crenshaw. I am sure this was related to the lopsided racial knowledge I held as a Black, middle class woman in her early 20s, living in the South during 1990s. It is true: I held considerable experiential knowledge about race. The little substantive sociocultural knowledge I possessed about race and culture focused on the missing histories of African diasporic communities I did not receive in school. With my father I explored works in this area—including Martin Bernal's (1987), *Black Athena*, and George G. M. James's, *Stolen Legacy* during my later high school years. However, the growing consciousness of both my racial, cultural, class, and gender identities, and the limited critical sociopolitical knowledge I had received in my schooling, pointed to gaping holes in my understandings about race.

In college I was introduced to the idea of miseducation (Woodson, 1933/2000). Historian Carter G. Woodson used the term miseducation to refer to the systematic way formal schooling undermines African American knowledge acquisition. This process, Woodson argued, detrimentally impacted Black identity formation, connections to self and others, and the resulting political and economic commitments Black people held to their communities. I was absolutely certain I had experienced miseducation in my own K–12 schooling. In addition to the limited, virtually nonexistent exposure I had to culturally inclusive curriculum, what I learned about race was mired in a paradox. I had learned both a little and a whole lot about race and racism.

Race and racism appeared in my official school curriculum (Apple, 2014). Officially, I learned very little sociocultural content knowledge about race in school. What I learned came as short units of study on the history of the U.S. I learned about the enslavement of African peoples—how they labored on plantations under harsh conditions, were separated from their families, and were often denied the right to literacy (Perry, Steele, & Hilliard, 2003). I do not recall learning much about the fight for racial equality in the U.S. and the Civil Rights movement it ignited. Aside from the two books I read by and about Black people in my upper-level Advanced Placement classes, one of which was Ralph Ellison's *Invisible Man* and the other, William Shakespeare's *Othello*, my school curriculum did not address people of color. When covering these texts in class or when discussing the history of slavery in the U.S, I do not remember having substantive discussions on race or racism and their relationship to my contemporary world or my school or the community where I lived. We did not interrogate the nature of racism, how its formation changes over time and its impact on the social landscape of the U.S. (Holt, 1995; Omi & Winant, 1986/2015). Racism was positioned as the individual actions of racist people from a distant past. The most important lesson I learned about race from my official school curriculum was that structural/institutional racism indeed held a place in the history of the U.S. And it was a place that had passed.

If my formal school curriculum around race taught me little about the nature and relevance of race and racism in the U.S., the hidden curriculum (Apple, 1971) of race was loud and present. Unlike the official school curriculum authorized and sanctioned by education systems, the hidden curriculum is the unintended knowledge that students learn as a result of the organizational arrangements and practices of schools themselves (Apple, 1971). By my senior year my school underwent racial demographic changes in the student body. The vast majority of the teachers remained White. Yet while the school still had a predominantly White student body, an influx of new Black students enrolled. Growing racial anxieties and tensions resulted between students, their families, and staff members. While these always existed, the new Black students had not grown up in our suburban community. They did not take the overt displays of racism as a matter of course. Racial conflict, sometimes physical, ensued between students. It was purported that a Black parent physically attacked a White administrator over concerns of racism. In my classes, some White teachers openly expressed fears about attending sporting events where our school would play other schools that had a predominantly Black student population. The irony was that before this change, when we played teams that had a reputation for being racist and experienced fans that hurled insults and discarded food items at us as we lined up to perform our marching band show at halftime, not one teacher said or did anything on our behalf. As I write this story I am struck by the way we dealt with these conditions. I remember the fury we felt and sometimes expressed, but more so the profound ambivalence that enshrouded our daily interactions in the school space. We knew these conditions were not right but recognized them as business as usual (Sleeter & Grant, 1986/2006). Living in Texas, specifically in the outlying White suburban community we called home, we were aware of overt racism. We knew that some, (but not all) White people in our school and larger community were racist. This knowledge was so deafening that it blunted our expectations for racial parity. Since it was assumed that some local areas were bastions of racism, including a school in our athletic district that had a local White Camelia Knight of the Ku Klux Klan in its city limits, we were angered, but not surprised when racism occurred. The primary way I remember Black students addressing racism was to recognize that we were always on potentially volatile racial ground. And when something racial occurred, we were most likely the ones to get in trouble because our responses were viewed as violent or aggressive. One had to be sure-footed when deciding when and how to address racist incidents.

As a result, Black students in particular became adept at negotiating the racial microaggressions from students, teachers, and staff that were present daily. Racial microaggressions refer to the slights, assumptions, prejudgments that co-terminously accompany people of color as they engage in the social world (Pierce, 1974; Solórzano, 1998; Sue, Capodilupo, Torino, Bucceri, Holder, Nadal, & Esqui-lin, 2007). These microaggressions were present in my honors level and Advanced Placement classes where Black students were in the minority. I listened and tried to argue back against racist comments made by students concerning the presumed cultural and intellectual deficiencies of African diasporic people. And on at least one occasion I was called the N-word in earshot of several other Black students, who said nothing, and my White Spanish teacher, who also ignored the incident. She later threatened to send me to the office when I confronted my racist agitator.

These experiences affirmed that race mattered and racism existed, but that neither was worthy of serious consideration by the adults in the school. In fact, addressing them individually could land a "good" student like me in trouble if I responded with the natural emotions of an angered teenager. Yet because this racism was grounded in the everyday, seemingly idiosyncratic actions of overtly racist individuals—not all White students, teachers, or staff acted in these ways—I developed a micro-level lens for understanding racism. This is akin to what A. L. Brown and K. D. Brown (2010) and K. D. Brown and A. L. Brown (2010) referred to as "bad men doing bad things." I knew that legal racism no longer existed—or what logically amounted to institutional and structural racism. However, I did not have these terms to use, nor did I possess an interpretive framework that would have enabled me to recognize how the individual and the structural were con-nected, how the historical and the contemporary were implicated in these expe-riences. I entered college equipped with a bevy of experiences with racism but a weak interpretive framework to make sense of the relationship between individual and institutional racism both historically and in the present. It is not surprising that I did not hold a fully realized critical race literacy. I was unable to fully appre-ciate or decipher Derrick Bell's theoretical insights around the role and perma-nence of racism in the U.S.

Following my undergraduate education I deferred acceptance to a doctoral program in political science, moved to Long Beach, California, and accepted an elementary teaching position as a Los Angeles Teach for America (TFA) corps member. The then fledgling TFA program positioned itself as a social movement organized to improve the access all students had to a quality educational experi-ence. As a teacher, I immersed myself in making available for my elementary and later middle school students knowledge that was often left out of official curric-ulum. I viewed much of this sociocultural knowledge as relevant to the everyday lives of the students I taught (Ladson-Billings, 1994/2009). I also believed access to this would encourage the development of deeper, more critical thinking abilities in the students, as well as capture their attention by reinvigorating excitement about school and their own learning. During this time I read extensively. I was always seeking out knowledge I found personally intriguing and potentially useful in getting my students invested. In 1997 I stumbled upon and purchased an edited book focused on the key writings in the field of Critical Race Theory. I read through the chapters, feeling more nostalgia than keen insight for the pieces. I was knee-deep in making sense of the world of teaching, curriculum, and lesson plans. Still lacking a complex interpretive lens for examining racism, I was fascinated by the work—the ideas of intersectionality and race analysis and story-telling about race. Yet it was not immediately apparent how to make connections between this theory and the work I was doing in the classroom, even as I held a decidedly critical and socio-politically conscious stance as a teacher. It was clear that the schooling and the teaching process was fully racialized. I entered teaching for decidedly political reasons and was deeply troubled by what I found in the schools where I taught and in U.S. schools in general. Black and Brown students were overrepresented in schools and the targets of reforms designed to improve educational outcomes. I found official school curriculum often uninspiring and disconnected from the lives of the students positioned as most in need of improving their academic achievement. At the time my goal was to learn more about how I might offer school knowledge that was relevant to these students and that aligned with their sociocultural identities as raced, classed, and gendered beings.

In hindsight, it seems self-evident how I might have linked my interests with the study of Critical Race Theory and Derrick Bell's work, specifically. At the time, however, this was not the case. Critical Race Theory, mired in legal and policy concerns, was intriguing but not fully discernible as a vehicle for examining education and curriculum. This was in part connected to my inability to theorize racism as a complex social construct that shifted temporally and spatially, while serving to maintain a foundational set of practices and discourses that upheld Whiteness and advanced anti-Blackness. My failure was rooted in a theoretical dilemma of interpretation: I did not have experience thinking theoretically about race and racism concurrently and across varied levels.

My experiences as a classroom teacher brought me to a new vista. I no longer wanted to study political science but instead wanted to examine how sociocultural markers of identity impact the way teachers thought about and approached their work. Race was one of those markers but I did not yet have a way to think about race playing a primary, foundational role in organizing social relations. In my doctoral studies I was immediately introduced to the idea and function of a theoretical framework as an organizing frame for making sense of phenomena. Engaging with ideas in this way, through the concept of a theoretical framework, initiated a radically new way for me to think about the social world and myself. At the same time I was introduced to a powerful framework for thinking about knowledge. Not knowledge as pieces of discrete, connected bodies of information, but rather knowledge as bodies of information that coalesce to constitute organized rules for looking at and understanding the world. Knowledge not only informed what we presumed to know about self and the world but also framed the possible ways we might maneuver in and respond to that world. In this equation, knowledge and action formed a symbiotic relationship. Thinking about knowledge and what I came to understand as discourse—the rules by which one is able to see and act in the social world (Foucault, 1972) fueled my research interests. I had no doubt that knowledge was a sociocultural construct, imbued with power and implicated by the very factors that comprised the identity markers (e.g., race, class, gender) I initially wanted to examine with teachers in the first place.

Thus, when I was reintroduced to the work of Derrick Bell and Critical Race Theory, I had a much stronger, scaffolded way to enter the conversation of race, racism, and education, specifically. My ability to interpret, in a more complex way, how race and racism operated in U.S. society and schooling was proportional to my understanding of how to utilize a theoretical framework, and, in this case, one theorized around race. My introduction to Critical Race Theory and its application to education included understanding how scholars drew from this work theoretically (Ladson-Billings & Tate, 1995; Solórzano, 1997) and methodologically (Parker & Lynn, 2002). Key constructs in the theory, including Whiteness as property in relation to education concerns (Ladson-Billings & Tate, 1995) and counterstorytelling (Chapman, 2005; Solórzano & Yosso, 2001) were of particular importance in my own learning. Another clear lesson learned was the power of placing race at the center of one's analysis (DeCuir & Dixson, 2004; Dixson, 2006; Dixson & Rousseau, 2006).

What this collective work illuminated, regardless of the CRT construct addressed, was Derrick Bell's primary thesis concerning the nature of race in the U.S. Bell argued that race occupied a permanent, organizing role in the sociopolitical nature of U.S social relations. This stance came as a result of analyzing how the U.S. had historically dealt with race. Bell noted that since the ratification of the Constitution, the U.S. government has compromised the rights of Black people in service to White property. However, racial remedy is advanced only when it stands to benefit dominant White interests. This idea of interest convergence (Bell, 1995; Donnor, 2005) helped to explain both the salience of Whiteness and the perpetuation of anti-Blackness through the sacrificing of Black rights in promotion of White interests. It also spoke to Bell's (1991–1992) doctrine of racial realism that elucidates the guiding rules for how race functions in society. I would argue that one cannot possess critical racial literacy without understanding these foundational ideas.

My reintroduction to Critical Race Theory and Bell's work during my doctoral studies accompanied a more theoretical engagement with the topic of race and racism. While I did not focus my dissertation on this topic, my research examined how sociocultural knowledge organized around discourses of risk and the "at-risk" student. These discourses were raced, classed, and gendered, with specific bodies and actions positioned as more or less risky than others. In the years since conducting this work I have written extensively about the racial aspects that informed the study and my engagement in the field with my participants (Brown, 2011, 2013, 2014, in press). Placing race at the center of my analysis punctuated how race was always present, whether fully acknowledged or realized. It also helped to elucidate the salient role race played in the knowledge constructed about students and achievement.

Given the pervasive place that race holds in social relations, why does so much confusion exist around its role, function, and impact? Why do schools, at all levels, struggle to equip students to understand race and racism in a robust, multidimensional way? These questions served as the impetus for me turning my scholarly and pedagogic attention squarely on the topic of race. As currently configured, what students appear to learn about racism is, at best, the individual, biased actions of people, and at worst, a phenomenon that no longer exists. As an untenured assistant professor I began a co-conducted research study of the then most recently state-adopted social studies textbooks in Texas regarding how they addressed racial violence targeted towards African Americans (A. L. Brown & K. D. Brown, 2010; K. D. Brown & A. L. Brown, 2010). This study highlighted the limitations in official school curricula around the topic of racism. While the textbooks addressed the racial violence, they generally positioned racism as a historical phenomenon, enacted by aberrant or otherwise abnormal people. Racism was not presented as institutional and structural, nor was it discussed as rooted in the democratic project upon which the U.S. was founded. Racism was also not addressed as endemic to Whiteness, a project that not only benefited those who enacted it but all Whites who were the beneficiaries of unearned White privilege. If this is the knowledge students accessed about racism in their official K–12 curriculum, it is not surprising that they come to universities with gaps in their sociocultural knowledge about race.

I noticed gaps in my students' racial knowledge early in my university teaching. I was responsible for teaching a mandatory foundations course for all students prior to beginning the teacher education program. These students comprised one third of the total student population. Another third of the students took the course as an Ethnic Studies elective, and the remaining students took it to meet either a diversity course requirement or elective. This was not my first time teaching such a course. I had experience teaching similar classes during my doctoral studies and in other professional development settings.

My early experiences teaching the course as a junior faculty member of color and without tenure proved challenging. My students generally enjoyed my course, indicating increased learning (even transformed understandings, in some cases) regarding the sociocultural nature of schooling in the U.S. Yet, upon asking a subset of students who took the course and planned on entering the teacher education program questions about what they learned in the courses, I was surprised to find that students cited learning knowledge that I covered in the course, as well as knowledge that I critiqued, questioned and actively worked to dismantle. Students expressed they learned more about the role that race played in schooling (and society). This discovery, however, accompanied strongly held beliefs in the meritocracy narrative that holds that hard work overcomes the barrier to social mobility in the U.S. Students also expressed that certain students, families, and communities—primarily those of color—needed targeted remediation to address their education needs. These discussions generally placed blame and responsibility on individuals, without providing any explanation of the larger racist, classed, and gendered contexts that implicated the conditions in which these people navigated. Additionally, the students expressed superficial understandings of racism that accounted for it as an individual level action only. My students shared that the course made them aware of the sociocultural knowledge teachers need to have in order to work effectively with all students. However, this knowledge was less about transforming how teachers approach their teaching, curriculum, students and the communities from which they come, and more about recognizing the challenges students face that make effective schooling and teaching exceedingly difficult, daresay even impossible.

These findings led me to critically examine my class. I examined my approaches to teaching, curriculum, and the goals I held for student learning. Based on this I made several changes in the structure and organization of the course. I shifted the course from meeting biweekly for one and half hours to meeting weekly for three hours. This allowed me time to draw from a range of pedagogic activities including the use of multimedia in the instructional space. Given I had between 13–15 weeks to teach, I also decided to focus my content on only a few key ideas that I wanted students to walk away understanding. One of these was the role that race, as an individual and structural level factor, played in creating inequitable educational opportunities. To help students see these connections I presented examples from U.S. history that illustrated the accumulated investment and divestment of economic and political capital that accrued from varying groups on the basis of race. Students were asked to grapple with the implications of Whiteness and White privilege over time, including around questions of democracy and equity of opportunity, specifically in schooling. Additionally, students explored the nature and role of historically entrenched discourses of race, such as colorblind ideologies, deficit thinking, anti-Blackness, that impact how students, communities, teaching, and curriculum are constructed and addressed. These discourses, as my students have found, link to material practices that illuminate how everyday realities are integrally connected to larger historical and institutional conditions that privilege and malign in racialized ways. My critical reflections on how I might trouble and help students develop a deeper understanding of race and racism, then, led me back to Critical Race Theory, and, most importantly, to the work of Derrick Bell around cultivating a critical racial literacy.

DERRICK BELL ON ACQUIRING A CRITICAL RACIAL LITERACY

As this chapter has attempted to show there is a clear need and impetus to cultivate a critical racial literacy. This need is indicative of the challenges and gaps that constitute the dominant discourses on race and racism. These discourses position race as a contentious construct and racism as a historically relevant, yet deeply individual, activity, enacted by backward, aberrant people. If students struggle to understand race and racism as sociopolitical constructs that are informed by historical context and operate concurrently at individual and institutional levels, they lack key elements in the acquisition of a critical literacy of race.

A hallmark of the history of social relations in the U.S. is the inconsistent application of basic human rights and legal protections proffered in the nation's founding documents. This history, marred by a jagged, unjust enactment of liberty, challenges any claim to the existence of unfettered human freedom in America. In the U.S., the freedom to live, thrive, and flourish is integrally connected to the sociocultural context that fashions the everyday fervor of life. Race stands at the forefront of this context. There is no denying that one must have a critical racial literacy to both understand and engage issues of race and racism as well as aspire to live in accordance with the nation's highest ideals. Cultivating a critical racial literacy is necessary for all who seek to live humanely and in true community with others. This is not an overstatement, given that the notion of human freedom, as shaped by the contours of U.S. statehood, has proven untenable for peoples of color since the country's founding.

Derrick Bell's incisive critique of race and its integral, permanent place in U.S. society provides clarity to a concept that is both slippery and elusive. Through his careful reading of the history of political and legal intervention in the U.S., Bell illuminated the function and role of race as a tool utilized to divest Blacks of their rights and even humanity, while simultaneously investing Whites with sociopolitical, economic, and symbolic power and privilege. This, Bell argued, is not done unintentionally or from ignorance. Rather, this symbiotic relationship is enacted as part of a larger project of Whiteness and anti-Blackness in the name of sacrificing Black life, livelihood, and liberty for White interests.

In considering the pervasive hegemonic discourse of race and racism as historic and implicated generally in the individual actions of aberrant others, what does Derrick Bell tell us about deciphering and developing a critical understanding of race and racism? In an article adapted from the book, *Faces at the Bottom of the Well*, Bell (1992–1993) theorized the Three Is as a framework to understand the role, function, and lasting significance of race and racism in the U.S. The Three Is refer to Information, Interpretation, and Inspiration.

To establish the necessity for employing the Three Is, Bell (1992–1993) situated his argument in the context of a real-life incident of a teacher who employed a mock slave auction in a first grade classroom in Pennsylvania to teach about the history of slavery in the U.S. The incident was ill-received by Black parents and other education stakeholders. Bell acknowledged that while the teacher had the "right idea" (p. 1037) concerning the need to teach about the history of slavery, the conceptualization and implementation of the lesson, along with the belief of some students and parents that this unsavory history was inappropriate curriculum, illuminated a breach in critical racial literacy.

For Bell (1992–1993) the first I—*information*—addressed a fundamental concern; the absolute need for people to acquire factual knowledge about the country's racial past. Bell recognized the power of knowledge, drawing a distinction between possessing general knowledge of, versus deeper understandings about, the U.S. history's racial past. The former recognizes knowing that an event or condition existed or occurred, while the latter is both aware of, and holds knowledge about, the nature and dynamics of the event and condition. For example, Bell recognized the difference between knowing "of" slavery—the awareness that it existed in the U.S., and understanding "about" slavery—including, the nature of its practice, its relationship to the body politic, and its impact on, and legacy to, the nation-state. The distinction Bell drew between holding "facts about—as opposed to the fact of" (p. 1038) calls attention to the difference in degree and utility he saw in possessing robust versus superficial knowledge. In a society where the expectations for learning about race and racism are limited and marginalized, Bell highlighted two kinds of knowledge implicated by forgotten, neglected, and otherwise marginalized racial sociocultural knowledge: content knowledge about race and racism in the U.S. and self-awareness. Bell recognized the pervasiveness and power of both as they each inform how one reads and acts in the world (Freire, 1970/1993).

First, problems with sociocultural content knowledge have long plagued K–12 schooling (Woodson, 1993/2000), particularly when associated with race and racism. Across the twentieth century, scholars acknowledged how curriculum about groups of color in the U.S. suffered from inaccuracies, invisibility, and marginalization (Banks, 1993; King, 1995; Woodson, 1933/2000). This information reified Whiteness, while concomitantly reinscribing what Sylvia Wynter (2005) termed the "unbearable wrongness of being" perpetually placed on Black life.

Second, Bell recognized the problems connected to a lack of self-awareness that also contributed to gaps in understandings about race and racism in the U.S. While seemingly grounded in individual level responses, Bell viewed self-awareness as integrally connected to larger structural factors that shaped perspectives of self and others. Drawing from the example of knowledge about slavery, Bell argued that both White and Black people suffer from limited racial knowledge that manifests in how these individuals orient themselves to discussions of race and racism in the U.S. In the case of some Whites, Bell (1992–1993) suggested there is a desire to ignore and deny race and racism. This self-delusion is "both easy and comforting" (p. 1038) as it concurrently allows for distancing one's self from the dirty legacy of slavery and the ongoing significance of racism. This self-delusion is fostered and maintained through the perpetuation of dominant social narratives. These stories obscure the role of race and racism, and this is perhaps best observed in the context of meritocracy, perhaps one of the most salient stories told about life and the potential for social mobility in the U.S. Alongside with, and bolstering, this tale is a narrative of racial progress, a story that boasts of an American racial landscape that if at a previous time it did, no longer impedes opportunity. Narratives of meritocracy and racial progress, propelled by one another, support the assertion that success is limited only by the individual characteristics of a person.

Colorblindness, another hegemonic discourse key to the U.S. social narrative, provides a convenient veil to renounce the import of race, making it possible to see, but not place serious attention on or consideration of, the role it plays in a social context (Bonilla-Silva, 2006). The limits in racial knowledge brought about by denial of the significance of race, however, do not only occur to Whites. Bell argued that in the face of the legacy of slavery in the U.S., some Black people feel profound stigmatization that leads to rejections of the ongoing significance of race and any attempt to bear witness to its unsavory past. Bell (1992–1993) noted that the heritage of U.S. slavery, "burdened black people with an indelible mark of difference as [they] struggled to be like whites" (p. 1038). This approach to racial progress, shrouded in assimilation dreams, required refutation and forgetting as the cost for reaping the crumbs of Whiteness.

The gaps in information brought on by lapses in content knowledge of race and in self-knowledge exist along with the challenge of *interpretation*, the next I in Bell's framework for critical racial literacy. In this context, interpretation is concerned with reading and making sense of the role of race in the U.S. and the implications of this history on contemporary events and social relations in the country. While dependent on information, interpretation extends from the idea of possessing knowledge about a topic, to knowing how to construct and explicate meaning about this knowledge base. Interpretation, then, draws from specific knowledge in order to build a framework of understanding that translates what this knowledge conveys about the topic of inquiry. To interpret is to explicate, construct, and explain.

Bell offers the example of interpretation of slavery in American law to illustrate the power and necessity of interpretation in understanding race, historically and in the contemporary context. Bell (1992–1993) contended that Americans often fail to "see little present significance in the fact that the Framers of this country's Constitution saw fit to recognize slavery" (p. 1040). This, despite the fact that "while the Constitution is proclaimed as the model charter of individual freedom … the Constitution as originally written contained no less than ten provisions intended to recognize and protect property in slaves" (p. 1040). Bell continued, making the following provocative claim:

> Just how much reliance can we place in assurances that American slavery is an artifact of history with no contemporary relevance? Unfortunately, history contains any number of post-slavery instances where black rights were sacrificed in order to protect the political or property interests of whites. (p. 1041)

The question Bell poses is not simply rhetorical. He asks the reader to interpret with him factual knowledge from America's past. In so doing, he provokes the reader to apply a critical interpretivist lens to this knowledge that considers the accumulated effect (materially, symbolically) of history. This approach calls for an understanding of how the present is in the past and the past, a progenitor to the contemporary, an accrual of the future.

The paradox that Bell presented around U.S. slavery and in the founding ideas and documents of the country offers a useful example of moving between the interstices of content knowledge and meaning making, or interpretation. What do the facts presented by Bell mean in relation to slavery in the U.S.? How can one make meaning of this history? What are its implications in the present? Bell recognized that to understand racism in the U. S. one needed a way to construct meaning from discrete bodies of past and contemporary knowledge about racism. This meant moving across history and asking questions beyond just "what happened?" to considering what were the factors associated with this event happening? Who was impacted by this event? What was the impact of the event? Is there a pattern of similar events occurring over time? Who is privileged or marginalized by such events? How are this privilege and marginalization realized, enacted? What are the implications of this event and its impact (i.e., privileges and marginalization) to the present? Do such events continue to occur? In what ways are these contemporary events similar to or different from events that have occurred in the past? Asking these and other pertinent questions enables one to dig deeper into wellsprings of knowledge that beg us to make connections, spinning webs of meaning making and significance.

The third I, *inspiration*, moves in a different direction than do the previous two Is. Inspiration is a hopeful gesture in the face of conditions that may, but do not necessarily, make any outcome certain. To engender inspiration is to influence, to provoke in the direction of change. Bell's read of racism in the U.S. historical arc is not one of hopeful optimism. Rather, it is one of sobering realism that recognizes the (im)possibility of transcending the conditions that continue to plague societal relations around race. Bell was fully aware of the challenge he asked of himself and all of us in acknowledging the depth and lasting import of America's racial past while simultaneously working in earnest to bring light and creative engagement to its legacy in the present. Harkening back to the histories of struggle and survival that are the inheritance to African diasporic people living in the U.S., Bell (1992–1993) boldly proclaimed that stepping into such a stance is not novel, nor should it inherently fill one with despair. It required a willingness to engage with the "both" and the "and" when traversing untenable conditions. Drawing from the ideas of his former student, Erin Edmonds, Bell (1992–1993) concluded:

> It is not a matter of choosing between the pragmatic recognition that racism is permanent no matter what we do, or an idealism based on the long-held dream of attaining a society free of racism. Rather, it is a question of *both, and*. *Both* the recognition of the futility of action—where action is more civil rights strategies destined to fail—*and* the unalterable conviction that something must be done, that action must be taken. (p. 1049)

Bell's read of U.S. history shatters any naïve hope held out for the successful execution of a "just right" racial remedy. The problem is not one of political will or faulty policy implementation, nor is the solution how to find and craft better legislation. The trouble rests on the premise that legislation or some other mandate can effectively topple a society fully vested in the maintenance of White power and property interests. Bell recognized the importance of understanding the endemic nature of racism in the U.S., while simultaneously summoning the need to enact a critical praxis of race that calls for decisive action. The inspiration Bell advanced is a hope that fuels persistence in the face of on-going, unending struggle. Redress, as the ultimate end goal, loses significance in place of efforts to excavate, illuminate, and challenge problematic understandings of race in the U.S.

TOWARD A CRITICAL RACIAL LITERACY: PUTTING THIS WORK INTO RESEARCH AND TEACHING PRACTICE

The genius of Bell's work in general, and specifically around critical racial literacy and the three Is, lay in its rigor, clarity, and simplicity. His implacable read of American history—legal, political, and economic—sets a backdrop to his decisive analysis that race will continue to matter in a society that has perpetually relinquished its highest ideals. Applying the three Is to the (auto)ethnographic account of my experiences with the sociocultural knowledge of race, it is apparent that information and interpretation were of particular importance to my story. Content knowledge about race was missing from my official K–12 curriculum, while experiential knowledge played a particularly salient role. This condition, however, helped to ground my own interpretation of racism as an individual level, abnormal social response. Lacking a way to make sense of racism as a complex process that operated at multiple levels, my racial knowledge was limited to the interpretive framework I had access to at any given time. As my interpretive lenses became more robust, my ability to understand and read racism deepened. This knowledge defined not only how I understood race but also how I acted in relation to this knowledge in my everyday life as a student, a researcher, a teacher. My own story illuminates the power that a critical race theoretical framework leveraged for me by deepening my ability to understand, research, and teach about racism.

In presenting my narrative of race, I intended to highlight the usefulness of Derrick Bell's critical racial literacy and his framework of the three Is, both as a theoretical construct and in one's everyday practices. My account illustrated how *information*, *interpretation*, and *inspiration* operated in, and implicated my understandings of, race and racism in the U.S. First, the limited sociocultural content knowledge I held about racism, coupled with my experiences of individual and collective acts of racism, were evident to me as such, but were viewed ultimately as just that—individuals who engaged in racism. What I needed was more knowledge about racism as a symbiotic historical and contemporary artifact in the U.S. Second, in spite of my own relatively strong self-awareness about race and my identity as a Black person who abhorred and sometimes directly challenged (but definitely expected) overt acts of racism when they occurred, I lacked tools to interpret these actions as more than simply individual/collective racism. Racism, to my mind, was reserved for socially backward people, socialized by their equally abnormal families and communities to hold racist beliefs and act in racist ways. Over time, as I acquired more information about race and theoretical clarity around both the permanence of racism and the intersection of micro-and macro-level instantiations of racism as key to U.S. social relations, my understandings transformed. Third, inspiration fueled my eventual exploration of my own information, interpretation, and approaches to teaching about racism.

How, then, might the three Is speak to everyday work in researching and teaching about race and racism? An initial step is understanding that in order to approach an inquiry of race—empirically or instructionally—one needs to possess information about the nature of race and the role racism has, and continues to play, in the U.S. Recognizing the legacy of racism as part and parcel of the American democratic project is both eye-opening and instructive. This history, presented along with examples taken from U.S. history on how race was used to sacrifice the rights of some at the expense of others, can transform curriculum that positions racism as historical and extraordinary. Learning about specific incidents in the history of the U.S. that illustrate the role and nature of racism will help to establish a knowledge base *about*, rather than simply *of*, racism.

Providing students with the opportunity to deepen their self-awareness around the sociocultural knowledge of race is also a needed exercise. One way to engage this directly is to ask students to critically reflect on their content and experiential knowledge of race and racism (Berry, 2009; Milner, 2003). Milner (2003) has argued that preservice teachers need to acquire more complex understandings of race, and this begins with investigating the self. Asking students or researchers to journal or critically reflect on their experiences with race and racism provides an entry point to accessing this knowledge. When this experiential knowledge is recognized as valid forms of knowing, openings are made possible for further reflection and deepening growth (Baszile, 2008). However, rules of racial realism often lead to the marginalization and even penalization of students and researchers of color when sharing their experiences of racism (Bell, 1992).

Equipped with content knowledge and self-awareness, one must explore how to make meaning of this history through deep engagement with theory that helps to organize the functioning of racism in the U.S. context. These discussions should focus on adopting and using theory as a meaning-making tool for information. Applying a set of critical questions like the ones discussed previously when looking at the history and implications of race is a first step. These questions initiate a way of thinking about, and approaching, racism that lends easily to the adoption of a theoretical framework to make connections across and between pertinent information on racism. Such a framework also enables one to consider the kinds of questions that are (im)possible to ask when applying a particular framework. Thus, whether adopting a theoretical framework to use when crafting a research study and collecting and analyzing data or providing instruction around how to utilize a theoretical framework to make sense of racism as an individual and institutional set of practices, interpretation is vital.

Finally, the role of inspiration is the necessary ingredient that fuels the challenging work of excavating the role of racism and/or helping others to acquire a critical racial literacy. This work is not distinct or dichotomous and often occurs concurrently. Speaking to the entrenched nature of racism and the actions of racial redress that have consistently failed to transform the full racial grammar in the U.S. while investing Whites with economic and political privilege is a difficult pill for many to swallow. Whether in the context of teaching or researching about racism, it is vital that the idea of struggle and engagement remains at the heart of the work. The willingness to ask difficult questions and present troubling conclusions if and when these are necessary should not mitigate against the act of speaking truth to race. These counterstories of resistance challenge any assumption that people cannot, do not, or should not see and intervene in racially inequitable conditions. These actions do not always operate in ways acknowledged as critical or transformative (Solórzano & Delgado Bernal, 2001), yet they are indicative of the daily expressions of humanity exerted in the face of oppressive conditions (Kelley, 1993).

As a teacher and researcher whose scholarship has centered on the study of race and racism, this work was, and continues to occur, in the midst of deep struggle. It sometimes manifests in student resistance to the information or lenses of interpretation I provide, and sometimes as emotionally draining and toiling work for me personally as a researcher and teacher (of color). In either instance, I am propelled to action not because I anticipate full transformation of the conditions I address, but rather because I seek to work more authentically as an expression of the very humanity I wish to bear witness to and affirm. I close with these words by Derrick Bell (1992) that sum up the promise of acquiring or helping others to find a critical racial literacy. "It is a story less of success than of survival through an unremitting struggle that leaves no room for giving up. We are all part of that history and it is still unfolding" (p. 200).

REFERENCES

Apple, M. W. (1971). The hidden curriculum and the nature of conflict. *Interchange, 2*(4), 27–40.

Apple, M. W. (2014). *Official knowledge: Democratic education in a conservative age.* London, England: Routledge.

Banks, J. (1993). The canon debate, knowledge construction, and multicultural education. *Educational Researcher,* 4–14.

Baszile, D. T. (2008). Beyond all reason indeed: The pedagogical promise of critical race testimony. *Race Ethnicity and Education, 11*(3), 251–265.

Bell, D. A. (1979). *Brown v. Board of Education* and the interest-convergence dilemma. *Harvard Law Review, 93*(3), 518–533.

Bell, D. (1987). *And we are not saved: The elusive quest for racial justice.* New York, NY: Basic Books.

Bell, D. (1989–1990). Racism: A prophecy for the year 2000. *Rutgers Law Review, 93*, 93–108.

Bell, D. (1991–1992). Racial realism. *Connecticut Law Review, 24*(2), 363–379.

Bell, D. (1992). *Faces at the bottom of the well: The permanence of racism.* New York, NY: Basic Books.

Bell, D. (1992–1993). Learning the three I's of America's slave heritage. *Chicago-Kent Law Review, 68*, 1037–1050.

Bell, D. A. (1995). *Brown v. Board of Education* and the Interest Convergence Dilemma. In K. Crenshaw, N. Gotanda, G. Peller and K. Thomas (Eds), *Critical Race Theory: The key writings that formed the movement.* (pp. 20–29). New York: The New Press.

Bell, D. (1996). *Gospel choirs: Psalms of survival in an alien land called home.* New York, NY: Basic Books.

Bernal, M. (1987). *Black Athena: The Afroasiatic roots of classical civilization.* New Brunswick, NJ: Rutgers University Press.

Berry, T. R. (2009). Women of color in a bilingual/dialectical dilemma: Critical race feminism against a curriculum of oppression in teacher education. *International Journal of Qualitative Studies in Education, 22*(6), 745–753.

Bonilla-Silva, E. (2006). *Racism without racists: Color-blind racism and the persistence of racial inequality in the U.S.* Lanham, MD: Rowman & Littlefield.

Brown, A. L., & Brown, K. D. (2010). Strange fruit indeed: Interrogating contemporary textbook representations of racial violence towards African Americans. *Teachers College Record, 112*(1), 31–67.

Brown, K. D. (2011). Elevating the role of race in ethnographic research: Navigating race relations in the field. *Ethnography and Education, 6*(1), 95–109.

Brown, K. D. (2013). The love that takes a toll: Exploring race and the pedagogy of fear in researching teachers and teaching. *International Journal for Qualitative Studies in Education, 26*(2), 139–157.

Brown, K. D. (2014). When one door opens, another one closes: Experiences and the contradictions of centering race in ethnographic research. In A. D. Dixson (Ed.), *Researching race in education: Policy, practice and ethnography* (pp. 219–232). Charlotte, NC: Information Age.

Brown, K. D. (in press). Race and emotions in the researching of teachers and teaching. In M. Zembylas & P. Schutz (Eds.), *Methodological advances in research on emotion and education.* New York, NY: Springer.

Brown, K. D., & Brown, A. L. (2010). Silenced memories: An examination of the sociocultural knowledge on race and racial violence in official school curriculum. *Equity and Excellence in Education, 43*(2), 139–154.

Chapman, T. K. (2005). Peddling backwards: Reflections of *Plessy* and *Brown* in the Rockford public schools de jure desegregation efforts. *Race Ethnicity and Education, 8*(1), 29–44.

Coates, T. (2015). *Between the world and me.* New York, NY: Spiegel & Grau.

DeCuir, J. T., & Dixson, A. D. (2004). "So when it comes out, they aren't that surprised that it is there": Using Critical Race Theory as a tool of analysis of race and racism in education. *Educational Researcher*, 26–31.

Dixson, A. D. (2006). The fire this time: Jazz, research and critical race theory. In A. D. Dixson & C. Rousseau, *Critical Race Theory in education: All God's children got a song* (pp. 213–230). New York, NY: Routledge.

Dixson, A. D., & Rousseau, C. (2006). *Critical Race Theory in education: All God's children got a song.* New York, NY: Routledge.

Donnor, J. (2005). African-American football student athletes in major college sports. *Race Ethnicity and Education, 8*(1), 45–67.

Eisner, E. W. (1979). *The educational imagination: On the design and evaluation of school programs.* New York, NY: Macmillan.

Foucault, M. (1972). *The archaeology of knowledge & the discourse of language.* New York, NY: Pantheon.

Freire, P. (1993). *Pedagogy of the oppressed* (Rev. ed.). New York, NY: Continuum (Original work published 1970)

Guinier, L. (2004). From racial liberalism to racial literacy: *Brown v. Board of Education* and the interest-divergence dilemma. *The Journal of American History, 91*(1), 92–118.

Holt, T. C. (1995). Marking: Race, race-making, and the writing of history. *The American Historical Review, 100*(1), 1–20.

Hughes, S., Pennington, J. L., & Makris, S. (2012). Translating autoethnography across the AERA standards: Toward understanding autoethnographic scholarship as empirical research. *Educational Researcher, 41*(6), 209–219.

James, G. G. M. (2015). *Stolen legacy: The Egyptian origins of western philosophy.* Eastford, CT: Martino Fine Books.

Kelley, R. D. G. (1993). "We are not what we seem": Rethinking Black working-class opposition in the Jim Crow South. *The Journal of American History, 80*(1), 75–112.

King, J. (1995). Cultured-centered knowledge: Black studies, curriculum transformation, and social action. In J. A. Banks & C. M. Banks (Eds.), *Handbook of research on multicultural education* (pp. 265–290). New York, NY: Macmillan.

Ladson-Billings, G. (2009). *The dreamkeepers* (2nd ed.). San Francisco, CA: Jossey-Bass (Original work published 1994)

Ladson-Billings, G., & Tate, W. (1995). Toward a Critical Race Theory of education. *Teachers College Record, 97*(1), 47–68.

Milner, H. R. (2003). Reflection, racial competence, and critical pedagogy: How do we prepare pre-service teachers to pose tough questions? *Race, Ethnicity and Education, 6*(2), 193–208.

Omi, M., & Winant, H. (2015). *Racial formation in the U.S.* (3rd ed.). New York, NY: Routledge. (Original work published 1986)

Parker, L., & Lynn, M. (2002). What's race got to do with it? Critical Race Theory's conflicts with and connections to qualitative research methodology and epistemology. *Qualitative Inquiry, 8*(1), 7–22.

Perry, T., Steele, C., & Hilliard, A. (2003). *Young, gifted and black: Promoting high achievement among African American students*. Boston, MA: Beacon Press.

Pierce, C. (1974). Psychiatric problems of the Black minority. In S. Arieti (Ed.), *American handbook of psychiatry* (pp. 512–523). New York, NY: Basic Books.

Sleeter, C. E., & Grant, C. A. (2006). *Making choices for multicultural education: Five approaches to race, class and gender* (5th ed.). New York, NY: John Wiley & Sons (Original work published 1986)

Solórzano, D. G. (1997). Images and words that wound: Critical Race Theory, racial stereotyping and teacher education. *Teacher Education Quarterly, 24*, 5–19.

Solórzano, D. G. (1998). Critical Race Theory, race and gender microaggressions, and the experience of Chicana and Chicano scholars. *International Journal of Qualitative Studies in Education, 11*(1), 121–136.

Solórzano, D., & Delgado Bernal, D. (2001). Examining transformational resistance through a Critical Race and Latcrit Theory framework: Chicana and Chicano students in an urban context. *Urban Education, 36*(3), 308–342.

Solórzano, D. G., & Yosso, T. J. (2001). Critical Race and LatCrit Theory and method: Counter-storytelling. *International Journal of Qualitative Studies in Education, 14*, 471–495.

Sue, D. W., Capodilupo, C. M., Torino, G. C., Bucceri, J. M., Holder, A., Nadal, K. L., & Esquilin, M. (2007). Racial microaggressions in everyday life: implications for clinical practice. American psychologist, 62(4), 271–286.

Woodson, C. G. (2000). *The mis-education of the Negro*. Chicago: African American Images (Original work published 1933)

Wynter, S. (2005). On how we mistook the map for the territory, and re-imprisoned ourselves in our unbearable wrongness of being, of Désêtre. In L. Gordon & J. A. Gordon (Eds.), *Not only the master's tools: African American studies in theory and practice* (pp. 107–169). Boulder, CO: Paradigm.

CHAPTER TEN

Derrick Bell ON Race AND Memory

From Abolition to Obama

ANTHONY L. BROWN

INTRODUCTION

Delgado and Stefancic (2001) argued that *revisionist history* is a signature theme of critical race theory (CRT). They defined *revisionist history* as a reexamination of America's historical record by "replacing comforting majoritarian interpretations of events with ones that square more accurately with minorities' experiences" (p. 20). This approach to history is a cornerstone to the CRT framework, first locating a moment in history that tells a particular dominant racial narrative that has sustained over time and then deconstructing the presumptions society holds about this history. These racial narratives typically are "watershed moments," marking a new and more equitable racial reality.

By *race narrative*, I am referring to stories that enclose and delimit how a racial history is understood over time. Such narratives hold in place dominant stories that become unquestioned and define current conceptions of race and racism in the present. These narratives depict certain political and social actors such as presidents, judges, and politicians as exercising a particular kind of agency needed to promote racial equality that allowed America to live up to its highest ideals of democracy and egalitarianism. The power of racial narratives is that they can affect how we make sense of the present. Our interpretations of the past help to define how and why actors took action, as well as describe the intentions of the characters in the storyline. In this case, history transforms into folklore, where the overarching stories we tell about a moment in time become normalized by the telling of the story. We learn these racial narratives in K–12 settings, museums, children's literature, libraries, and speeches. Critical historian Michel-Rolph Trouillot (1995) called this "the production of history."

An example of racial narratives of this kind is the dominant master narrative of Rosa Parks and the Montgomery Bus Boycott. Most of us have been told that Mrs. Parks was a "tired seamstress" who, on December 1, 1955, decided that she would no longer sit at the back of the bus. For most of my life, this how I heard the story. After a while, the story was no longer about the details that led up to the bus boycott and what her actions meant in relation to the Movement. She was reduced to being a "tired seamstress" who was brave and of course iconic to the Movement. What I later learned about Rosa Parks was that what she did on this day in Montgomery was part of a long-term and strategic civil rights effort. I never knew this information, nor that she attended the Highlander Folk Schools and was the secretary for the local chapter of the NAACP. The narrow rendering of Rosa Parks became a majoritarian racial narrative.

This kind of reinterpretation of the past is certainly a hallmark of the intellectual corpus of legal scholar Derrick Bell. His work has turned upside down our thoughts about America's past racial histories, challenging the intentions and implications of histories that for long were heralded as triumphant moments in America's racial history. In this chapter, I will accomplish three goals. The first is to outline the key theoretical tenets that undergird Derrick Bell's work. From here, I show how Bell's historical revisionism is part of a long tradition in Black intellectual thought committed to revising the histories of African Americans. Then my attention focuses on what I am calling Derrick Bell's *genealogy of Americans' racial history*. In this section of the chapter, I draw on Bell's analysis of three historical moments. First, I discuss the abolition of slavery in the North. Second, I examine the drafting of the Emancipation Proclamation. Third, I explore Bell's well-known historical critique—*Brown v. Board of Education*. Finally, I discuss the 2008 presidential election of Barack Obama. In the final section of this chapter I argue that beyond Bell's critique of the triumphant racial histories of the U.S., his racial chronicles create a speculative context that helps to reconceptualize key moments in American history. I conclude this chapter summarizing the main tenets of Bell's historical revisionism and its implications to the teaching of history in K–12 settings.

DERRICK BELL'S THEORETICAL TENETS OF HISTORICAL REVISION

Derrick Bell's notion of historical revision draws from three theoretical premises about race and power. The first is that racial inequality for African Americans in the U.S. has always advanced the interests of White elites. In his groundbreaking analysis of the landmark case *Brown v. Board of Education*, Bell (1980) referred to this as *interest convergence*. He also called this his three rules of race relations. The First Law of Race Relations is: "Racial remedies are the outward manifestations of unspoken and perhaps unconscious conclusions that such remedies—if adopted—will secure, advance, or at least not harm societal interests deemed important by whites in power" (Bell, 1992, p. 263). Bell's body of work looks to history to show that the intentions to mobilize racial change from bondage to freedom, to voting rights and civil rights, was never a matter of America living up its highest ideals of democracy. He has shown that the remediation advanced to Blacks through the Emancipation Proclamation, the Reconstruction Amendments, and Civil Rights actually secured and advanced the economic, social, and political interests of Whites.

His Second Law of Race Relations is that:

> The benefits to blacks of civil rights policies are mainly symbolic rather than substantive, and when the crisis that prompted their enactment ends, they will not be enforced for blacks, though, in altered interpretations, they may serve the policy needs of whites. (Bell, 1992, p. 265)

The Third Law of Race Relations is that: "Injustice that so dramatically diminishes the rights of blacks because of race also drastically diminishes the rights of many whites, particularly those who lack money and power or are part of an unpopular minority group or movement" (Bell, 1992a, p. 268).

These three laws of race relations are consistent throughout Bell's analysis of American racial history. From a historical standpoint, these laws of race relations are important to the production of African American history. If much of what we define as Black History (e.g., The Declaration of the Emancipation Proclamation, Passage of *Brown v. Board*, and the efforts of Civil Rights) is merely symbolic in the way Bell argued through his laws of race relations, then the context and meaning of Black History must be reconceptualized as a historical arc enveloped by both powerful White interests and Black political agency. This seemingly pessimistic take on the histories heralded as landmark racial narratives calls for a new conceptual lens to America's racial past. Before I explore the different ways Bell has employed his theories to key moments in American history, it is important to situate Bell's work in a long history of African American scholars concerned with revising the history of African Americans.

BLACK REVISIONIST HISTORIES IN THE BLACK INTELLECTUAL TRADITION

The notion of historical revision is certainly not a new idea within African American thought. In fact, some may argue that the entire arc of African American history is revisionist in nature, responding to a normative construct of Blackness (Gates, 1988). At a fundamental level, Black historical revisionism was a philosophical project. The continuity across time has been to revise and repudiate the myths told about Black people, Africa, Africans, and the African Diaspora—what philosopher Charles Mills (1998) called revisionist ontology. Consistent across time, historical revision in Black intellectual thought has been concerned with the ontological meanings of Blackness and how the production of history and myth contribute to a form of race-making (Grant, Brown, & Brown, 2015; King, 2014). Historically, the traditions of Black intellectual thought grappled with the issue of historical revisionism in at least three ways.

The first is to address the issue of absence and silence within the American historical record. Essentially, arguing that African Americans have played a central and pivotal role in American nation-building. Some of the earliest textbooks written in the late nineteenth century sought to recognize the contributions of African Americans in Civil War memory (Ernest, 2004; Wilson, 1890/1994). This approach to Black revision has remained to this day with scholars noting the forgotten legacies of American history (Brown, 2010; Brown & Brown, 2010). Joseph T. Wilson's (1890/1994) book *The Black Phalanx* best illustrated this approach to historical revisionism. His 582-page volume detailed the Black soldiers' honors in battle from the Battle of 1775 through the Civil War. The narratives highlighted in this text placed Black men in the trenches of some of the most important battles in American history. His dedication in the book to these Black soldiers provides some indication of his impetus to write this book:

> SOLDIERS: As a mark of esteem and respect for your patriotic devotion to the cause of human freedom, I desire to dedicate to you this record of the services of the negro soldiers, whom you led so often and successfully in the struggle for liberty and union during the great war of 1861–'65.

> Your coming from the highest ranks of social life, undeterred by the prevailing spirit of caste prejudice, to take commands in the largest negro army ever enrolled beneath the flag of any civilized country, was in itself a brave act. The organization and disciplining of over two hundred thousand men, of a race that for more than two centuries had patiently borne the burdens of an unrequited bondage, for the maintenance of laws which had guaranteed to them neither rights nor protection, was indeed a magnificent undertaking. (Wilson, 1994 [1890], dedication page)

This approach to revising the forgotten histories has been a staple of the Black freedom movement—from Carter G. Woodson to the work of African American historians and curriculum scholars up to the present (Grant, Brown, & Brown, 2015).

The second approach is to revise the prominent interpretations of the historical record of African Americans. For example, for decades, White historians argued that African Americans were "happy slaves" on the plantation (Banks,

1969; Reddick, 1934). There was little-to-no record of slave insurrection and resistance until the work of Carter G. Woodson and Charles Wesley (1928) in their textbooks and Herbert Aptheker's (1943/1969) groundbreaking history of slave revolts. The revisionist slave historians (Blassingame, 1979; Gutman, 1975; Stuckey, 2013) have documented African Americans' persistence to be free, their unyielding desire to hold their families together, and the unique cultural ways Black life was expressed beyond bondage. These scholars attempted to reconceptualize a historical time and place in African Americans' history. Scholars of curriculum have similarly drawn from this notion of historical revisionism to rethink the portrayal of moments in history and historical figures (Alridge, 2006; Brown & Brown, 2010; King, 1992).

The third approach to African American historical revision is to show that history has a reproductive capacity that tied to the material and discursive realties of African Americans in the present. In other words, there is a *critical* dimension to historical revision concerned with productive capacities of historical knowledge in mobilizing policies and practices in the present. This is quintessentially Derrick Bell. While the other two approaches are certainly part of Bell's project, this critical dimension to history comes closest to his form of historical revisionism. To put it simply, how one makes sense of the past racial histories and policies in the U.S. informs how they conceptualize their present racial realities. So Bell is not just about revising the historical record, he undertakes a reanalysis of the past legal histories that requires a complete rethinking of our current racial realities. His work examines racial remedies from slavery through the Civil Rights movement, exploring the intentions and politics that informed racial remedies, as well as whether such reforms had a lasting impact on racial inequality in the U.S. over time. In the sections that follow, I show how Bell illustrated this kind of interpretation of America's past racial histories.

RACIAL REVISIONIST AMERICAN HISTORY — BELL'S HISTORICAL PESSIMISM

White Interests and Black Freedom: Abolition and Slavery

One of the common narratives of American's racial progress is the abolition of slavery in the North. Much of the narrative even to this day portrays slavery as evil and institutionalized by White southerners who insisted that the bondage of millions of Blacks was a State right and a matter of Manifest Destiny. For example, I never learned in schools that states such as New York, Rhode Island, and Connecticut had a significant number of enslaved Africans before the Civil War. The prevailing meta-narrative portrays America's slave history in regional terms with the North symbolic with freedom. Even those "good" Whites such as Harriet Beecher Stowe and William Lloyd Garrison were from the North and typically portrayed as tireless fighters against slavery in the U.S. Again, the duality of good and bad, free and enslaved was essentially defined by the demarcation of the Mason-Dixon line. However, never did I learn in schools how and why African Americans were free in the North. In the end, the North had the right moral fortitude to abolish slavery.

My presumption was simple, Whites in the North had the right belief system and White folks in the South were morally corrupt. This narrative is still quite common in schools to this day. However, in his essay "Racial Remediation: An Historical Perspective on Current Conditions," Bell (1976) provided a different account for the abolition of slavery in the North. Drawing from the work of slave historians, Bell found that

> the major motivation for abolition of slavery in the North was the economic advantages emancipation promised white businessmen who could not efficiently use slaves, and laborers who did not wish to compete with slaves for jobs. In addition, abolition both lessened the ever-present fear of slave revolts, and the concern that blacks, slave or free, would reside in the "free" states in large numbers. (p. 7)

In the end, the abolition of slavery in the North was hardly freedom. In Bell's words,

> The exclusion of emancipated blacks from the political process in all the Northern states and their consignment to menial jobs and an inferior social status reflect the distinction most whites drew between abolition of slavery and acceptance of the former slaves. (p. 7)

Bell even further maintained that our analysis of "free" Blacks in the North must be examined within the racial barriers that defined their lives. To simply understand history through the binary of the North as symbolic of freedom and the South being symbolic with enslavement is patently false. Bell (1992c) here explained what Northern abolition meant in terms of the experiences of African Americans:

> Those blacks living in the pre-Civil War North, though deemed "free," had to live with the ever-present knowledge that the underground railroad ran both ways. While abolitionists provided an illegal network to aid blacks who escaped slavery, Southern "slave catchers" likely had an equally extensive system that enabled them to kidnap free blacks from their homes or the streets, and spirit them off to the South and a life in bondage. In *Prigg v. Pennsylvania*, the Supreme Court asserted that masters or their agents had a constitutional right of "self-help" to seize fugitive slaves and return them to the South as long as they could accomplish their mission without a "breach of peace." (p. 1046)

Bell made clear that whatever romantic or false historical knowledge we had about "freedom" in the North must be reexamined in the context of White interests and the failure to preserve the basic freedoms of Black life in the North.

White Interests and Black "Freedom": Emancipation Proclamation

Remaining consistent with his thesis of racial remediation, Bell's analysis of the Emancipation Proclamation also asks that we rethink our preconceived ideas about the historical interpretation of Black freedom. As historians explain, the story of Lincoln as the "Great Emancipator" has become part of the dominant collective memory of U.S. chattel slavery (Schwartz & Schuman, 2005). In summary, the Confederacy fought hard and long to preserve U.S. slavery, and Lincoln, through his issuance of the Emancipation Proclamation and personal will to end slavery, helped to set in place its eventual abolition. Derrick Bell, on the contrary, explained that White interests mostly undergirded this grand and triumphant narrative of Black freedom. The first interest was to preserve the Union. As Bell (1976) explained:

> President Lincoln was no friend of slavery, but his primary objective was to save the Union. To preserve the Union he wrote Horace Greeley in August 1862, he would end slavery, see it maintained, or end part and keep part. When signed into effect on January 1, 1863, the Emancipation Proclamation reflected Lincoln's statement to Greeley. By its terms, the order, justified as a necessary war measure to suppress the rebellion, covered only those areas still under the control of the Confederacy. (p. 8)

Bell powerfully locates this history within his theories of race and power. Here, Bell is not simply rearticulating a problematic record of history. He is locating this history within the problem of racial remediation, where Whites' interests are the impetus for racial reform. The second prominent interest tied to the Emancipation Proclamation, according to Bell, was the need for Black troops to fight with the Union. In this context, the interest to increase manpower led to the mobilization of Black inclusion. Bell, however, claimed that what occurred in the Civil War was a pattern in past U.S. wars. He stated,

> Parenthetically, in every war from the War for Independence to World War II, blacks had to petition for permission to fight for this country. In each instance, an affirmative response came only when it became apparent that filling the ranks was more important than maintaining the color line. (p. 9)

The issuance of the Emancipation Proclamation stands as one of the most heralded moments in American history, where benevolent Northern Whites challenged the prevailing ideologies of race and racism. Bell, however, shows again that White economic and political interests were a fundamental incentive for the writing of the Emancipation Proclamation, not the core ideas of the document: Black freedom.

THE POST-CIVIL-WAR AMENDMENTS: RETHINKING RADICAL RECONSTRUCTION

Bell also set his sights on Radical Reconstruction, a moment also viewed as the legal precedent to abolish slavery and extend citizenship rights to African American men. What Bell first shows is that after the fervor of the Emancipation Proclamation and the end of the Civil War, White elites began to express their ambivalence about African Americans now potentially in their "midst." To make the point he showed that a lingering discourse of pragmatism and necessity was the impetus for the passing of the fourteenth amendment. In his essay "Reconstruction's Racial Realities" Bell (1992a) drew on the words of Senator Jacob Howard, a Radical Republican, who was the key architect for the Fourteenth Amendment. The following quote from Senator Howard illustrates the tenor of the discourse during this time.

> For weal or for woe, the destiny of the colored race in this country is wrapped up with our own; they are to remain in our midst, and here spend their years and here bury their fathers and finally repose themselves. We may regret it. It may not be entirely compatible with our taste that they should live in our midst. We cannot help it. Our forefathers introduced them, and their destiny is to continue among us; and the practical question which now presents itself to us is as to the best mode of getting along with them. (p. 262)

Bell explained that the ambivalence expressed in Howard's words reflects the kind of thinking about racial remediation that would remain throughout the twentieth century, particularly pertaining to civil rights. Without understanding the kind of interests that were at stake during this time one might conclude that Radical Reconstruction was solely about extending freedom and civil rights to African Americans. But as Bell explained, Radical Reconstruction created the conditions for Republicans to control Congress, "by threatening to reduce the representation of states who denied the right to vote to males over the age of twenty-one" (p. 263).

Bell (1992a) explained that the Fourteenth Amendment is emblematic of what he called his *First Rule of Race Relations*, which, in essence, means that racial remedies are the "outward manifestations" of "unspoken conclusions" (p. 263) and that such remedies will advance, or not harm, the interests of Whites. Bell explained that because the Fourteenth Amendment offered federal protection against state interference with basic rights to *all* persons, corporate lawyers realized that such protections could also block state efforts to protect workers from abusive policies for industrial growth. As a result, the Fourteenth Amendment protections were used to nurture the interests of capitalists and not the interests of Blacks' basic civic rights.

For the next half of the twentieth century, Bell's (1992a) thesis would remain consistent. In particular, his Second Law of Race Relations, which maintains that Blacks' "civil rights policies are mainly symbolic rather than substantive" (p. 265), and when the specific crisis or set of interests wane the enforcement of such policies will no longer be a priority.

BROWN V. BOARD OF EDUCATION: INTEREST-CONVERGENCE AND HISTORY

The master narrative of *Brown v. Board of Education* is recognized as a triumphant racial icon. My own historical understanding of the landmark case illustrates the classic imagery of *Brown*. For instance, my earliest understanding of race and racism came through two prominent narratives—the narrative of White oppression and the narrative of African American resistance. Within these racial narratives, *Brown* was a watershed moment that ended Jim Crow racial segregation and catalyzed the Civil Rights Movement. I interpreted *Brown* and the subsequent marches, acts, and racial reforms from the 1950s to the 1970s as directly tied to my racial reality. I lived in a social world where I could drink from drinking fountains, attend integrated schools, and live in integrated communities.

The historical narrative of the Civil Rights Movement presented a world in striking contrast to my own. From my historical understanding, *Brown* was a vital legal catalyst to the Civil Rights Act of 1964 and the Voting Rights Act of 1965. I was in essence an heir to what the social engineers of *Brown* "fulfilled." I learned this history in K–12 history textbooks, museums, documentaries, and almost all facets of my learning about the Civil Rights Movement. I held close to this narrative even though I was well aware of the pervasive effects of racial inequality. Not for a moment, however, did I believe that the very foundation of the modern Civil Rights Movement occurred because of the interests of White elites. In my mind, *Brown* was the doing of courageous Black activists and the actions of some White agents who sought to change the world. Years later, mostly through the work of Derrick Bell, I realized that my current understanding was largely a majoritarian racial narrative. Whereas, according to Bell, *Brown* was a perfect moment when Black interests to challenge the legal precedent of *Plessy v. Ferguson* converged with the interests of White elites to shape the image of America.

Hess (2005) explained that *Brown* as the racial narrative of *iconic triumph* has remained as the common narrative told in U.S. society. Here Hess states about the Smithsonian Museum rendering of *Brown*,

> While rightfully extolling the hard-won victory of *Brown* in the context of the 1950s, the Smithsonian exhibit ignores the persistence of racial inequality in the United States evidenced by the achievement gap, the income gap, the access to health care gap, and so on. In addition, the exhibit glosses over the fact that the vast majority of schools are still segregated. In the exhibit there is no simmering crisis with respect to race and schooling, no ongoing lack of educational opportunity, no divisiveness over educational outcomes and their origins. An instantiation of the "official knowledge," the museum instead presents *Brown* as an icon of American democracy, a case to be remembered with reverence and extolled as achievement. (p. 2047)

The iconic imagery of *Brown* has remained the prominent narrative in school text-books and the entire production of knowledge around this history. Legal historian Mary Dudziak (2004) explained that even in legal history, *Brown* is a linear tale of legal struggle.

> The struggle is [won] by lawyers to change an unjust legal regime. Its denouement is the Court's simple opinion in *Brown*. The treatment is consistent with a consensus narrative in American lawbooks: *Brown* is a straightforward story of the triumph of a progressive Court and progressive Constitution, after a hard-fought battle of lawyers and litigants. (p. 33)

However, before Hess and Dudziak, it was Derrick Bell's thesis of racial remedi-ation that again provided one of the most persuasive examinations of *Brown*. As numerous scholars explain, it was Bell's challenge to the prevailing majoritarian narrative that would help to further develop his racial theory, what he called the *interests convergence dilemma* (Delgado & Stefancic, 2001; Guinier, 2004).

For Bell, *Brown* is another legal triumphant racial narrative, similar to previ-ous ones, where White benevolence is central to the storyline of racial remediation in the U.S. Bell examined these presumptions on two grounds. The first was that the protections offered by the Fourteenth Amendment were not determined by the racial harm to African Americans (Bell, 1980). In Bell's words:

> I contend that the decision in *Brown* to break with the Court's long-held position on these issues cannot be understood without some consideration of the decision's value to whites, not simply those concerned about the immortality of racial inequality, but also those whites in policy-making positions able to see the economic and political advances at home and abroad that would follow abandonment of segregation. (p. 524)

In the context of *Brown*, the political advances were both international and domes-tic. The international interests of *Brown* were tied to the global politics of the Cold War. At the time, the U.S. struggle with Communist countries gave the impression to the world that the U.S. was a true democracy. The blemish of the Jim Crow South suggested that the U.S. was a hypocritical nation. For Bell, *Brown* was the perfect racial policy to rectify the U.S.'s image problem.

Dudziak's (1988) study of *Brown* showed that Bell's assertions about the Cold War imperative and Civil Rights were dead on. Dudziak (2004) stated,

> *Brown* was also a major international story. The decision was on the front page in the daily newspapers in India. Under the headline "A Great Decision," the *Hindustan Times* of New Dehli suggested that "American democracy stands to gain in strength and prestige from the unanimous ruling. ... The practice of racial segregation in schools ... has been a long-standing blot on American life and civilization." (p. 35)

Bell also argued that *Brown* emerged out of the political advances of White elites to quell the growing domestic tensions of the Civil Rights Movement. At the time, close to a million African American men had fought in World War II, and the U.S. government needed a radical racial policy to reassure "American blacks that the precepts of equality and freedom so heralded during World War II might yet be given meaning at home" (Bell, 1980, p. 524). In addition, in the context of domestic concerns, some Whites understood the potential profit in desegregating the South. Some Whites wanted to advance new racial policies that would enable the South to transition from being a rural plantation society to becoming a more advanced industrialized region.

Bell's analysis helped to deconstruct the shallow sentimentalism attached to this iconic racial narrative—showing that *Brown* was more of a sophisticated prop to stabilize the imagery of American exceptionalism, rather than a victorious moment when Americans did the right thing. For Bell, *Brown* was not motivated by an invigorated new legal moral compass that called for a new direction in American racial society, it was mobilized by White elite interests. Therefore, when *Brown* had served its propagandistic purposes of a global and domestic imagery, maintaining civil rights for Blacks no longer became a priority soon after the passing of *Brown*. For Bell, this was most reflected by the efforts of schools for the next twenty-five years to desegregate. To illustrate this point, Bell argued that in cases such as *Milliken v. Bradley* and *Dayton Board of Education v. Brinkman (Dayton I)*, the Court elevated the concept of local autonomy that enabled schools to employ local control relating to this issue of desegregation. Bell (1980) stated, "Local control however, may result in the maintenance of a status quo that will preserve superior educational opportunities and facilities for whites at the expense of blacks" (pp. 526–527).

Again, Bell's method of historical revisionism powerfully shows that the same attention to the past reveals not a triumphant narrative of America overcoming its racial past but a history mired in interests—serving more as a symbol rather a true moment where racial inequality was redressed.

Bell's interest convergence thesis has had quite the impact on scholars seeking to understand the complexity of racial inequality (Dudziak, 2004; Guinier, 2004). In education, scholars have drawn from the notion of interest-convergence to show that any efforts to change the conditions for historically underserved populations are implicitly tied to the interest of Whites (Bolgatz & Crowley, in press; Donner, 2005; Gillborn, 2010). Even in the field of history education, some scholars have begun to look at the extent to which a convergence of interests informed the passing of Civil Rights policies over time (Brown & Urietta, 2010; Crowley, 2013). Crowley (2013) found in his textual analysis of Lyndon B. Johnson's presidential documents that the *Voting Rights Act* (VRA) helped to advance four levels of interests. The first was to bolster the Democratic Party's electorate. Crowley stated,

The 1964 Civil Rights Act passed against intense opposition from southern senators and signified a shift in the Democratic Party electorate that persists today. While scanning the newspaper headlines about the landmark legislation the day after its passage, Johnson remarked to aide Bill Moyers, "I think we delivered the South to the Republican Party for your lifetime and mine" (In Califano, 1991, 55). The 1964 presidential election, although a landslide victory for Johnson, offered signs that Johnson's prediction might come true.

As Democratic support for civil rights legislation pushed away many southern White voters and southern Democrats such as Strom Thurmond switched to the Republican Party, the Democrats needed to secure votes elsewhere. The VRA, championed by President Johnson shortly after events in Selma forced his hand, created millions of loyal Democratic voters through federal protection for the voting rights of African Americans. Once again, advances for the Black population only occurred when White elites were to benefit as well. Similar to Derrick Bell, Crowley also found that the Cold War imperative had an impact on the drafting of the VRA. Throughout the phone transcripts with Dr. Martin Luther King, Jr., Johnson repeatedly expressed the need to have a policy such as the VRA that could better inform the international image of America within a Cold War context.

The usage of Bell's thesis within Crowley's analysis powerfully shows the utility of employing a theoretical notion of historical revisionism. Bell's race theorizing shows that at the heart of revisionist history is not just the limited ways a historical narrative is told but how racial narratives such as *Brown* are imbued with contexts. In the section that follows, I show how Bell examined the ascension of Barack Obama to become the president of the United States.

OBAMA: ON ELECTIONS AND FREEDOM

The 2008 election of Barack Obama certainly served as the single most significant symbol of racial change in American history. Immediately after the election, journalists and media pundits asked whether this historic change marked a new racial landscape, what some were referring to as a "post-racial moment" (Smith & Brown, 2014). Bell found that even in the case of the 2008 presidential election, a convergence of interests made this history possible. The bulk of historical revisionist work tends to look back in time to rethink historical facts; however, for Bell, rethinking of the past helps to reveal racial realism over time in the present. Bell (2009) argued that similar to past racial histories, crisis and interest propelled the election of Barack Obama. To put it simply, Bell maintained that Barack Obama's ascension came at a time of inept leadership and in the midst of an unprecedented economic crisis.

In his words, "An important component of his victory, though, is that the country is domestically and in foreign affairs in the worst shape it has ever been" (Bell, 2009, p. 5). However, Bell (2009) conceded that comparison between the 2008 presidential election and previous racial remedies is not quite the same in that in this context it was not a small elite group of White males extending their own interests, it was "sixty-five million voters who believed that their interests converged with the dramatic promises Obama made" (p. 2). In the end, Bell's thesis calls that we remember the first Black president not as a moment when America's racial conscience allowed it to set aside its racial hang-ups and vote for a Black man, but more a matter of crisis and contingency that made this history possible.

BELL'S HISTORICAL FICTION AND THE METHOD OF RACIAL CHRONICLES

Through Bell's speculative fiction the past, present, and future places are the historical locations to express his thesis of racial realism. His racial chronicles highlight fictional characters such Geneva Crenshaw and Professor Golightly, each representing the spectrum of ideological tensions within African American thought. The method of storytelling enables Bell to use the genre of fictional writing to help the reader explore different aspects of America's racial history, with specific attention to civil rights. In his best-selling book, *And We Are Not Saved*, Bell (1987) takes his readers back in time to examine racial contradictions within mainstream consensus histories. For example, in the chapter "The Real Status of Blacks Today," Geneva Crenshaw goes back in time to speak before the Constitutional Convention of 1787. This section of text highlights Bell's method of revising the past:

> "Gentlemen," I said, "my name is Geneva Crenshaw, and I appear here to you as a representative of the late twentieth century to test whether the decisions you are making today might be altered if you were to know their future disastrous effect on the nation's people, both white and black." (p. 26)

Bell created a historical context to foreshadow America's racial future. In this context, Geneva Crenshaw is located within three temporal spaces: the past, the present, and the future. The past being 1787, the present being the late 20th century, and the future being two centuries after the Constitutional Convention. All through the chapter, she debates the "founding fathers" and even challenges America's first president. In this exchange with George Washington, Geneva Crenshaw is able to go back to the past and address the real contradictions of the Constitutional Convention. Here, with cogent argumentation and verbal dexterity, Geneva Crenshaw is able to bring to the fore the latent issues of race:

> "Thank you, General Washington," I responded. "I know that you, though a slave owner, are opposed to slavery. And yet you have said little during these meetings—to prevent, one may assume, your great prestige from unduly influencing debate. Future historians will say

of your silence that you recognize that for you to throw the weight of your opinion against slavery might so hearten the opponents of the system, while discouraging its proponents, as to destroy all hope of compromise. This would prevent the formation of the Union, and the Union, for you, is essential."

"I will not respond to these presumptions," said General Washington, "but I will tell you now what I will say to others at a later time. There are in the new form some things, I will readily acknowledge, that never did, and I am persuaded never will, obtain my cordial approbation; but I did then conceive, and do now most firmly believe, that in the aggregate it is the best constitution, that can be obtained at this epoch, and that this, or dissolution, awaits our choice, and is the only alternative."

"Do you recognize," I asked, "that in order to gain unity among yourselves, your slavery compromises sacrifice freedom for the Africans who live amongst you and work for you? Such sacrifices of the rights of one group of human beings will, unless arrested here, become a difficult-to-break pattern in the nation's politics." (p. 32)

The temporal and spatial contexts of these interactions between Geneva Crenshaw and George Washington helped to create a speculative setting, where the reader is taken to a new space to reconceptualize the problems with historical events. What makes this unique is that the issues Geneva Crenshaw raises are ideologically in line with much of the discourse among African Americans during that time that called into question the troubling contradictions of American democracy. This is quintessentially revisionist and counter narrative in nature because now history is called into question by creating a fictional context that enabled voices to be present that were actually absent during these early deliberations of the founding of this nation.

Bell's racial chronicles are able to produce a theater of race to re-imagine unresolved historical questions and tensions that existed during this time. By reconstituting the plot, characters, and storyline of history, Bell invites the reader to explore the pertinent racial issues related to race in this country. This kind of revisionist history is methodologically powerful because he relocates the voices that challenged the contradictions of this period.

CONCLUSION: BELL AND RE-THINKING OF BLACK HISTORY

For 40 years, Derrick Bell has asked us as a society to look back and rethink our presumptions about race and history. Bell challenged whatever naïve or simplistic perspectives we have had about the past regarding race relations in the U.S. His work, together, offers a genealogy of racial remediation. In almost every key moment in American history, White interests mediated African Americans' freedoms. As he consistently reminds us, there were real good people that fought, struggled, and died for the great cause of social justice, but despite these efforts our analysis must go deeper and ask contextual questions about what made these histories possible. In essence, he is asking us as consumers of history to not be overly romantic about what happened in the past.

As Bell's works marches us through American racial history in the "land of the brave and home and the free" one sees a rather consistent thesis—race is permanent and real. In this sense, Bell's revisionist history provides a racial lens or conscience—what he called *racial realism*. For Bell, *racial realism* is an ideological perspective that is fully aware of the limitations of civil rights litigation that "could do little more than bring about the cessation of one form of discriminatory conduct that soon appeared in a subtle though no less discriminatory form" (Bell, 1992b, p. 373).

However, I propose that in order for Bell to help us understand race in this manner, he has consistently turned to America's racial past. Bell has always been careful to focus on triumphant historical narratives that highlight America's effort toward a new racial history. Our collective memory of emancipated Africans, the passing of *Brown* and the twentieth century civil rights policies helped to construct a meta-narrative that race has overcome different epochs of racial division. As this pertains to K–12 schooling and the teaching of Black history, we must re-examine the historical moments that provide a conception of Black equality and freedom. Bell's framework offers a cogent analysis of multicultural and Black history discourse that often relies on the historical moments Bell examined. In keeping with Bell's thesis of racial realism, the dominant narratives of American history that produces a veil of ignorance that helps to engender the gradual disappearance of race. This is particularly troubling in K–12 settings, where young people hear the same old stories year in and year out about the triumphant racial histories of America. Over time, this process helps to produce a cultural memory (Assmann & Czaplicka, 1995), where students learn that race no longer matters and their current condition can only be an outcome of a kind of deficient individualism.

Bell's theoretical analysis of history asked that we rethink and reexamine the histories that presume race to be a settled issue. In this sense, such histories help to interrogate watershed moments of racial remediation, thus helping to produce a collective consciousness to challenge the notion that race is a relic of the past and no longer pertinent in the present. Such an analysis of history would thus create the conditions for a kind of racial realism poised to see the world of race reform as mired in ideological interests. I conclude this chapter with Bell's (1985) words because they powerfully convey the point that he has made all along about American racial history:

> The contemporary myths that confuse and inhibit current efforts to achieve racial justice have informed all of our racial history. Myth alone, not history, supports the statements of

those who claim that the slavery contradiction was finally resolved by a bloody civil war. The Emancipation Proclamation was intended to serve the interests of the Union, not the blacks, a fact that Lincoln himself admitted. The Civil War amendments, while more vague in language and ambiguous in intent, actually furthered the goals of northern industry and politics far better and longer then they served to protect even the most basic rights of freedmen. The meager promises of physical protection contained in the civil rights statutes adopted in the post-Civil War period were never effectively honored. (p. 9)

In the end, Bell's racial realism reminds us that we were never saved, and as a result we are not saved today.

REFERENCES

Alridge, D. (2006). The limits of master narratives in history textbooks: An analysis of representations of Martin Luther King, Jr. *Teachers College Record, 108*(4), 662–686.

Aptheker, H. (1969). *American Negro slave revolts.* New York, NY: International (Original work published 1943)

Assmann, J., & Czaplicka, J. (1995). Collective memory and cultural identity. *New German Critique, 65*, 125–133.

Banks, J. (1969). A content analysis of the Black American in textbooks. *Social Education, 33*, 954–957.

Bell, D. A. (1976). Racial remediation: An historical perspective on current conditions. *The Notre Dame Lawyer, 52*(1), 5–29.

Bell, D. A. (1980). *Brown v. Board of Education* and the interest-convergence dilemma. *Harvard Law Review, 93*(3), 518–533.

Bell, D. (1985). The civil rights chronicles. *Harvard Law Review, 99*(1), 4–83.

Bell, D. (1987). *And we are not saved: The elusive quest for racial justice.* New York, NY: Basic Books.

Bell, D. A. (1992a). Reconstruction's racial realities. *Rutgers Law Journal, 23*(2), 261–271.

Bell, D. A. (1992b). Racial realism. *Connecticut Law Review, 24*(2), 363–379.

Bell, D. (1992c). Learning the three "I's" of American slave heritage. *Chicago-Kent Law Review, 68*(3), 1037–1049.

Bell, D. (2009). On celebrating an election as racial progress. *Human Rights, 36*(4), 2–5.

Bennett, L. (2000). *Forced into glory: Abraham Lincoln's White dream.* Chicago, IL: Johnson.

Blassingame, J. W. (1979). *The slave community: Plantation life in the antebellum south* New York, NY: Oxford University Press.

Bolgatz, J., & Crowley, R. M. (in press). The Voting Rights Act of 1965? In Whose Interest? *Social Education.*

Brown, A. L. (2010). Counter-memory and race: An examination of African American scholars' challenges to early 20th century K–12 historical discourses. *Journal of Negro Education, 79*(1), 54–65.

Brown, A. L., & Brown, K. D. (2010). Strange fruit indeed: Interrogating contemporary textbook representations of racial violence towards African Americans. *Teachers College Record, 112*(1), 31–67.

Brown, A. L., & Urietta, L. (2010). Gumbo and menudo and the scraps of citizenship: Interest convergence and citizen-making for African Americans and Mexican Americans in US education. In A. P. De Leon & E. W. Ross (Eds.), *Critical theories, radical pedagogies and social education* (pp. 65–83). Rotterdam, The Netherlands: Sense.

Crowley, R. M. (2013). "'The goddamndest, toughest voting rights bill": Critical Race Theory and the voting rights act of 1965. *Race Ethnicity and Education, 16*(5), 696–724.

Delgado, R., & Stefancic, J. (2001). *Critical Race Theory: An introduction.* New York, NY: New York University Press.

Donnor, J. K. (2005). Towards an interest-convergence in the education of African-American football student athletes in major college sports. *Race Ethnicity and Education, 8*(1), 45–67.

Du Bois, W. E. B. (1935). *Black reconstruction in America, 1860–1880.* New York, NY: Atheneum.

Dudziak, M. L. (1988). Desegregation as a cold war imperative. *Stanford Law Review, 41*(1), 61–120.

Dudziak, M. L. (2004). *Brown* as a cold war case. *The Journal of American History, 91*(1), 32–42.

Ernest, J. (2004). *Liberation historiography: African Americans writers and challenges of history, 1794–1861.* Chapel Hill, NC: University of North Carolina Press.

Gates, H. L. (1988). The trope of a new Negro and the reconstruction of the image of the black. *Representations, 24*(24), 129–155.

Gillborn, D. (2010). The white working class, racism and respectability: Victims, degenerates and interest-convergence. *British Journal of Educational Studies, 58*(1), 3–25.

Grant, C. A., Brown, K. D., & Brown, A. L. (2015). *Black intellectual thought education: The missing traditions of Anna Julia Cooper, Carter G. Woodson and Alain Locke.* New York, NY: Routledge.

Guinier, L. (2004). From racial liberalism to racial literacy: *Brown v. Board of Education* and the interest-divergence dilemma. *The Journal of American History, 91*(1), 92–118.

Gutman, H. (1975). Persistent myths about the Afro-American family. *Journal of Interdisciplinary History, 6*(2), 181–210.

Hess, D. (2005). Moving beyond celebration: Challenging curricular orthodoxy in the teaching of *Brown* and its legacies. *Teachers College Record, 107*, 2046–2067.

King, J. E. (1992). Diaspora literacy and consciousness in the struggle against miseducation in the Black community. *Journal of Negro Education, 61*(3), 341–355.

King, L. J. (2014). When lions write history. *Multicultural Education, 22*(1), 2–11.

Loewen, J. (2007). *Lies my teacher told me: Everything your American history textbook got wrong.* New York, NY: The New Press.

Mills, C. (1998). Revisionist ontologies: Theorizing white supremacy. In C. Mills (Ed.), *Blackness Visible: Essays on philosophy and race.* Ithaca, NY: Cornell University Press.

Reddick, L. (1934). Racial attitudes in American history textbooks of the south. *Journal of Negro History, 19*(3), 225–265.

Schwartz, B., & Schuman, H. (2005). History, commemoration, and belief: Abraham Lincoln in American memory, 1945–2001. *American Sociological Review, 70*(2), 183–203.

Smith, W., & Brown, A. L. (2014). Beyond post-racial narratives: Barack Obama and the (re) shaping of racial memory in US schools and society. *Race Ethnicity and Education, 17*(2), 153–175.

Stuckey, S. (2013). *Slave culture: Nationalist theory and the foundations of Black America,* New York, NY: Oxford University Press.

Trouillot, M. R. (1995). *Silencing the past: Power and the production of history.* Boston, MA: Beacon Press.

Wilson, J. T. (1994). *The Black phalanx: African American soldiers in the war of independence, the War of 1812, and the Civil War* (1st Da Capo Press ed.). New York, NY: Da Capo Press (Original work published 1890)

Woodson, C. G., & Wesley, C. H. (1928). *Negro makers of history.* Washington, DC: Associated.

Afterword

The Ethics of Derrick Bell:
Oh, How He Loved

WILLIAM F. TATE

"Greater love has no one than this, that one lay down his life for his friends."
—JOHN 15:13 (NEW AMERICAN STANDARD BIBLE)

Derrick Bell lived a life of love. His professional life is best characterized as one of sacrifice on behalf of others. Sadly, after his death, he was "Fox-Newsed." I use this term to describe 24-hour cable television talk shows that distort the truth, while attempting to appear to engage in objective investigative reporting. The show's report is framed as the logical presentation of facts. Rather than provide the results of a deep and thoughtful investigation, the show largely provides the opinion of a small number of individuals characterized as experts. The talk show makes a rational appeal (logos), then fails to generate factual evidence. Instead, it offers testimony (ethos) from questionable experts. The rhetorical appeals are conflated and the resulting information is not verifiable. While Fox News is the focus here, the 24-hour cable news cycle has generated a culture of sensationalism, entertainment, and opinion at the expense of depth and verification (Kovach & Rosensteil, 2010). Verifying the truth is a challenge that extends beyond the reporting of one particular cable news station.

In the months leading up to the 2012 presidential election, Fox News host Sean Hannity organized a panel discussion to critique Derrick Bell's perspectives on race and the United States (Hannity, 2012). Professor Bell was not the main target of critique. The primary aim of the panel was to provide a historical narrative about President Barack Obama's intellectual development and socialization.

Professor Bell was a Harvard Law School professor while President Obama attended the law school. Using quotes out of context and snippets of video, Hannity and his guest panelists, David Webb, a Sirius XM Patriot Host, and Michael Myers, executive director and president, New York Civil Rights Coalition, characterized Professor Bell as being both racially polarizing and anti-Semitic. Professor Bell was described as the archetype of the unpatriotic and unethical faculty member populating today's elite institutions of higher education. The panelists and host offered no historical perspective on Professor Bell's life—personal or professional. No serious evidence was provided about his ethics or reasoning. Instead, he was treated as a pawn in a larger game to attack the character of a sitting president.

As I watched the show, and more recently its digital recording, I am reminded of how the media are capable of reframing a life story. The show was a shameful treatment of a man who dedicated his life to principles of democracy, freedom, and justice. Moreover, Professor Bell was willing to sacrifice his personal advancement and standing to support justice. Nearly a month later, I was a panelist at the annual meeting of the American Educational Research Association held in Vancouver, Canada, organized to discuss the contributions of Derrick Bell to the field of education. My remarks focused on the man and his ethics. While Professor Bell was not alive to defend his character, ethics, and legal reasoning, it was a great honor for me to share my thoughts. My aim in this afterword is to recount these remarks as a tribute to a great American.

MILITARY SERVICE TO COUNTRY

The Fox News exposé failed to reveal one of Professor Bell's important contributions to his country. The oversight is curious in light of the show's host. Sean Hannity is a professed patriot with best-selling books focused on the topic, showing commendable philanthropic support of scholarships for the children of slain U.S. military personnel. Derrick Bell was a veteran; he participated in the ROTC as an undergraduate at Duquesne University and then served as a lieutenant in the United States Air Force (Butterfield, 1990).

Bell was stationed in Korea and Louisiana. He was one of the more than 600,000 African Americans who had served in the armed forces by the end of the Korean conflict ("The Beginnings of a New Era for African-Americans in the Armed Forces," n.d.). Facing war in Korea was not his only fear. Bell (1987) described being lost on a road during station duty in Louisiana where his worst fear became fact. He faced a state policeman who threatened to hold him responsible for various crimes in the area. "It was only by showing him my uniform with its gold lieutenant's bar and my military orders that I managed to calm him ... Gaining a measure of protection through my officer's uniform was the first of

Fig 1: Derrick Bell, United States Air Force, military service in Korea and Louisiana. Reprinted with permission from Lisa Marie Boykin.

many techniques I have adopted in my life as supplement—more accurately, substitute—for the respect racism denied me as a person" (p. 182). Bell was changed by his traumatic and impactful experiences and motivated by his experiences and the conditions in the South.

Like other African American soldiers of that period, Bell was subjected to war on two fronts—North Korea and a segregated United States. The NAACP's *The Crisis* magazine ("Korean War," 1950) captured the two-front war, stating:

> In its first meeting since the beginning of hostilities in Korea, the board of directors of the Association voted support of the efforts of the United States and the United Nations to halt Communist aggression in Korea. This board resolution, which condemns unreservedly this breach of the peace by the armed forces of the government of North Korea aided and abetted by the Soviet Union, was passed at the regular monthly meeting on September 14. We are acutely aware, the resolution continues, that victory over disruptive and sinister Communist forces cannot be achieved by guns alone. If America is to win the support of non-Communist Asia and Africa it will have to demonstrate that democracy is a living reality which knows no limitation of race, color, or nationality. Expressing hope for an early victory, the resolution calls upon this government and the American people to take prompt and effective action to end all forms of racial discrimination and segregation in our military and civilian life. (p. 586)

Derrick Bell and many other soldiers served and sacrificed for their country without the benefits of full citizenship. Stationed in a small Louisiana town, Bell was not allowed to sit with other parishioners at the local Presbyterian Church (Rosen, 1994). Instead, he was relegated to the segregated upper level of the church. Bell requested permission to sing with the choir but was shipped to Korea without resolution of the petition. What kind of man is willing to sacrifice his life for a country that does not offer all the rights of full citizenship? Bell could see a different America not as he experienced at the time of his service. Rather, he was part of a generation that hoped and dreamed for a just America. He lived his life envisioning justice for all.

Why did Hannity fail to mention Professor Bell's service to the United States or the challenges of that era? At the time of Hannity's show, Professor Bell's biographical background, including his military service, had been available from Internet sources and digital archives for years. Hannity's failure to accurately disclose this fact distorted the picture of Derrick Bell the man and his ethics. Derrick Bell was a patriot willing to sacrifice his life for a country that did not fully embrace his humanity. He fought for decades to secure and promote the civil rights of the traditionally underserved.

ETHICS, RELIGION, AND THE WAR ON RACIAL INJUSTICE

Derrick Bell referenced biblical concepts to frame dilemmas in the law and social policy throughout his academic career. In a 1976 *Yale Law Review* article, Bell used Matthew 6:24 and the parallel text in Luke 16:13, "No one can serve two masters. Either you will hate the one and love the other, or you will be devoted to the one and despise the other. You cannot serve God and mammon," as premise for his critique of the litigation tactics of the NAACP Legal Defense and Education (LDF) in school desegregation cases. The approach is an early indicator of how he linked ethics, religion, and the fight for racial justice. Some context is warranted. Matthew 6:24 is focused on materialism. The driving question beyond the text is, "What do you value?" The overarching principle is straightforward: the way we envision and use our resources is an indicator of what we value. Why would Professor Bell use a scripture text that highlights values and two masters in an analysis of the NAACP LDF's desegregation strategy? Linguistic context is required to fully appreciate the approach.

In the Greek, *kurios* (master) is translated lord, and refers to a slave owner (MacArthur, 1985). Not to be confused with an employer, who may have many employees who complete their assigned work in reasonable fashion. In contrast, the slave owner has complete control of the slave. The slave's obligation is not part-time to his master. The commitment of service is full-time and without deviation. There is no service left for others. To give partially to another person would render the master less than a true master. The biblical argument is that we all have a master, something or someone we serve. This argument is applied in Bell's discussion of the civil rights communities' approach to education and school desegregation litigation. They valued integration and not the aims of parents seeking a quality education for their children.

Integration was the master. All NAACP LDF's resources were to be dedicated to this aim. Derrick Bell was a part of this organization and supported its aims. Cases to integrate education in the south were dangerous. Only the most committed would stay the course. Derrick Bell was willing to give his life for the cause. Here he is pictured serving the LDF in support of James Meredith's attempt to integrate the University of Mississippi.

Fig 2: Derrick Bell, left, working as an attorney with the NAACP LDF, leaves federal court in Jackson, Miss., on Jan. 16, 1962 with NAACP LDF colleague, Mrs. Constance Baker Motley and James Meredith, center, an Air Force veteran suing the State of Mississippi for admission to the all-white University of Mississippi. Reprinted with permission from the AP.

As a member of the LDF team, Bell worked on both higher education and K–12 school segregation cases. Professor Bell (1976) offered insight into the thinking of civil rights attorneys fighting for school desegregation:

> The civil rights lawyers would not settle for anything less than a desegregated system. While the situation did not arise in the early years, it was generally made clear to potential plaintiffs that the NAACP was not interested in settling the litigation in return for school board promises to provide better segregated schools. Black parents generally felt that the victory in Brown entitled the civil rights lawyers to determine the basis of compliance. There was no doubt that perpetuating segregated schools was unacceptable, and the civil rights lawyers' strong opposition to such schools had the full support of the named plaintiffs and the class they represented. (pp. 476–477)

Bell (1976) offered two reasons for the NAACP LDF's commitment to desegregation and integration ideals over their clients' desire for educational quality without regard to racial balance that are relevant to this discussion. First, for many in the civil rights community, success in attaining racial balance in schooling had become a symbol of the nation's commitment to equal opportunity. Moreover, the education desegregation effort was seen as interdependent to proposed reforms in housing, employment, and other fields where the negative effects of racial discrimination were present. Second, the legal community consisted of upwardly mobile Blacks and Whites, where integration was valued and seen as a positive in their day-to-day interactions. Their thinking was that once less-affluent Blacks and Whites experienced desegregated schools they would come to the same conclusion. Bell cited the argument of education scholar Ron Edmonds, who posited that the school desegregation lawyers were seeking to support the values of middle class Americans' assimilation goals, and not the values of parents living in concentrated segregation seeking an effective school for their child.

Derrick Bell (1976) did not seek to please his colleagues. He worked for the NAACP LDF early in his legal career. His *Yale Law Review* article is critical of his former colleagues. He made it clear that the clients' values should be central to school desegregation litigation. His position did not align with the civil rights orthodoxy of the day. Instead, he remained true to his value system and fought for justice for all. He lived a life consistent with Philippians 2:4, "Let each of you look not only to his own interests, but to the interests of others."

The Sean Hannity Show has a long history of supporting religion in the public square. How did the show's organizers not see the ethics of Derrick Bell? They missed an opportunity to discuss Bell's life of service, a man that lived his faith, at times with great cost to himself and his family.

FAMILY MAN

I have attempted to rationalize why the *Hannity Show* would not discuss Derrick Bell's family life. Perhaps they were taking the high road. Family is off limits. However, the show has vilified Black communities as dysfunctional. Well, here is a man that operated with honor, love, and support for his family. In 1960, Professor Bell married Jewel Hairston, who was an educator and civil rights activist. The couple had three sons: Derrick III, Douglas Dubois, and Carter Robeson (see Figure 3).

Fig 3: Jewel Bell (left), the Bell's three sons, Derrick Bell (right), and an unidentified person (rear) in the 1960s. Reprinted with permission from Lisa Marie Boykin.

The Bell's marriage spanned 30 years, until his wife's death in 1990. In a conversation with her husband, while struggling with cancer, Mrs. Bell instructed him to marry again (Chira, 1992). In 1992, he followed this advice, and married Ms. Janet Dewart (see Figure 4). They remained married until his death. Not a word was mentioned on this front.

The discussion of Bell's character should have included his loving actions. Failure to do so provided an incomplete and inaccurate portrayal of an honorable life.

WORDS OF DERRICK BELL

The Hannity program was titled, "The Words of Derrick Bell: Controversial Harvard Professor Exposed." Where was the expert testimony about how he loved and cared for his family, friends, and students? Why not have at least one guest that knew the man? I do not have answers for these questions. My colleagues and I

Fig 4: Derrick and Janet Dewart Bell. Reprinted with permission from Lisa Marie Boykin.

offer this book project as a testimony to the character, merit, and contributions of a man who loved us. We hope our interpretation of his words reflects the sacrificial love he displayed throughout his life.

Oh, how Professor Bell loved us.

REFERENCES

The beginnings of a new era for African-Americans in the armed forces. (n.d.). Retrieved from http://www.nj.gov/military/korea/factsheets/afroamer.html

Bell, D. A. (1976). Serving two masters: Integration ideals and client interests in school desegregation litigation. *The Yale Law Review, 85*(4), 470–516.

Bell, D. A. (1987). *And we are not saved: The elusive quest for racial justice*. New York, NY: Basic Books.

Bernstein, F. (2011, October 7). Obituary: Derrick Bell/law professor and racial advocate. *Pittsburgh Post-Gazette*. Retrieved from http://www.post-gazette.com/news/obituaries/2011/10/07/Obituary-Derrick-Bell-Law-professor-and-racial-advocate/stories/201110070234

Butterfield, F. (1990, May 20). Old rights campaigner leads a Harvard Battle. *The New York Times*, p. 18.

Chira, S. (1992, October 28). At lunch with: Derrick Bell, The charms of a devoutly angry man. *The New York Times*. Retrieved from http://www.nytimes.com/1992/10/28/garden/at-lunch-with-derrick-bell-the-charms-of-a-devoutly-angry-man.html?pagewanted=all

Hannity, S. (Producer). (2012, March 12). The words of Derrick Bell: Controversial Harvard professor exposed [Video file]. Retrieved from http://video.foxnews.com/v/1503325912001/the-words-of-derrick-bell/?#sp=show-clips

Korean War. (1950, October). *The Crisis*, 57(9).

Kovach, B., & Rosensteil, T. (2010). *How to know what's true in the age of information overload*. New York, NY: Bloomsbury.

MacArthur, J. (1985). *The MacArthur New Testament commentary: Matthew 1–7*. Chicago, IL: Moody Press.

Rosen, I. (1994). Bell, Derrick 1930–. Retrieved from http://www.encyclopedia.com/doc/1G2-2870800016.html

Contributors

Ana Antunes is originally from Rio de Janeiro, Brazil, but she now lives in Salt Lake City, Utah. She is a PhD candidate and an adjunct instructor at the University of Utah. Her research interests are post-colonial feminism, diaspora studies, and refugee studies. A self-titled, crazy cat lady, outside of academia she likes to spend time with her dogs and cats and believes everything is better with farofa.

Anthony Brown is associate professor of curriculum & instruction in social studies education at the College of Education, The University of Texas at Austin. He is also an affiliated faculty in the areas of cultural studies in education, the John Warfield Center of African and African American studies, and the Department of African and African Diaspora Studies. His research agenda falls into two interconnected strands of research, related broadly to the education of African Americans. His first strand of research examines how educational stakeholders make sense of, and respond to, the educational needs of African American male students. The second strand examines how school curriculum depicts the historical experiences of African Americans in official school knowledge (e.g., standards and textbooks) and within popular discourse. He has been published in *Teachers College Record, Harvard Educational Review,* and the *Journal of Educational Policy.*

Keffrelyn D. Brown (PhD, University of Wisconsin-Madison) is associate professor of cultural studies in education in the Department of Curriculum and

Instruction at The University of Texas at Austin. She is also affiliated faculty in the Department of African and African Diaspora Studies and the Center for Women and Gender Studies. Her research focuses on the sociocultural knowledge of race in teaching and curriculum, critical multicultural teacher education, and discourses surrounding the (educational) experiences of Black Americans in the US. She has published work in *Harvard Education Review, Teachers College Record, Race Ethnicity and Education, and Teaching and Teacher Education.* Keffrelyn is a former elementary and middle school English teacher and school administrator.

Rosie Marie Connor currently serves as the director of Institutional Advancement at Snow College. She is also an adjunct faculty member in the Communications and Social Sciences Departments. She has a bachelor's degree in agricultural communications from the University of Illinois, and a master's degree in public health from the University of Southern California. She is currently working on her doctorate in educational leadership and policy at the University of Utah. Her research interests include an examination of graduate education policies and their impact in addressing social, gender, and economic challenges that impact women of color in pursuing graduate degrees in STEM fields of study. Her volunteer and civic involvement includes activities and charitable causes that affect marginalized communities locally, nationally, and globally.

Kathryn Kay Coquemont is a PhD student in educational leadership & policy at the University of Utah. She also serves as the University of Utah's director of new student & family programs, an instructor in the leadership studies academic minor, and previously as the director of leadership development. Her commitment to social justice drives her research interests in Critical Race Theory, student success, and Asian American students.

Jamel K. Donnor is an assistant professor in curriculum and instruction in the School of Education at The College of William and Mary. His primary area of specialization is the cumulative impact of race and inequality on the learning opportunities of African Americans. His recent publications include: *Is the Post-Racial Still Racial?: Understanding the Relationship Between Race and Education,* published by *Teachers College Record,* and *The Resegregation of Schools: Race and Education in the Twenty-First Century* (Routledge). He is currently working on the co-edited volumes: *Scandals in College Sports: Legal, Ethical, and Policy Case Studies, The Charter School Solution: Distinguishing Fact From Rhetoric,* and the second edition of *Critical Race Theory in Education: All God's Children Got a Song,* all with Routledge.

Kahaulani Folau was born and raised in Salt Lake City, Utah. She is the third daughter of Oulono and Melsihna Folau. Her father is from Fasi, Tonga, and mother from Pingelap, Pohnpei. They both migrated to the US in the 1980s. Kehau has Polynesian, Melanesian, and Micronesian ancestors and identifies as Pasifika. After graduating from West High School she attended the University of Utah where she became the first graduate of Utah's Ethnic Studies program. She is currently pursuing her master's degree in the Educational Leadership and Policy Department at the University of Utah. She hopes that her formal education can provide avenues for her passion to enhance access to higher education and provide opportunities for her communities.

David Gillborn is professor of critical race studies and director of the Centre for Research in Race & Education at the University of Birmingham, England. He is founding editor of the peer-reviewed journal *Race Ethnicity and Education* and twice winner of the "Book of the Year" award from the Society for Educational Studies. He is known for his research on racism in educational policy and practice and, in particular, for championing the growth of Critical Race Theory internationally. David received the Derrick Bell Legacy Award from the Critical Race Studies in Education Association and was recently named to the Laureate Chapter of the *Kappa Delta Pi* international honor society, limited to 60 living educators who have made a significant and lasting impact on education.

Vinay Harpalani is associate professor of law at Savannah Law School. His scholarship focuses on race, education, and constitutional law, examining legal, social, and political dimensions of racial identity. He has published several law review articles on race-conscious university admissions and has written on a variety of topics in Critical Race Theory, including racial ambiguity, racial stereotypes, and "acting White." Professor Harpalani earned his PhD from the University of Pennsylvania. He received his JD from New York University School of Law, where he worked closely with the late Professor Derrick Bell. Previously, he was the inaugural teaching fellow at the Fred T. Korematsu Center for Law and Equality, Seattle University School of Law, and Visiting Assistant Professor of Law at Chicago-Kent College of Law.

Gloria Ladson-Billings is the Kellner Family Distinguished Chair in Urban Education at the University of Wisconsin-Madison. Ladson-Billings, along with William F. Tate, is generally credited for introducing Critical Race Theory into the field of education.

Allison Martin is a doctoral student at the University of Utah, where she is completing her EdD in educational leadership and policy. She is also an English teacher at a public high school. Her research centers on leadership for social justice and LGBTQ+ youth in public schools, and she has a forthcoming article that will be published in the *Journal of Cases in Educational Leadership*.

Laurence Parker is a professor in the Department of Educational Leadership & Policy in the College of Education at the University of Utah. His research and teaching specializations are in the areas of educational leadership, policy, and Critical Race Theory at the K–12 and higher education levels. His recent publications appear in *Qualitative Inquiry* and *Urban Education*.

Nicola Rollock is deputy director of the Centre for Research in Race & Education at the University of Birmingham, England. She is interested in race equality in education and the workplace and how racially minoritized groups negotiate and survive racism. She is author of several publications, including the book *The Colour of Class: The Educational Strategies of the Black Middle Classes*, which documents how Black British middle class families seek to navigate their children successfully through the education system. Dr. Rollock is Patron of the Equality Challenge Unit's Race Equality Chartermark and was selected as a 2015 Woman of Achievement by the Women of the Year Council for her contributions to the field of race equality.

Daniel Solórzano is a professor of social science and comparative education in the Graduate School of Education and Information Studies at the University of California, Los Angeles. His teaching and research interests include Critical Race Theory in education; racial microaggressions and other forms of everyday racism; and critical race pedagogy. Over his 44-year career, Solórzano has taught at the Los Angeles County Juvenile Hall, in the California Community College, the California State University, and the University of California Systems. Dr. Solórzano has authored over 100 research articles and book chapters on issues related to educational access and equity for underrepresented student populations in the United States. In 2007 Professor Solórzano received the UCLA Distinguished Teacher Award. In 2012 Solórzano was presented with the American Education Research Association (AERA) Social Justice in Education Award. Also in 2012 Solórzano was awarded the Critical Race Studies in Education Association Derrick A. Bell Legacy Award. In 2013 Solórzano was given the Mildred Garcia Exemplary Scholarship Award from the Association for Studies in Higher Education (ASHE). In 2014 Solórzano was selected as a Fellow of the American Education Research Association.

William F. Tate IV is the Edward Mallinckrodt Distinguished University Professor in Arts & Sciences at Washington University in St. Louis. He currently serves as dean of the graduate school and vice provost for graduate education.

His academic and research appointments have included American Culture Studies, Applied Statistics and Computation, Education, Public Health, and Urban Studies. A past president of the American Educational Research Association (AERA), he received a Presidential Citation from AERA for "his expansive vision of conceptual and methodological tools that can be recruited to address inequities in opportunities to learn." Tate is an AERA fellow and recipient of the Distinguished Contributions to Social Contexts in Education Research-Lifetime Achievement Award (AERA-Division G).

Laura Tyler-Todd is a third-year PhD student in the department of Education, Culture, and Society at the University of Utah. Her research interests include critical literacies, culturally relevant curriculum, and critical pedagogy. She currently teaches seventh grade language arts—in a small Rocky Mountain ski town—and enjoys creating moments of laughter and humorous disequilibrium with her students. She has been a K–12 public education teacher for 10 years. When she is not motivating students to read, she is mountain biking, reading, fly fishing, eating, hiking, or skiing.

Index

abolition, 167–68, 169

academic achievement, 11, 102

academy, 114. *See also* faculty of color; faculty of color, female

access, to public education. *See also* desegregation; integration
  vs. outcome, 14

achievement gap, in England, 102

Act 35, 12

activism
  Bell's, 134–35, 137
  and CRT, 101, 134–35, 138
  and "The Rules," 100–6

affirmative action, 42
  anti-affirmative action laws, 50
  and intangible factors, 47
  used for Whites' advantage, 8

Ahmed, Sara, 125n8, 126n21

Alexander, Andrew, 97

Altbach, P. G., 114

ambition, ethical, 28, 134

And We Are Not Saved (Bell), 3, 131, 135, 144, 175–76

"The Chronicle of the Sacrificed Black Children," 4–7

anti-affirmative action laws, 50

anti-Blackness, 9–14, 149, 152. *See also* racism

antiracism, and "The Rules," 100–6

Antunes, Ana Carolina, 68

Apple, M., 105, 112

Aptheker, Herbert, 167

Artz, Andy, 31

Asian Americans, 60–64

assessment, educational, 101–2

associational rights, 81

authenticity, 95–96, 98

authority
  confronting, 26, 28
  in speaking about race/racism, 92–95

(auto)ethnography
  Brown's, 144–52, 156
  described, 142

Awkward, Michael, 135, 137

Bakke v. Board of Regents, 48

BAME (Black, Asian, and minority ethnic), 120

Banks, James, 43
Baszile, D. T., 142
battle fatigue, 115, 124
Bell, Derrick
  And We Are Not Saved, 3, 131, 135, 144,
    175–76
  attacks on, 103, 181–82, 184, 186
  background, 131
  "The Chronicle of the Sacrificed Black
    Children," 4–7
  Confronting Authority, 26
  death, 36
  Ethical Ambition, 28
  experience with desegregation cases, 13
  Faces at the Bottom of the Well, 91, 111, 131,
    135–36, 144–45, 153 (*See also* "The
    Rules of Racial Standing")
  family, 187
  Gospel Choirs, 135
  health, 34–35
  influence of, 17, 36, 131
  and love, 181–87
  military service, 182–84
  protests, 134, 137
  Race, Racism, and American Law, 3, 39
  "Racial Remediation," 168
  "Reconstruction's Racial Realities," 170
  resilience, 34
  "The Space Traders," 57–58, 60, 92
  *Teacher's Manual: Race, Racism, and
    American Law*, 39
Bell, Janet Dewart, 28, 35, 136, 187
Bell, Jewel Hairston, 28, 135–36, 187
Bell Fellows, 20–21, 24
Bernal, Martin, 145
Birbalsingh, Katharine, 96
Black, Asian, and minority ethnic (BAME), 120
"Black Lives Matter," 14
Black Phalanx, The (Wilson), 166
Blacks. *See also* faculty of color; men, Black;
  women, Black
    mental health, 121
    as witnesses to racism, 104–5
Blair, Tony, 97
Blanco, Kathleen, 12
Blears, Hazel, 99
Boone, Joseph, 135

Bourdieu, P., 112–13
Branch, Elizabeth, 134–35
Brazil, race in, 70
Breitbart.com, 103
Britain
  Blacks' defense of White racism in, 95–98
  Blacks' experience in, 115–24
  Commission for Racial Equality (CRE), 97
  Daily Mail, 97–98, 103, 106n1
  educational assessment in, 101–2
  elitism in, 126n19
  English Baccalaureate, 102
  English Defence League, 100
  Equality and Human Rights Commission
    (EHRC), 97
  faculty of color in, 114
  Lawrence, 101, 116, 124n4, 125n18,
    126n20
  race politics in, 99–100
  racial profiling in, 99
  racism in, denial of, 116
Brown, A. L., 147
Brown, K. D., 147
Brown v. Board of Education, 9, 171–74
  Bell's analysis of, 29, 83, 87, 165, 186
  effects of, 86
  effects on Whites, 85
  as iconic triumph, 171–72
  and image of America, 24, 84, 171–72
  implementation of, 85
  and interest convergence, 5, 24, 81, 165,
    172–74
  and persistence of educational inequity, 44
  problems with, 5, 86
  "*Separate Is Not Equal*" exhibit, 39
  Smithsonian's rendering of, 171
  uniqueness of, 84
  used to assert rights of White families, 8
  value to Whites, 82 (*See also* interest
    convergence)
  Wechsler on, 81
bullying, 120–21

Cabral, Valerie, 35–36
Cameron, David, 94–95, 99
Cann, Colette, 91

"Can We At Least Have *Plessy?*"
(Ladson-Billings), 5
Capital One-New Beginnings, 12
Carpenter, John, 91
Carter, Robert, 44, 48, 51
Celestial Curia, 135–36
charter schools, 7, 11–13, 67
Choice Foundation, 12
"Chronicle of the Sacrificed Black Children,
part 2" (Ladson-Billings), 5–7
"Chronicle of the Sacrificed Black Children,
The" (Bell), 4–7
Civil Rights Act, 173–74
civil rights law/policies, 7
and interest convergence, 173–74
as symbolic, 165, 170
used for Whites' advantage, 7–8
and White interests, 5 (*See also* interest
convergence)
civil rights litigation. See also *Brown;
McLaurin*
limits of, 177
Civil Rights Movement, 81, 86, 171
Civil War, 169
class, and educational disparities, 11
class song, 30–31
Coates, Ta-Nehisi, 9
Cold War, 174. *See also* Communism
colorblindness, 58–59, 86–87, 154
Commission for Racial Equality (CRE), 97
Commission on Social Mobility & Child
Poverty, 126n19
Communism, 84, 172, 174
Confronting Authority (Bell), 26
Connor, Rosie, 64
conservatives, Black, 95–96
conspiracy, racism as form of, 101
Constitution, U.S., 24–25, 29–30
contracts, fixed term, 118, 125n11
convergence of interest. *See* interest
convergence
Cooper, Anna Julia, 132
Coquemont, Kathryn K., 60
counterstories, 112, 149, 158
"The Space Traders," 57–58
by students, 60–76
courses, Bell's, 19–21, 25

Court of Bell, 22
Crenshaw, Geneva (fictional character), 93,
131–32, 135–36, 145, 175–76
Crenshaw, Kimberlé, 132–33
crime
as representative of group, 98–100
and segregation, 8
critical constitutional pedagogy, 24–26
critical engagement, 30
critical pedagogy, 50–51
Critical Race Theory (CRT). *See also*
counterstories; knowledge, experiential
and activism, 101, 134–35, 138
Bell on, 26
and centrality of race and racism, 58–59
challenge to dominant ideology, 59
and confronting authority, 28
counterstorytelling in, 149 (*See also*
counterstories)
in education, 17, 43
and feminism, 132–35
and gender, 132–33
and historical context, 59
and interdisciplinary perspective, 59
and interest convergence, 29
measurement of progress, 134
methods of, 58
revisionist history in, 163 (*See also* history)
and social justice, 59, 101
and truth, 26–28
Whiteness in, 149
Critical Race Theory in Education (CRTE), 43
critical racial literacy, 141, 149, 152–57,
159. *See also* information; inspiration;
interpretation
critical racial testimony, 142
Crowley, R. M., 173–74
CRT (Critical Race Theory). *See* Critical Race
Theory
CRTE (Critical Race Theory in Education), 43
cultural deficit frameworks, 50
curriculum, 144–47, 150, 153. *See also*
education; schooling

Daily Mail, The (newspaper), 97–98, 103, 106n1
*Dayton Board of Education v. Brinkman
(Dayton I)*, 173

Delgado, R., 163
democracy, American, 176
desegregation. See also *Brown;* integration
    and foreign policy, 24, 84, 171–72
    and local control, 173
    NAACP's commitment to, 185–86
    potential profit of, 173
    vs. quality of education, 14, 185–86
    and White interests, 173
discipline, in charter schools, 12
discourse, 149
diversity. *See also* equity, racial
    images of, 126n21
    promises *vs.* reality, 112, 117, 122–23
Donnor, J., 114
double-consciousness, 18–19, 24–26, 29
double standards, 98–100
Du Bois, W. E. B., 18, 26, 132
Dudziak, M. L., 84, 172

E.Bacc (English Baccalaureate), 102
EDL (English Defence League), 100
Edmonds, Erin, 156
education. *See also* curriculum; schooling;
    schools, public
    access, 14 (See also *Brown;* desegregation;
        integration)
    and American Dream, 84
    CRT in, 17, 43
    and equity, 13
    as field, 113
    and justice, 13
    race narrative in, 177
    Warren on, 84–85
educational equity cases, and intangible
    factors, 47
Educational Management Organizations
    (EMOs), 12, 14
elitism, in Britain, 126n19
Emancipation Proclamation, 169
engagement, critical, 30
England. *See* Britain
English, as official language, 74–75
English Baccalaureate (E.Bacc), 102
English Defence League (EDL), 100
Equality and Human Rights Commission
    (EHRC), 97

equal opportunity, effects of, 59
equity, educational, 42, 47. *See also* inequity,
    educational
equity, racial. *See also* diversity; inequity, racial
    promises *vs.* reality, 118, 120–23
    race as tool for promoting, 86
    threats to Whites, 83
Ethical Ambition (Bell), 28
ethics, Bell's, 186
Eugene, Oregon, 134–35
experimentation, in schools, 12, 14
expulsion rates, 10

Faces at the Bottom of the Well (Bell), 131,
    135–36, 144–45, 153
    "The Rules of Racial Standing," 91–106,
        111
faculty, in U.S., 114–15
faculty, White female, 119–20
faculty of color, 112
    career experiences, 115–24, 125n12
    home-domiciled, 114, 124n1
    promotion, 117–19
    in U.K., 114
    in U.S., 114–15
faculty of color, female, 114–24
fathers, Black, 94–95
fatigue, 115, 124
feminism
    and Bell, 135–38
    and Black men, 132, 135, 137
    and CRT, 132–35
    intersectionality, 132–33
field, 113
First Line Schools, 12
Fisher v. University of Texas et al., 42, 48
Folau, Kehaulani, 73
folklore, 163
Fourteenth Amendment, 170, 172
Fox News, 103, 181, 184, 186
Framework for Understanding Poverty, A
    (Payne), 11
Franklin, Benjamin, 29
freedom, Black, 168–69, 176
free speech, and White supremacy, 94
Freire, Paulo, 14, 17, 19, 21, 50–51
Freirean Problem-Posing Process, 50–51

gender, 115–24, 132–33. *See also* faculty of color, female; men, Black; women, Black
generative codes, 50–51
Giles, M. S., 115
Goldfeder, Mark, 33
Gospel Choirs (Bell), 135
grades, in Bell's courses, 24
Gratz v. Bollinger, 48
Greenhouse, L., 111
Greenhouse, S., 7
Grutter v. Bollinger, 48
Guardian (newspaper), 124n5
Guinier, L., 143

Hall, J. D., 86
Hannity, Sean, 181–82, 184, 186–87
Harper, S. R., 10
Harris, Cheryl, 93
Harvard University, 135, 182
Haskins, Tommy, 26–28
Hess, D., 171
Hey, V., 125n12
historical context, and CRT, 59
historical revisionism. *See also* history, revisionist
    Bell's, 164, 167
    in Black intellectual tradition, 165–67
    and Obama's election, 174–75
history
    Bell's analysis of, 164–78
    and Bell's fiction, 175–76
    critical dimension, 167
    production of, 164–65
history, Black, 165–66. *See also* race narratives
history, revisionist. *See also* historical revisionism
    in Black intellectual tradition, 165–67
    in CRT, 163
    defined, 163
history, U.S., 152
    Bell's read of, 156
    Eurocentric versions of, 43
    and interest convergence, 176–77
    need for knowledge about, 153
    and race/racism, 157–58
Howard, Jacob, 170
Hughes, R. L., 115

Hughes, S., 142
humanism, radical, 33

ideology, dominant, 59
incarceration, linked to suspensions, 10
inequity, educational
    persistence of, 44
    understanding, 82, 87 (*See also* interest convergence)
inequity, racial
    Black males as cause of, 94
    persistence of, 171
    redressing, 143
information, 144, 153, 157
inspiration, 144, 155–58
integration. See also *Brown;* desegregation
    as focus of NAACP, 185–86
    overemphasis on, 18
    vs. quality of education, 14, 185–86
integration, voluntary, 82, 85–87
interdisciplinary perspective, and CRT, 59
interest convergence, 5, 24–25
    in *Brown*, 5, 24, 81, 165, 172–74
    and civil rights policies, 173–74
    and Critical Race Theory, 29
    genesis of theory, 83
    in "The Space Traders," 57
    and understanding contemporary racial inequity, 82, 87
    and U.S history, 176–77
interests, White, 169. *See also* interest convergence
interpretation, 144, 148–49, 153–55, 157
intersectionality, 132–33

Jackson, J. F. L., 114
James, George G. M., 145
James, Joy, 132
Jim Crow, 46–47. See also *McLaurin;* segregation, legal
Johnson, Lyndon B., 173–74
Jones, Brittany, 30
justice. *See also* social justice
    and education, 13
Justice Department, 81, 134

King, Deborah, 133–34
King, Martin Luther Jr., 8

KIPP (Knowledge is Power Program), 12
knowledge
    acquisition of, 145
    and action, 149
    disrupting dominant White notions of,
      142
    lack of, 144
    price of, 106
    robust *vs.* superficial, 153
    thinking about, 149
knowledge, experiential, 59, 95, 112, 145, 158
knowledge, sociocultural, 15, 144–45, 147–48,
    151, 153, 158
Knowledge is Power Program (KIPP), 12
Korean conflict, 182–84

Ladson-Billings, Gloria, 17, 114
language, in public schools, 74–75
Lawrence, C. R., 134
Lawrence, Stephen, 101, 116, 122, 124n4,
    125n18, 126n20
law school, humanizing, 30–33
legal protections, 152
Leonardo, Z., 94
Lincoln, Abraham, 169
Littlejohn, Richard, 98
Lomotey, K., 114
Lorde, Audre, 43–44
Louisiana, Bell's experiences in, 182–84
Lundquist, J., 114

magical realism, 135
Makris, S., 142
Mandela, Nelson, 124n4
Marable, Manning, 43–44
margins, positioning on, 113–14
marriage, Bell's view on, 29
Marshall, Thurgood, 48
Martin, Allison, 71
McLaurin, George, 39–50
*McLaurin v. Oklahoma State Regents for Higher
    Education*, 39–50
meaning making, 155
men, Black, 125n18
    fathers, 94–95
    and feminism, 132, 135, 137

    pathologized, 120
    relationships with women, 136–37
    violence against, 101, 116, 122, 124nn4,5,
      124–25n6, 126n20
mental health, 121
Meredith, James, 185
meritocracy, 58–59, 62, 151
microaggressions, racial, 43–45, 49, 147.
    See also racism, everyday
Milliken v. Bradley, 173
Mills, Charles, 166
Milner, H. R., 158
Mirza, Munira, 95–96
miseducation, 145–46
Misra, J., 114
misrecognition, 112–13
Missouri ex rel. Gaines v. Canada, 46
Montgomery Bus Boycott, 164
multiculturalism, 97, 99
multiple jeopardies, 133–34
Muslims, 99
Myers, Michael, 182

National Association for the Advancement of
    Colored People (NAACP), 81
    Bell's conflicts with, 18
    Bell's membership in, 134
    on Korean conflict, 183
    litigation tactics, Bell's critiques of, 184–86
    and *McLaurin*, 42, 46, 48
National Center for Education Statistics
    (NCES), 114
National Museum of American History, 40
neighborhood schools, 10
neoliberal agenda, 6–7
New Orleans, Louisiana, 12–13
news cycle, 8, 181
Newton, Huey, 101
New York Times Book Review, The, 111

Obama, Barack, 29, 94, 103, 174–75, 181–82
objectivity, 59, 112
Office of Civil Rights, 10
Ohio, 7
Oklahoma, University of, 46. See also
    McLaurin

On Being Included (Ahmed), 125n8
ontology, revisionist, 166
open debate, and White supremacy, 94
oppression, gendered, 133–34
Oregon, University of, 134–35
O'Reilly, Bill, 103
O'Shea, Peggy, 10–11
over-policing, 14

Palin, Sarah, 103
*Parents Involved in Community Schools v. Seattle
    School District No. 1 (PICS)*, 8, 82, 85–87
Parks, Rosa, 164
patriarchy, 132
Patterson, James T., 84
Payne, R., 11
pedagogy, critical, 50–51
pedagogy, critical constitutional, 24–26
pedagogy, problem-posing, 50–51
pedagogy, radical humanist, 18–19, 33
Pennington, J. L., 142
perfect, as enemy of good, 28–30
Phillips, Melanie, 97
Phillips, Trevor, 97–98
physicians, black female, 64 66
*PICS (Parents Involved in Community Schools v.
    Seattle School District No. 1)*, 8, 82, 85–87
Pinellas County, Florida, 10
Plessy v. Ferguson, 5, 171
poetry, spoken-word, 73–76
police brutality, 141. *See also* violence, against
    Blacks
policy, everyday racism in, 49
political state power, 144
Porter, R. K., 94
poverty, 9, 11
power, institutional, 44, 92
power, state, 144
pragmatism, Bell's, 29
Presumed Incompetent (Gutiérrez et al.), 115
Prigg v. Pennsylvania, 168
privatization, 6–7, 10–13
problem-posing Critical Race dialogue, 51
problem-posing pedagogy, 50–51
profeminist, 132–33, 136–37. *See also* feminism
professors, Black. *See* faculty of color

progress, measuring, 134
promotion, of faculty of color, 117–19
prophecy, 101
Prospect (magazine), 96
protests, Bell's, 134–35, 137

race. *See also* racism
    in analysis, 149–50
    authority to speak on, 92–95
    (auto)ethnographic narrative of, 144–52
    in Brazil, 70
    centrality in American society, 58–59
    confusion about, 150
    in curriculum, 145–47, 153
    as defining feature of American social
        landscape, 142
    denial of, 154
    knowledge about, 153
    master narrative of (See *Brown*)
    minimizing importance of, 123
    need for knowledge about, 153
    permanent role of, 149
    relation with gender, 132
    as social construction, 43
    as tool for promoting racial equity, 86
    as tool to divest Blacks of rights, 152
Race, Racism, and American Law (Bell), 3, 39
race dialogue, 93–94
race martyrs, 99
race narratives, 163–64. *See also* history
    abolition, 167–68
    in education, 177
    Emancipation Proclamation, 169
    slavery, 167–69
race neutrality, effects of, 59
race relations
    Bell's rules of, 165, 170
    in Britain, 124n4 (*See also* Lawrence,
        Stephen)
race relations industry, 95
racial gesture politics, 122–23
racial literacy, 143. *See also* critical racial literacy
racial profiling, in Britain, 99
racial realism, 51, 149, 158, 177
racial remediation, 169, 172
"Racial Remediation" (Bell), 168

racism
    authority to speak on, 92–95
    awareness of, 8
    Blacks as witnesses to, 104–5
    in Britain, denial of, 116
    centrality in American society, 58–59
    in curriculum, 145–46, 150, 153
    in debate about race/racism, 92
    as defining feature of American social
        landscape, 142
    definitions of, 43–44
    denial of, 154
    experiences of, 146–47 (*See also* knowledge,
        experiential)
    as form of conspiracy, 101
    impact on relationships, 136–37
    as individual actions, 151
    knowledge about, 153
    minimizing importance of, 123
    and minoritized critics of minoritized
        communities, 95–98
    permanence of, 40, 51, 82, 100, 143–44
        (See also *Faces at the Bottom of the Well;*
        racial realism)
    recognizing, 143
    reporting, reaction to, 103, 120–21, 126n21
    superficial understandings of, 151
    and teacher education, 150–52
    teaching, 50–51
    in textbooks, 150
racism, everyday, 44, 49–50. *See also*
    microaggressions, racial
racism, gendered, 115–24
racism, institutional, 40, 43–45, 49–50, 126n20
racism, overt, 146–47
racism, systemic, 9
radical humanist pedagogy, 18–19, 33
radical realism, 40
Radical Reconstruction, 169–70
"Reconstruction's Racial Realities" (Bell), 170
Recovery School District, 12–13
religion, Bell's use of, 184–86
ReNew Schools, 12
research, 116
researcher, in cultural analysis, 142. *See also*
    (auto)ethnography

resegregation, 10, 81–82
Revesz, Richard, 21
Rhee, Michelle, 7
rights, 149, 152, 155, 157
Rivers, S., 114
roach powder analogy, 25, 29–30
Roberts, John, 85
Robinson, Monique, 25
"Rules of Racial Standing, The" (Bell), 91–106,
    111
    authenticity, 95–96
    as basis for antiracist activism, 100–6
    and Blacks as witnesses to racism, 104–5
    double standards, 98–100
    impact of, 92–93, 102
    and minoritized critics of minoritized
        communities, 97
    and price of knowledge, 106
    prophecy, 101
    simplicity of, 102, 104

sacrifice, 13
safe spaces, 94
schooling. *See also* curriculum; education;
    schools, public
    problems with sociocultural knowledge,
        153
    as racialized, 148
    undermining of African American
        knowledge acquisition, 145
schools, public. *See also* curriculum; education;
    schooling
    closure of, 14
    enmity aimed at, 7
    language in, 74–75
    symbolic value, 84
    transfer of funds from, 11
Schrag, Tania, 24
*Schuette v. Coalition to Defend Affirmative
    Action*, 42, 48
science fiction, 91
scripture, Bell's use of, 184–86
Seattle, Wash., 85–87
second-sight, 18–19, 30
segregation. *See also* desegregation; integration;
    resegregation

after *Brown*, 9
and Communism, 84
and crime, 8
hyper-segregated schools, 10
segregation, legal, 46–47. *See also*
   McLaurin
self-awareness, 153–54, 158
separate but equal, 5
"Separate Is Not Equal" exhibit, 39–42, 49
Sewell, Tony, 96
Shanker, Albert, 11
simplicity, of Bell's work, 102, 104, 156
sincerity, 26
Sinha, Maneka, 31–32
slavery, 154–55, 166–69
Smedley, A., 9
Smedley, E., 9
Smith, E. J., 10
Smith, W. A., 115
Smithsonian Museum, 171
social justice, 59, 101
social media, and awareness of racism, 8
socioeconomic class, and educational
   disparities, 11
soldiers, Black, 166, 169
   Bell, 182–84
South, Bell's experiences in, 182–84
Southeast Asian Americans, 62–64
"Space Traders, The" (Bell), 57–58, 60, 92
   spin-off counterstories, 60–76
speaking out, 120–21, 126n21
speech, free, 94
state power, 144
status quo
   and colorblindness, 87
   and judicial system, 83
Stefancic, J., 163
Stevens, Cat, 30
storytelling, Bell's method of, 19, 112, 175–76.
   See also counterstories
Straw, Jack, 122, 124n4, 125n18
students, Bell's interactions with, 31–33
students of color, 112
success, defining, 102
Supreme Court, U.S. *See also Brown*;
   Constitution

significance of, 84
on voluntary school integration, 82
suspensions, school, 9–10
Sweatt v. Painter, 40, 46, 48

tacit, 113
Tate, William, 17
teacher, Bell as, 135
   approach, 21–24
   critical constitutional pedagogy, 24–26
   dedication, 33–36
   evolution of, 19
   grading, 24
   interactions with students, 31–33
   last course, 34–35
   radical humanist pedagogy, 33
   teaching philosophy, 17–18, 33
teacher certification, alternative, 7
teacher education
   considered unnecessary, 7
   foundations course, 150–52
   and understanding of race, 158
teachers
   backlash against, 7
   in New Orleans, 12
   of students of color, 10, 14
   turnover, 10
*Teacher's Manual: Race, Racism, and American
   Law* (Bell), 39
teacher-student contradiction, 31
Teach for America, 147
teaching, as racialized, 148
test scores, in New Orleans, 13
Texas, textbooks in, 150
textbooks, 150, 166–67
They Live (film), 91–92
Thompson, Anthony, 35
three Is, 144, 153, 156–57. *See also* information;
   inspiration; interpretation
Todd, Laura, 66
Trouillot, Michel-Rolph, 164
truth, 26–29
Twenty-Seventh-Year Syndrome, 136–37

UCLA Civil Rights Project, 81–82
U.K. *See* Britain

unemployment rates, for Black college graduates, 9
University and College Union (UCU), 125n9

violence, against Blacks, 101, 116, 122, 124nn4,5, 125n18, 126n20, 141, 150
voices, Black, 93–94
Voltaire, 28
Voting Rights Act (VRA), 173–74
voucher programs, 7, 11

Warmington, Paul, 95, 96
Warren, Earl, 84–85
Washington, Booker T., 18
Washington, George, 175–76
Webb, David, 182
Wechsler, Herbert, 81
Wells-Barnett, Ida, 132
Wesley, Charles, 167
Whiteness
    and authority of racism, 105
    crafting identity of, 141
    in CRT, 149
    as image problem, 126n21
    project of, 152
Whiteness Studies, 105
Whites
    as antiracist, 104–5
    appropriation of Civil Rights Movement's narrative, 86
    interests of (See interest convergence)
    use of colorblindness, 86–87
White supremacy, 43–46
    in cultural deficit frameworks, 50
    in definitions of racism, 44
    focus on, 51
    and free speech, 94
    and minoritized critics of minoritized communities, 95–98
    in photograph of McLaurin, 49
Wilson, Joseph T., 166
Wisconsin, 7
women, Black
    Black female physician faculty, 64–66
    Crenshaw, 131–32, 135–36, 145
    female faculty of color, 115–24

invisibility of, 120
multiple jeopardies, 133–34
relationships with men, 136–37
stereotypes of, 64–66
Twenty-Seventh-Year Syndrome, 136–37
women, in law, 135
women, White, 119–20
Women's Studies, 132–33
Woodson, Carter G., 145, 166–67
Wynter, S., 113, 153

Yale Law Review, 184, 186
Younge, Gary, 124n5

sj Miller & Leslie David Burns
GENERAL EDITORS

Social Justice Across Contexts in Education addresses how teaching for social justice, broadly defined, mediates and disrupts systemic and structural inequities across early childhood, K–12 and postsecondary disciplinary, interdisciplinary and/or transdisciplinary educational contexts. This series includes books exploring how theory informs sustainable pedagogies for social justice curriculum and instruction, and how research, methodology, and assessment can inform equitable and responsive teaching. The series constructs, advances, and supports socially just policies and practices for all individuals and groups across the spectrum of our society's education system.

Books in this series provide sustainable models for generating theories, research, practices, and tools for social justice across contexts as a means to leverage the psychological, emotional, and cognitive growth for learners and professionals. They position social justice as a fundamental aspect of schooling, and prepare readers to advocate for and prevent social justice from becoming marginalized by reform movements in favor of the corporatization and deprofessionalization of education. The over-arching aim is to establish a true field of social justice education that offers theory, knowledge, and resources for those who seek to help all learners succeed. It speaks for, about, and to classroom teachers, administrators, teacher educators, education researchers, students, and other key constituents who are committed to transforming the landscape of schools and communities.

Send proposals and manuscripts to the general editors at:

sj Miller   sj.Miller@colorado.edu
Leslie David Burns   L.Burns@uky.edu

To order other books in this series, please contact our Customer Service Department at:

(800) 770-LANG (within the U.S.)
(212) 647-7706 (outside the U.S.)
(212) 647-7707 FAX

or browse online by series at:

WWW.PETERLANG.COM